Dangerous Imagination, Silent Assimilation

first edition

by Cara St.Louis and Harald Kautz-Vella

Autumn, 2014

London, Berlin, and Oslo

TABLE OF CONTENTS

First Edition

Part One – Cara St. Louis on Social Engineering for Cultural Revolution in the 20th Century

Part Two – Harald Kautz-Vella on the Chemical Composition of Chemtrails, Demonic Foundations, Morgellon's Disease, and Sentient Oil

3

FOREWORD by Ole Dammegard

Through the ages every generation has had to face difficult challenges. At this point in time, these challenges have taken on extreme proportions, on a scale never seen before. When faced with threats and intimidation, most individuals have chosen to lower their eyes, take a step back and accept the oppressors. Others have given up, believing that nothing can be done to change the outcome and that the best thing is to bury their heads in the sand, pretending that everything is okay. Anxiety, hopelessness, frustration and despair have become a mainstream way of living.

Yet, in what might appear as very scary times, some souls have felt an inner urge to stand up and express themselves in brave attempts to change the world for the better. Facing their own fears, sometimes even experiencing intimidation, threats and at great personal loss, they have managed to keep their inner balance and stay focused on exposing what they see as the real truth. Not for any personal gain, but with the inner conviction that the future for all mankind can and will be bright, as long as we manage to transcend the current, massive obstacles. They have managed to turn the problem into a solution and even seen it all as a possibility for spiritual growth.

In my humble opinion, authors Cara St.Louis and Harald Kautz-Vella, are such strong individuals, who believe in good and who will not succumb. Instead, they have chosen to do everything they can to spread vital information. Determined to share their knowledge about chemtrails and other unpleasant truths, they have appeared on international radio, speaker forums and in media, searching for ways to get the word out there.

In this book they will take you on a journey into both history and unknown territories, in their quest to unveil the Matrix and expose what is going on behind the dark veils of so called power. It is a high time for us all to wake up to what is really going on as well as to valiantly expose the structures behind the global conspiracy that threatens to destroy the beauty in the world. This book will guide you, inform you and show you possible ways forward.

To quote the authors: 'No' is the sacred word that has more power than any other. I would like to add: Once our No is strong and established - it will also liberate our YES.

Ole Dammegard
Researcher, International speaker and inventor, from Light On Conspiracies.com
Author of the books 'Coup d'etat in Slow Motion', 'Shadow of Tears',

and 'Re-Mind Me'

6

FOREWORD by Dr. Michael Vogt

"The dominant historiography is the historiography of the dominant class"

... This wise observation of Karl Marx acquires a completely new and novel quality in the face of new methods of manipulation of our brains.

Take for instance the recent elections in Greece. The electorate enjoyed that rare opportunity, to execute a real choice; real enough to have turned it into a thunderous 'NO' to the EU dictatorship from Brussels with it's capitalist exploitation of the country by the EU by now solely controlled by banking interests and high finance.

That Brussels has problems with the will of the people, is historically a well known fact. Almost none of the people enjoyed a free choice when it came to the introduction of the Euro currency, the EU Constitution, the Treaty of Lisbon, and the ESM Bailout (which, by the way, is prohibited by the Treaty of Lisbon). The German people were never given a choice, in any of these. All of these tiptoe steps were undertaken without any democratic legitimacy and are gradually leading us into an increasingly fascist financial dictatorship.

Martin Schulz, the President of the European Parliament who, suffice it to say, has not been elected by the people, has in a television interview expressed a whole new understanding of democracy within the EU, when he commented on the pre-election period in Greece. His view is notable for several reasons:

Firstly, Schulz pointed out that if the choice in Greece came up with a "wrong" result it could adversely affect every EU citizen. (Of course, these self same luminaries did not care an iota what effects the nonsensical and purely ideological introduction of the Euro currency has had on millions of Europeans). He stated that an election that could change the status quo of the 'powers that be' was unacceptable and must be changed.

What does that mean in plain language? Elections in a country where the interests of EU-citizens are affected (meaning, the interests of banks and large fincancial coporations), must be abolished. At least, if elections result in a "false" outcome , they should have no meaning. Elections may only be relevant if they support the "correct political agenda". And what is correct or incorrect, is, of course, determined by the EU bureaucracy. The whole agenda is thus on fast track towards a eurocratic dictatorship. For, either the ruling elites accept the vote of the people, even if it is an uncomfortable one for their agenda, or elections become obsolete, and the hidden financial dictatorship turns into an open one, a new form of fascism through consolidation of interests of big business and the ruling elites.

So here, on one hand, the president of the EU Parliament treats all viewers to an understanding of 'democracy' that clearly shows how finally the mask has been dropped.

On the other hand is also noteworthy that the interviewing journalist does not immediately reply to Schulz, with the question: if the "non-acceptance" of such an electoral outcome, does not actually constitute the end of elections and, as such, the end of freedom? (Apart from the question: 'Since when did the interests of EU citizens ever seriously play a role in Brussels?')

Perhaps the ARD correspondent (First German TV channel) was too surprised and perplexed as to the plain fascist openness of a President of Parliament. However, his colleagues should have been progessionally obligated themselves to question this on the very same day. But the entire mainstream remained silent on an announcement that active preparations were under way in Brussels to remove the democratic impact from elections in individual member states. So, in consequence it would mean that free, fair and open-ended elections would in future be abolished. The cryptic remark by Schulzs that the effects of elections in one state should not adversely effect EU citizens in other states can only be interpreted as a further step into an EU totalitarianism. The mainstream journalists did not see fit to either demand an explanation or comment, nor express some criticism as to this state of affairs.

And finally, this process is remarkable because of the lack of response by the people up and down the EU countries. That a conformist media, which is shaping opinions to aim at a conformist people, thinks that elections, because of their uncertain outcome, are rather annoying and unnecessary, is quite understandable. But it is a remarkable fact that there is no ourcry amongst the people in Germany and Europe as a whole, when the supreme representative of the EU bureaucracy, on camera, openly entertains the idea to abolish elections and hard fought for democratic rights, when the outcomes of elections provide for an uncomfortable result that does not fit the EU agenda.

So here we see an unelected EU bureaucrat publicly expressing the view that 'wrong' outcomes of elections are not acceptable, and no voice of protest is heard, nor any call for resignation for someone who quite obviously has a problem with a democratic expression of the will of the electorate.

Have the people in this country missed this one, one wonders? Have the effects of brainwashing by the conformist media in continuation of the agenda of re-education become so perfected that the people have succumbed to the continuous barrage of it's mainstram outlets?

This is patently not the case, since an ARD's (First German TV channel) own survey reported on the very same day that the reputation of the federal government was good with 59% approval ratings (satisfied or very satisfied) and noted this to be a "record high." However, the same people voted in the chat of the ARD webwite just a few inches below the carefully manicured and probably faked 'Hooray!' message as follows: amongst 70,000 votes submitted it showed just 2.4% and 3.7% respectively were "very satisfied" or "satisfied" with the federal government, 3.6% were less satisfied and 89.5% (!) voted "not satisfied"! **Thus, a staggering 90% of this representative group of voters revealed complete dissatisfaction with the Merkel administration.** Here, in plain sight for all to see, manifested the true mood and voice of the people.

And this by no means stands as an isolated case: A popularity poll conducted by the popular commercial TV channel 'n-tv' asking the 'credibility' question for Mrs. Merkel of 50,000 votes cast a meagre 5% agreed with yes (= credible) and an overwhelming 95% reponded in the negative (= not credible).

Furthermore, the NDR (North German Broadcasting corp.) had to learn in a specially commissioned survey ragarding their own 'appropriate, truthful, unbiased and comprehensive coverage' of the Ukraine conflict recently, that a clear majority of respondents did not think they were being comprehensively and truthfully informed by the mainstream media.

This is a clear and unequivocal expression of the distrust of the populace, the true sovereign ruler, towards politics and it's mainstream media.

Of course, Bertold Brecht is correct, when he writes about the interpretative authority of the ruling elites:

> "*Always does the winner write the history of the vanquished.*
> *The slain becomes disfigured by the slayer.*
> *The weak is made to leave this world, and what remains is the lie.* "

But does this explain it all?
Does it, for instance, explain the massive contradiction between the knowledge of the people that they are being lied and cheated, that they think Merkel and Co. are utrustworthy, that they are dissatisfied with the work of their

political representatives, and that they are being exploited and forced into poverty by them? And to top it all off, they are being brazenly told that the upper EU-echelon is happily marching them towards a Pan-European dictatorship? Does it explain how everything seems to happen in plain sight and with the clear knowledge of the poeple, while at the same time a majority reacts in numb near-paralysis to this very same class of leading people?

The late Peter Scholl-Latour, the well known senior mainstream TV expert on Middle Eastern affairs, commented on the reporting of the ongoig conflict in Ukraine thusly: "We live in an age of mass dumbing down, particularly the dumbing down perpetrated by the mass media." Could it be that this dumbing down of the masses correlates with a homemade intentional inability of the people to move on the basis of their insights and findings to actual consequences, indeed to be able to come to conclusions? Is it more than just mass hypnosis by the media intent on obfuscating and distributing the facts via the mainstream outlets? Could there be real array of instruments at work for mass hypnosis the tools of which that keep the people in a constant state of mental imprisonment?

The two courageous environmental activists, Cara St. Louis and Harald Kautz-Vella, provide a rich array of answers to the desperate questions alluded to. Why is it that,despite the plethora of facts, answers, brilliant analyses and insightful observations...in spite of all the knowledge about the lack of credibility of politics and mainstream media alike... do the people, even in the knowledge hat they are being lied to, tremain in a state of passivity and tolerant obedience? Is this the Stockolm Syndrome at work? These two authors understand the mechanisms brilliantly. In the following pages they help shed a light on these instruments of mass hypnosis and dumbing down and the profound effects on the populations of industrialised societies around the world.

After having read through the pages of this present book the reader will feel imbued and fortified with a knowledge that ultimately leaves no room for despair, but calls us and encourages us to become more vociferous and express with more strength and conviction a statement of sanity and sovereignty. Say "No" to the machinations and of the rulers.[1]

Michael Friedrich Vogt

Historian, Screenwriter (The Secret Files Rudolf Hess)
Professor of Public Relations/Communications Management
Dissenting and Freethinker Internet TV-Journalist
Managing Director/Host TV-Channel www.Quer-Denken.TV

---

[1]

Introduction

Debility.
Dependency.
Dread.

Welcome to the three Ds of the 21st century. Have a good look. This tri-cornered hat we are now wearing took a good century to fashion...quite a bit more than that actually, however, we are focusing on the 20th century for the purposes of this discussion because this is the century that saw the deepest push. 1899 saw the end of the Kali Yuga, the darkest of ages in the long cycle of ages, according to the Austrian philosopher, Rudolf Steiner, and so the Adversaries would have had to catch the 20th century on the way out of the birth canal and try to strangle that baby to death. Why? It is the rise, the beginning of the inevitable, sure and steady turn for the next Golden Age. Already, humanity is awakening. Already, we are taking hold of the magical capacities from which we have been artificially severed. Already, the DNA from which we have been separated, that which has been inactivated, is coming back to life. There is no such thing as 'junk DNA.' Our chakras begin now to number something more like seventy than seven. Many visionaries and healers report this transformation.

It is good news that 'they' have not completely succeeded. What 'they' have managed to do quite well is put us in a trance, a state of deep somnambulance...we are sleep walking when we are not actually sleeping...and, since the supposed end of the last World War, their battle tactics have been two-fold: application of ever more intense external pressures in order to move us materially from one place to another, from one situation to another and, yes, application of internal pressures to try to bend us away from our will to theirs. In fact, we are probably more awake in the dream world than we are in the so-called waking world at the moment. Bear in mind that the program has long-since ceased to be a matter of herding large groups of people in whatever direction is desired. That was the point from about the end of the 19th century until the middle of the 20th century. That system is quite in place. Now, in its ripening incarnation, the Program has become an all-out full-spectrum-dominance drive to change us from human beings into the things-they-want-us-to-become. Passive. Mindless. Compliant.

I came to the decision to explore and present this subject matter when I realized, as I travelled, spoke, wrote and lectured, that perhaps 80% of the time, listeners and readers were unable (yes, *unable*) to move beyond two questions as they related to the Aerosol Assault we are undergoing:

What's the difference between a contrail and a chemtrail and couldn't chemtrails just be contrails?

Wouldn't too many people would have to know about this? It can't possibly be happening.

The answers to those two front lines of questioning really are easy. What's more, experts and activists have been answering those questions for nearly two decades. And there is an entry-level period of time when everyone asks those questions, even if only for the briefest moment in order to digest them or dismiss them. Fair enough. I'm bringing up the general situation, the mental loop we cannot seem to escape. It is clear at that crucial juncture that, individually and collectively, some sort of reset button is activated. The mind then circles back around and perhaps later on broaches the very same two questions again, the questions are answered, the answer is not what we wanted to hear because going forward would mean accepting that something truly evil is afoot, and the mind circles back around through the revolving door...and so on. But there is even more to it than that. There is a truly Pavlovian, trained response unfolding here which, as I said, has been a century in the making. It is this trained response we must now address. This physical inability to get past those two questions and integrate the avalanche of evidence before us may well be the problem to solve right now.

You see, we love our children more than we fear our enemies. That is very human. Often, it is this human capacity, this deep love for our children, that drives us to open our eyes and move forward or stop something. It is this profoundly human trait that has saved us thus far, for aeons. For various reasons, our adversaries must stop the children but in going after the children they often activate what is most invincible in human beings. That is really the location of the front line, the trenches, where we engage in hand-to-hand combat with our Predator. The children born from the last twenty-five years onward are particularly under assault because these children came here, incarnated at this time, to fight this fight. They are endowed in mighty, mighty ways. This will be discussed at length. It is also the inner will, which is the will of the soul and virtually immortal, that has stood the test. Strip us of everything and the will, the actual universal stream which supports natural law, cannot be brought down. It is the conundrum of our enemies, our Predator. The Soul Will resides in the Heart Mind, the heart vibration, a frequency they cannot even locate much less attack.

So, to elaborate just a little, this 3D scenario came by its name via the Korean War and the Mind Control Agenda that unfortunately gained so much traction during that period. It was as if fifty-plus years of data were thrown into a sorter and collator called a POW camp and from these situations were refined and distilled ever more demonic mind control processes. Thinking like what we might imagine a Korean War POW thinks like, in turn, we encounter then idea of Debility...helpless in the face of physical conditions, starvation, or wounds engendered a weakened, feeble state, as it always does in war. Add sleep deprivation and psychological manipulation, and so on, until an individual can barely raise his or her 'powerless' head off a cot. The message is one of abject debility, as in I cannot take care of nor help myself. Debility leads quite smoothly to dependency. One is entirely dependent on one's captors for everything: food, water, shelter and so forth. In this century we refer to this as socialized medicine and the welfare state. Socialism. How many, many ways we have been made dependent. And, finally, at that point, what makes us emotionally malleable and profoundly controllable? Dread. That is to say, terror. Terrorism. Living in a constant atmosphere of fear, terror and unpredictability. The 3D world, indeed.

Because grown human beings simply cannot emotionally or intellectually tolerate the idea that they are prisoners of war, they begin to identify with their captors in every way, misguided loyalty to a brutal parent so to speak, and we develop Stockholm Syndrome. Stockholm Syndrome is now a global condition. We are all suffering from it because we are all prisoners of war. It is much akin to the story of the little elephant whose leg was secured, with a great heavy chain, to a post. And as the elephant grew, the chain was replaced by lighter and lighter tethers until one day there was nothing around its leg holding it to the post. However, it had become so trained, so accustomed, to its being there that it did not realize it could move, leave, run away, stop whenever it wanted to do so. It stayed put because it had been conditioned to believe that staying put was 'normal' and its only option.

Our reality, our world, is a great big construct. It used to be our construct. Now it is theirs. It is an illusion, a scheme, a holograph put into place very carefully over time, mostly in the last hundred years, to keep us standing right by that post. We are convinced we are dependent on the state (the adversaries, the government as parent and so forth) for everything. The more time goes by, the more they take away from us so that, in the end the absolute illusion of 3D will become more true than it really is. Look down and see that the chain is no longer there.

Most importantly, we must be taught to see the great big illusion-making machine that keeps us in a constant state of dread. Think of 'the man behind the curtain' in The Wizard of Oz which is truly what that book was about. Think about the old Star Trek episodes in which one could enter a scripted hologram. All one had to do to stop it was say, 'Computer, End program.' The war on terror is a war on us, the inhabitants, not on terrorists, who mostly do not exist except in green-screened TV studios, Hollywood propaganda mills, and popular music factories.

We must be methodical now and examine the facts one step at a time, building a staircase to sanity. There can be no panic here. We must visit the beginning of the modern human abattoir of the psyche, The School. This has nothing to do with education and should never be mistaken as such. No, although it is quite possible and easy to trace many of the philosophical tenets underpinning the mass hypnosis of the human race back to Greece, the salient moment in time that was the formation of the Prussian Education System. The idea of school as prison or factory itself is ancient but had never been successfully launched anywhere due to it being so crazy and inherently damaging. We will start right there.

Having said that, I think it's important to note that, in my estimation at least, we cannot lay the blame for the universal embrace of this system on the poor old Emperor of Prussia. After all, he just wanted a military that would dive off a cliff if he asked it to. What debauched despot doesn't? He wanted robots who never questioned the state (himself) and were sure that everything he uttered was pure truth. No, we must examine how and when this Experiment was unleashed upon the world, by whom (or what), and why. Remember, we have said that capturing our children is Goal One. Where better than in the concentration camp we call 'school'?

Once the brain-washing bath was drawn, how then to compel the children to enter the water and stay there? Mandatory surrender :

compulsory education from 1850 until this very day. We're going to talk about that. Mandatory incarceration in a concentration camp: compulsory schooling. In some countries, like Germany, anything less than this is punishable by prison.

The 20th century could also be characterized as both an operating table and a laboratory. The 'science' *Behaviourism* was built as toolkit by Dr. John Watson who said, like the Jesuit Ignatio Loyola, 'Give me a baby and I can make any kind of man.' With the conscience-free program of this man, one of the most insidious assaults on human beings (and all other living entities) since the Inquisition was launched. It was a science, no doubt, if endless experimentation and collection of data define a science. The experiments were shocking; the results and conclusions used with true malice. Some of the other nefarious influences of the 20th century, such as Freudian Psychoanalysis, never saw the benefit of such quantitative and qualitative applications as 'testing' of hypotheses or procedure or paradigm. Theories were concocted and, no matter how improbable or unfounded, psychoanalysis fans just embraced them.

It must be stated immediately that behaviourists fashioned a practical application that, used to modify an individual's choices, was quickly applied to groups, nations and the world. The costs and social consequences have been incalculable. One of the first, if not the first, experiments performed on babies at Johns Hopkins University demonstrated the technique for conditioning fear into a human child. One does wonder why that would be the first goal? Ipso facto, behaviour turns out to be predictable and therefore, controllable. After all, the behaviourists claimed, organisms are merely machines comprised of flesh and blood. They require fuel, can be used in various forms of work, be repaired or redesigned (hello, transhumanism), and, critically, they can be compelled into performing an action. The rogues gallery will include Pavlov, Loeb, Boas, Mead and a handful of others.

Alas, within the context of the first two decades of the 20th century, a fertile field had been created, one which Business and Industry was eager to plough. Thanks to both the schooling system in place, the results of the grotesque experiments of the behaviourists and the overlay of false foundations in anthropology, those who would exploit humanity, certainly could and did. It was a heady time indeed for the truly greedy, like children in a candy store. Industrialists hired specialists to explore the possibilities – not the possibilities toward a more humane world but the possibilities within the context of slavery, power and profit. Men began to think and understand that they could control life forms like objects. This is still very much a plan in action today and the mechanisms have become slick and simplified but powerful and effective. We are Human Resources.

The scientific revolution, running in tandem with the industrial revolution, introduced the mind-set that everything was a sort of 'mechanical' part of a giant machine, which helped give rise to modern capitalism (imperialism), compartmentalisation, and assembly-line thinking right back down into the schools, where people are groomed into compliance. These 'parts,' these 'human resources' were seen not as living, breathing people anymore but rather more like a box of cheap baking powder. One used it until it was used up, a teaspoon here, a quarter cup there. Sovereign human beings were now cogs in a great big machine, each had a tiny mind-numbingly repetitive and staggeringly simple part to play on the assembly line (or in an office, for that matter), and were in reality completely cut off from the 'whole.' With no context, there was no logic, no argument, no power. This was the goal, in fact, of the industrialists and was achieved primarily via Henry Ford and a servant system called Taylorism.

The reduction of tasks in this way created alienation, low self esteem, and dissatisfaction. In a fragmented environment, there can be no expression of one's own capacities and we are convinced that we are diminished individuals in every way. We can't ever be that really but we have no memory of that or conscious access to our own power. It is not difficult to regain that knowing but we are urged to forget, to go to sleep. Starting to get the picture? Thus the 20th century was set up to fracture every part of what it is to be whole human being and live within a truly human context. Recently, in the German public education system for example, the presentation of the humanities became bits and pieces taken completely out of context. This is the technique of disempowerment. People who don't understand context cannot argue for their own lives and freedom.

These would become the 20th century's definition of 'rational principles.' Ration...as in to cut into parts, fractions, pieces. Ration...as in to dole out dribs and drabs of what it takes to be alive on the planet. Ration, cut in half, as in to sever one side of the brain from the other when it was never meant to be that way and, in fact, that is inflicted on us over time.

Rational principles meant for the individual worker, much to the delight of the industrialists; zero power, zero rebellion, zero creativity and zero empowering social movements. As Henry Ford said, he was much too smart to have rational principles imposed on *him* but the stupid workers wouldn't know what to do if the principles weren't imposed on *them*.

Indeed, this critical 20th century was forced to focus at its very beginning on brutality, turned on us like a laser. The hounds of hell were waiting to be released via the battle between Fascism and Marxism, evil twins born of the same egg; all-out assaults on the Folk Souls beginning with Russia and Germany and spreading out into the world like an oil spill from which we have yet to recover because we don't see it anymore. This is the Normalization Factor, a key tool in any form of abuse. (In fact, the study of epigenetics, which is a completely valid scientific paradigm and completely hidden, strongly indicates that environmental factors alone can change our genetics – our very DNA – over the course of only two generations. So much for Darwinism. Large newspapers were commandeered and used to sway entire nations toward the aims of just a few psychopathic banking families, again the same situation as today. These banking families also make up all of our royal families' biological lineage. Yet we continue to drool and fawn over these parasites due to the relentless administration of malicious behaviourist principles on our daily lives which create opportunities for ridiculous amounts of control for just a few. War brings amazing profit, gets rid of 'surplus' population, and distracts the masses so that those at the very top can continue to move the chess pieces around unnoticed. The only thing that will stop that is if people stop enlisting in the military. Simply refuse to go.

In terms of propaganda, the forces in America did not miss the opportunity either:

"Since President Woodrow Wilson openly enlisted the cooperation of Hollywood film makers to create propaganda to stir war fever among Americans, Hollywood and US media have been intimately linked with shaping consensus for US national strategy. ...The US Pentagon and the military industrial complex, together with the elites at the New York Council on Foreign Relations and other select organizations of power brokers, developed a form of culture and media warfare..." (Engdahl, FW, *Target China*)

And so the 'media' as such was invented and about five minutes later the control of the media began, snowballing until it was nothing more than a tool of the imperialists and elite industrialists and saboteurs of humanity. This method was so effective that, for example, the British, who had no quarrel whatsoever with Germany prior to WWI, were soon ready to tear the Germans limb-from-limb. The propagandist newspapers were even delivered to the trenches at the battlefront to keep 'morale' high and the war long. That translated to profits and the champion warmonger then, as now, was the Rothschild family. There are a handful of them.

World War II saw a deep refinement of the propaganda weapon.
It worked especially well -- the population had been through it once before
and the propaganda engineers had honed and streamlined their craft. There
were precedents set and lessons learned. The population 'knew' that the
media would be 'informing' them, that is to say, telling them who to hate,
who to love, what to think, what to do about it, who to trust and so forth.
An entire cadre of Nazi Operation Paperclip specialists, brilliant experts in
so many disciplines, such as psychology, descended upon the United States
just after the war with the express purpose of observing and analysing the
population and eventually mastering control of the same.

The Tavistock Institute in London was instrumental in starting
the propaganda war that led to the Great War. In Germany, on the heels of
the failed Marxist Bolshevik revolution in Russia, several intellectuals
formed a little club, a think tank, if you will, called The Frankfurt School.
It was their mandate to figure out how to achieve worldwide Marxism:
global collectivism. Combining the never-tested and wholly unscientific
principles of Sigmund Freud with Marxist philosophy, these psychically
damaged intellectuals set as their first task, as Freudo-Marxists, the
destruction of the nuclear family. This unit, they deduced, was the
backbone of the human race and, as such, one must shatter it utterly if one
were to reform the human population in general to their liking.
Psychopathy? You bet.

One of their more interesting 'scientific' observations: roughly
ten percent of the population was deranged. Hence, they decreed,
psychoanalysis would be necessary. However, one cannot simply cull that
particular ten percent from the world population and treat them. No, the
only solution was to 'treat' the world *in toto.* But how? Answer: the schools.
That is just what happened and is still happening. Again, crazy?
Unbelievable? Insane? Yes, yes, and yes. Nevertheless, this is what

happened and is happening.

The anthropologist with a political agenda, Franz Boas, together with his prized pupil, Margaret Mead, invented both anthropology and anthropological scenarios and principles that shored up the plans of both the Tavistock Institute and the Frankfurt School (after it moved to the United States in 1930 and became the Institute for Social Relations at Columbia University in New York). At roughly the same period in history, Sigmund Freud's nephew, Edward Bernays appeared like a nightmare from England and took up residence in the US, with his centrepiece essay, *Propaganda*, as his calling card. From the blatant attempt to manipulate people into doing what others wanted them to do when it is unlikely to have been their sovereign decision or aim sprung the fields of advertising, marketing and sales. In other words, trick people into doing what you want them to do and make them think it had been their idea all along. Of course, these practices were immediately recognized as unethical and often immoral. Therefore, the artificial construct of 'business ethics' was created as a shield.

There is much to say.

In order to understand why we cannot get past the two original propositions mentioned at the beginning of the introduction, the following two questions that must be thoroughly addressed:

How did we become people who would allow this to be done
to us?
How did we become people who would do this to each other?

I promise you, it was no accident. I promise you, once you understand the 20th century, you will understand that full spectrum dominance is upon us. One proviso. What I'm NOT going to do is talk about money, and here's why. That is The Way we have been most deeply trapped and controlled, it is Black Magic indeed and every time we pass money we are participating in a serious ritual, strengthening the stranglehold. It is a gaming addiction. It is so built into our very being that when the subject is broached we can think of nothing else. The reader will not find that subject here. However, a very broad and simple understanding of how black magic is used to govern will be presented.

Yet, one of our greatest and best hopes lies in understanding every other strand making up the straight-jacket called the 20th century I describe here because one yank on a piece of the yarn and the whole thing comes unravelled. If we talk about money, we are in a prison of an entirely different sort. So let's leave that for another book. Let's look, instead, at how we became people who would allow this to be done to us and people who are not only doing it to each other but somehow convinced it's a good idea.

Last but not least: we will remember that 'No' is the sacred word and that it has more power than any other.

Further Reading

http://www.princeton.edu/~achaney/tmve/wiki100k/docs/Stockholm_syndrome.html *Stockholm Syndrome.*

Namnyak, M.; Tufton, N.; Szekely, R.; Toal, M.; Worboys, S.; Sampson, E. L. *"'Stockholm syndrome': Psychiatric diagnosis or urban myth?". Acta Psychiatrica Scandinavica*

I. E. Farber, Harry F. Harlow and Louis Jolyon West. *Brainwashing,*

24

Conditioning, and DDD (Debility, Dependency and Dread)

Francis, Richard C. *Epigenetics: How Environment Shapes Our Genes*. *2012*

Chapter One

The Dangerous Imagination

Or how they taught us to submit....I say submit, and that is precisely what I mean. However, it's far worse than that. They taught us to injure ourselves and each other, quite on purpose and with a smile on our faces, convinced that we are/were doing the smartest and best thing. Voluntary self-mutilation and ultimately 'noble' self-extinction. Let's dig in because the rules of the game are simple and we don't have to play. We can always just put the toys down and walk away. It really is that simple in so many ways.

Schooling was intended to be "a 5th column into the burgeoning libertarian condition."[2] So said John Taylor Gatto, renegade American Educator and Philosopher. The method? Infiltration into the minds of children isolated too early and too completely from their parents. It has also been characterized as part of a movement one could describe as the Counter-Renaissance. It matters only a little how we choose to see it right now, as the main thing is that it is perhaps the most insidious tool of enslavement being foisted upon humanity. School, as it exists today, has nothing whatsoever to do with education. We must rip the mask from the face of the imposter. Education, certainly, is our birthright as human beings. School itself is a prison sentence.

PLATO

The idea, the concept, goes back to Plato. In *The Republic,* Plato

---

[2] Gatto, John Taylor. *The Purpose of Schooling: Truth vs. Disinformation...Everything You Know About Schooling is Wrong. See http://stopthecrime.net/docs/John%20Taylor%20Gatto.pdf, p1, as well as JohnTaylorGatto.com*

asserted that the state should train children from the age of three. Each citizen was guided by the state towards an ideal conception of 'justice.' Each citizen was placed into the social class and occupation best suited for him. Education had to be universalized so that all citizens could be effectively screened and placed. He insisted that it was the state's job to support and control schools and to make them mandatory: designed by the state for the benefit of the state.[3]

One notable feature of this method of 'educating' children is Plato's demand for strict censorship of literary materials, especially poetry and drama. He argued that early absorption in fictional accounts can dull a person's ability to make accurate judgements regarding matters of fact and that excessive participation in dramatic recitations might encourage some people to emulate the worst behaviour of the tragic heroes. Are these not the very vehicles of the Imagination? Worst of all, excessive attention to fictional contexts may lead to a kind of self-deception, in which individuals are ignorant of the truth about their own natures as human beings.[2] This rigid fear of the Imagination is a subject we will return to again and again. It is the reason our right and left brain hemispheres have been trained not to work together, as they used to, as they were intended to. One of those hemispheres, after all, is the apparatus of the imagination...*they think.*[4]

Plato's school for the masses had nothing to do with our romantic notions of education: unlocking vast and surprising human capacities or empowering hearts and minds. It never did, apparently. It had to do with maximum management of what we would now term 'human

---

[3]   Dillon, Ariel. *Education in Plato's Republic* http://www.scu.edu/ethics/publications/submitted/dillon/education_plato_repu blic.html p.1 *Underground History of American Education* by John Taylor Gatto online to read: http://johntaylorgatto.com/chapters/index.htm

[4]   *Ibid.*

resources' for the maximum benefit of the elite and/or the state. The other stuff; the enchanting shop window? Sold to us to keep us thinking the system was healthy and if we were unhappy there was something wrong with us. (Marketing, propaganda, sales).

If citizens express any dissatisfaction with the roles to which they are assigned, he proposed that they be told the "useful falsehood" that human beings (like the metals gold, silver, and bronze) possess different natures that fit each of them to a particular function within the operation of the society as a whole (but that are essentially unchangeable).[3]

Mass education for the state simply had not been tried on a large scale in more modern times because the idea was thought to be too outlandish, too crazy, too enslaving. Who in their right mind would go along with it? It is so important to trace the path of this line of thinking as, with a backward look, we can view it with complete justification as the chute in an abattoir and we, my friends, are the ambling, trusting cattle.

CALVIN

Let's move forward from Plato, then, to five centuries ago when John Calvin, seen as the most influential theologian of the last fifteen hundred years, was alive and working. We have our ideas who Calvin was and how bleak was his world view. The 'damned', the wretched, outnumber the 'saved' by orders of magnitude. Outnumbered by about 20 to 1, force was not an option in any attempt to overcome this majority, should that be wanted. Thus continued the Roman recipe for crowd control, anglicized, of 'bread and circuses.' Distraction and diversion became the order of the day. With powerful enough tools of confusion, one person could control twenty easily enough.

John Calvin said: salvation is already decided before birth. Justified sinners were going to heaven no matter what they did and 95%

were doomed no matter what they did. [5] This seems like absolute permission to use 95% of the population in any way with no consequences provided they never figure out what's going on. Hence, Calvin constructed the ideal of forced, mass education. Things of great persuasion had to be put in place to occupy the 95% such that they would never bother the 5% again. This theme saturates all angles of the spectrum in full spectrum dominance and certainly, Calvin wasn't the only one who thought of it. However, a compulsory schooling was thought to be a brilliant solution with which to warehouse, neutralize and exploit the 95%.

Distract, numb their minds, set them against each other...eat up their time, attention and energy. That plan is still in effect because it works. We think this is a new paradigm but it is an ancient tactic under which we have been enslaved for thousands of years. Now, in the 20th century, we must recognize that we have a Predator. So much is going so badly wrong in so many places that it is almost possible to pick the Predator out, for It will be in the only calm place. The Predator is using what is already in place and deepening it to unholy extremes. This is indeed the confusion, the inversion with which black magic operates, despite the fact that this comes from a so-called 'holy man,' John Calvin. We must grasp with what the walls of our prison are made.

SPINOZA

We move from Calvin to a thoroughly secular philosopher in Amsterdam, Benedict Spinoza, who published a book in 1670 that had a huge influence on the leadership classes of Europe, the United States and Asia. It's called *Tractate Religico Politicu.* It has been written that practically everyone who could read in colonial times read Spinoza.

---

[5] This philosophy is known as The Five Points of Calvin and includes what is called 'election,' meaning those who are pre-ordained for salvation. This theology was solidified by some of Calvin's followers at a meeting called The Synod of Dort.
https://www.princeton.edu/~achaney/tmve/wiki100k/docs/Synod_of_Dort.html

In his book, he wrote that people should not be characterized as 'damned' or 'saved' because there is no supernatural world. He also said there's an enormous disproportion between permanently irrational people who are absolutely dangerous and the people who have good sense. [6]Again, he said the ratio is about twenty to one.

We have to pay attention to that fraction, that figure. How was it derived and by whom originally? He also said 'permanently irrational people'. Hence, why devise a system of education at all? Spinoza's ideas have penetrated to all the continents. Here, I speak primarily about the US school system as a grandchild of the Prussian system but these techniques are now global.

Using different nomenclature, Spinoza falls into lock-step with Calvin. However, Spinoza actually says that an institutional school system should be set up as a *civil religion*.[7] It's a term found frequently in early colonial writing because Spinoza, as we have noted here, was very widely read. School: civil religion.

A civil religion (secular) would kill two birds with one stone. First, it would destroy the irrational and dangerous forms of official religion. So it had nothing to do with educating individuals whom he thought of as permanently irrational anyway. It would change who controlled them and reinforce the walls of their cage, that's all. The percentages remained stable.

Second, it would 'bind up' the energies of these irrational twenty to one (the damned of Calvin) and destroy their imagination. That bears repeating because it is crucial. **It would destroy, bind, their imagination.** Why would that be important? Do permanently irrational people have imagination? Does not imagination indicate a will to both conjure a

---

[6]   http://www.gutenberg.org/files/989/989-h/989-h.htm

[7]   http://plato.stanford.edu/entries/spinoza-political/ On Spinoza's account, under Moses, civil law and religion "were one and the same thing" (17, 213) Sections 3 and 4

different scenario and enact it? I would postulate that one must have some ability to order a series of variables in some way to use imagination in any way that might challenge those in control. So, yes, the imagination — like the children in whom it is nascent and unsullied — was the major target. It is also possible, perhaps probable, that the possession of imagination at all was what was being termed 'irrational.'

So, Spinoza said the same thing as Calvin. We have to destroy the imagination because its only through the imagination that the maximum damage (power and free will) is unleashed. Otherwise people can rebel, effect short-term change, but they can't do much harm to the fundamental structure because they can't think in any new or unhindered ways. In fact, the structure is too close and too ingrained for them to see it unless it is pointed out. The structure and its effects can be bewildering events that seem to have no origin.

Destroy the imagination and build a better cage; The Plan.

Even when the prescription is 'think outside the box,' the thought that follows is implanted. There is only the box, redesigned, painted, perfumed, and so forth, but it is still the box. It's a game. There is no box. They have unlocked the sacred door to our imagination and learned to use it against us. We think there is a box when there is not. We think our leg is chained when it is not. This is 'gaming' in a real way.

FICHTE

It would be not quite a century and a half from Spinoza in 1670 to Johann Fichte in Northern Germany in 1807-1809, where the very first successful institutional schooling in the history of the planet, was established.

Fichte says in his famous *Address to the German Nation8*, that the reason Prussia suffered a catastrophic defeat against Napoleon at Jena was because ordinary soldiers took battlefield decisions into their own hands. He called for a national system of training that would **make it impossible for the 19 out of the 20 to imagine** any other way to do things. A decade later Prussia had the first institutional form of mass schooling ever created.

One man did not think this idea, this crazy idea, was out of reach. Perhaps you anticipated that I would start with Frederick, Emperor of Prussia? Yes, but only insofar as he expressed a despotic, totalitarian desire. It had come to the emperor's attention that his troops were running away from the front lines in battle. They seemed to have been inexplicably overcome by an irresistible will to save their own lives. When a fellow wants his empire to grow, this behaviour is contraindicated, this abandoning of the battle lines. In 1805, Napoleon crushed Frederick's army. This could not be tolerated.

On the back of Fichte's admonishment to the nation, King Frederick of Prussia systematically established a schooling model designed to make sure that the spirit of ability within was permanently extinguished. Children were excised from their families, de-personalized and even isolated from each other at an early age. Seated in rows, they were easily silenced, controlled, and forced to engage in rote tasks whose sole purpose was to inculcate obedience. [9]

These practices shaped the curriculum of the Prussian public schools for over a century. That could logically only be considered a problem if one lived in Prussia, and then likely only if one were male. However, other powers with other goals and purposes took up the Prussian baton and ran with it. For example, we here in the United States had

---

[8]   http://ghdi.ghi-dc.org/pdf/eng/12_EnlightPhilos_Doc.8_English.pdf p.5

[9]   Richman, Sheldon. Separating School and State: How to Liberate American Families. Excerpt Chapter 3. http://www.sntp.net/education/school_state_3.htm

suffered a humiliating defeat in 1812 at the hands of the British. We were interested in this 'straight jacket' which had turned things around for the Prussian army.

Yes, the machine that was the Prussian military after the introduction of their new compulsory schooling system was very attractive indeed. It was really a well-received bonus that this system worked to crystallize a class system under siege and so easily inserted itself with blunt force into the liberty traditions. As with all other forms of social engineering aimed at cultural revolution which were the bulk of the 20th century living and operating environment, once an architecture was in place, it could be used by many small ruling groups for the purposes of dominance and control.

So, briefly, who was this mover of entire cultures?[10] The philosopher, Johann Gottlieb Fichte, supposedly from humble beginnings…the son of a ribbon weaver…but he managed to produce a philosophy that the Emperor of Prussia had converted to what we now refer to as The Prussian Education System. One wonders today if this was poor Fichte's goal. After all, many philosophers would find their work twisted and bent to serve a purpose for which it was never intended. Not so, J.W. Fichte, who like most children in his time, was home-schooled. One might have thought he was rising above his humble station, but that may be questionable. Let us add what John Taylor Gatto wrote on the incidence of formal education during Fichte's time and later:

"People who wanted their kids schooled had them schooled even then; people who didn't didn't. That was more or less true for most of us right into the twentieth century: as late as 1920, only 32 percent of American kids went past elementary school. If that sounds impossible, consider the practice in Switzerland today where only 23 percent of the student population goes to high school, though Switzerland has the world's

---

[10]   Johann Gottlieb Fichte: Briography. http://www.egs.edu/library/johann-gottlieb-fichte/biography/

highest per capita income in the world."

No matter what else Fichte was, it is important to note that he was also a Freemason. And, subsequent to the humiliating defeat of the Prussian army by Napoleon, he wrote one of the most important documents the modern world has known or of which we have become victims: "*Address to the German Nation.*" It led directly to the introduction on a practical level of compulsion schools in the west. Here was in place, of course, globally, any number of forms of 'forced training.' This was a completely different animal. [11]

In his second address regarding the 'New Education,' Fichte remarked, "If you want to influence [the student] at all, you must do more than merely talk to him; you must fashion him, and fashion him in such a way that he simply cannot will otherwise than what you wish him to will."[12]

Fichte blamed the education system for the weakness of Prussian soldiers, he said children would henceforth have to be disciplined through a new form of universal conditioning. Obviously, their parents could not be counted on to inculcate blind obedience to the state and a sheer ravenous will to win. No sentiment would remain alive.

Through forced schooling, everyone would learn that working for the State, even laying down one's life to its commands, was the greatest *freedom* of all. Do we not understand this sort of patriotism in the United States deeply? Semantic redefinition or neurolinguistic programming; no matter what one calls it, it is public relations genius and, frankly, allows **both** for heroics that may be deserved…assuming one has the power to critically make that choice…and mass slaughter over oil fields and such. This power was then later packaged and sold by Edward Bernays and a

---

[11]   *Address to the German Nation* p.67-8

[12]   *Addresses to the German Nation, 1807. Second Address: "The General Nature of the New Education".* Chicago and London, The Open Court Publishing Company, 1922, p. 21

cohort of propagandists (ad men and experimenters in mind control), who dominated the 20th century as it unfolded.

The first kind of natural authority in human life is parenting. And the fallacies used as justification for the State are dim copies of parenting indeed — they ride on the nascent relationship abilities by which young human beings relate to their parents. On a less romantic note, to a young child, the parents appear as magical beings who provide for our needs, if only one moans and cries, without one having to think about from where these things come. Parents (Governments, Emperors) are understood as well-meaning, having with their children (citizens, subjects) a relationship of mutual love; young infants have an absolute trust in their parents. Finally, it is almost universally accepted that parents have an authority to decide for their children, and even to punish them in certain cases. A system of mass education was desperately desired which would create just this sort of infantilized, compliant military. We call this patriotism or nationalism today. As it exists today, it was 'schooled' into us.

The system worked so well to transform the Prussian military that the country was often referred to as 'an army with a country.' Since the Aggressive Control Apparatus I refer to as the Adversaries or, more and more, the Predator, at the beginning of the 20th century had the USA in its sights as the military arm for world control, this system of education seemed ideal for creating a compliant citizenry. And, as noted above, we thought we had located a solution to the humiliation of 1812. The Prussian education model debuted in 1818. By the mid-19th century, our emissaries were singing the praises of a potentially Germanicized United States and a structure came together toward that end. Little has been written about that. In fact, we so romanticized the King of Prussia that he was invited to settle a border dispute with Canada and we named a town in Pennsylvania after him out of gratitude. Finally, let us add that in 1919, German public schools were described by German philosopher Kurt Eisner as "veritable drill academy[s] in which children could be intellectually crippled for life." [13]

Again, it must be noted that we can examine *Plato's Republic* and we can look deeply at the writings of John Calvin and Spinoza and Fichte but the responsibility for the depth of destruction and nefarious purposes to which our schools continue to have been dedicated lies squarely with those who embraced such even in the face of the very clear and vociferous opposition of the first parents faced with compulsory schooling. One also has to wonder in what way we viewed our human children (German, American, Japanese and so forth) if the entire purpose of their 'education' was to make them good cannon fodder, a sentiment just recently expressed again by the Council on Foreign Relations.

HORACE MANN

On the night of June 9, 1834, a group of prominent men "chiefly engaged in commerce " gathered privately in a Boston drawing room to discuss a scheme of universal schooling . Secretary of this meeting was William Ellery Channing, Horace Mann's own minister as well as an international figure and the leading Unitarian of his day. The location of the meeting house is not entered in the minutes nor are the names of the assembly's participants apart from Channing. Even though the literacy rate in Massachusetts was 98 percent, and in neighbouring Connecticut, 99. 8 percent, the assembled businessmen agreed the present system of schooling allowed too much to depend upon chance. It encouraged more entrepreneurial exuberance than the social system could bear. The minutes of this meeting are Appleton Papers collection, Massachusetts Historical Society[14]

13   Gurganus, A. (1992). A German Socialist's African Marchen: Kurt Eisner as Aufklarer. Journal of Black Studies, Vol. 23, No. 2, Special Issue: The Image of Africa in German Society, pp. 210-218

Horace Mann was curiously smitten by the Prussian system. However, clearly the resulting graduates were left infantilized and fearful, its members left weak and supremely conditioned to obey those in command. Yet it was this system that Horace Mann transplanted to the US in 1843 and which has spread around the world, anywhere in which despots and corporatocracies seek to gain mastery. [15]

Mann seemed to have understood the darker nature of the system yet he was mesmerized by its power. It is truly a 'ring of power' and those seduced by such always arrogantly convince themselves that they are really working for the greater good. Control was too appealing to resist. Mann called it the moral power over the "understanding and affections of the people." He and his colleagues believed that they should be the ones to determine values and ideas best perpetuated into the future. Such an old story and yet so buried that no average American understands the cage in which they and their children are living. It is critical to note that, primarily, Horace Mann was a lawyer working for the interests of the coal and railroad industries. He was not, as the legend suggests, an education reformer. He was carrying out the will of the industrialists.

Briefly, it is important to reveal that far from embracing the introduction of the compulsory Prussian-based education system into the United States, parents were adamantly against it. Many, many years went by before it was finally forced down the throats of parents in Massachusetts and the national guard had to be called out to 'walk' these first test children to school. "After the American Revolution, Massachusetts again spearheaded the compulsory-education movement. In 1852, the state set up

---

[14]   *Appleton Papers collection, Massachusetts Historical Society*

[15]   Cubberley, E. P. (1920).*Readings in the history of education: A collection of sources and readings to illustrate the development of educational practice, theory, and organization.* Boston, New York [etc.]: Houghton Mifflin company

the first modern government schooling system. It was not always smooth going for the enforcers, however. Some 80 percent of the people of Massachusetts resisted the imposition of public schooling. In 1880, it took the militia to persuade the parents of Barnstable, on Cape Cod, to give up their children to the system." [16] Parents rebelled, demonstrated and went to jail. They were convinced that this entombment of their children was nothing more than brain-washing. Turns out they were absolutely correct. Nevertheless, compulsory schooling became law.

In fact, when the passion for liberty burned brightest, there were no compulsory education laws in the US. Between the pre-Revolutionary period and the mid-1800s, the power to decide whether, when, and how to educate one's children lay entirely in the hands of the parents. "Schooling in that early period was plentiful, innovative, and well within the reach of the common people. What effect did it have? High and Ellig note that 80 percent of New Yorkers leaving wills could sign their names. Other data show that from 1650 to 1 795, male literacy climbed from 60 to 90 percent; female literacy went from 30 to 45 percent. Between 1800 and 1840, literacy in the North rose from 75 percent to between 91 and 97 percent. And in the South during the same span, the rate grew from 50-60 percent to 81 percent . Indeed, Senator Edward M. Kennedy's office issued a paper not long ago stating that the literacy rate in Massachusetts *has never been as high as it was before compulsory schooling was instituted.* Before 1850, when Massachusetts became the first state in the United States to force children to go to school, literacy was at 98 percent. When Kennedy's office released the paper, it was 91 percent." [17]

The first compulsory attendance law was adopted in Massachusetts in 1852. During the next 15 years, no other state followed Massachusetts. But, beginning in 1867, a steady stream of states began

---

[16]   Richman, S. Separating School and State, How To Liberate American Families. Chapter 3, p.1
       http://www.sntp.net/education/school_state_3.htm

[17]   Ibid.

adopting compulsory attendance laws and, by 1918, all states had enacted them. Over the years, the initial age of compulsory attendance became lower and lower. Now the age ranges from 5 years old through 18 years old although most states allow the children to stop when they are 16 if they so desire.

Coincident with the abject defeat of the populace to compulsory education, a professor at Harvard University released a book thoroughly discussing the state of American education and its goals. Once again, we rely on John Taylor Gatto when we pick up the trail via *The Innovative Educator*:

Prof. Alexander Inglis's 1918 book, Principles of Secondary Education, makes it clear that compulsory schooling in America was intended to be what it had been for Prussia in the 1820s. John Taylor Gatto explains that the work of Inglis's, who was a Harvard professor with a Teachers College Ph.D., positions school as a fifth column into the burgeoning democratic movement that threatened to give the peasants and the proletarians a voice at the bargaining table.[18] Modern, industrialized, compulsory schooling was to make a sort of surgical incision into the prospective unity of these underclasses. Divide children by subject, by age-grading, by constant rankings on tests, and by many other more subtle means, and it was unlikely that the ignorant mass of mankind, separated in childhood, would ever reintegrate into a dangerous whole." Inglis' basic functions of school follow:

6 basic functions of school

"1) The *adjustive* or *adaptive* function.

Schools are to establish fixed habits of reaction to authority. This, of

---

[18] http://theinnovativeeducator.blogspot.co.uk/2013/02/6-principals-of-secondary-education.html p.1

course, precludes critical judgement completely. It also pretty much destroys the idea that useful or interesting material should be taught, because you can't test for reflexive obedience until you know whether you can make kids learn, and do, foolish and boring things.

2) The *integrating* function. (conformity)

This might well be called "the conformity function," because its intention is to make children as alike as possible. People who conform are predictable, and this is of great use to those who wish to harness and manipulate a large labour force.

3) The *diagnostic and directive* function.

School is meant to determine each student's proper social role. This is done by logging evidence mathematically and anecdotally on cumulative records. As in "your permanent record." Yes, you do have one.

4) The *differentiating* function. (sorting)

Once their social role has been "diagnosed," children are to be sorted by role and trained only so far as their destination in the social machine merits – and not one step further. So much for making kids their personal best.

5) The *selective* function. (hygienic function)

This refers not to human choice at all but to Darwin's theory of natural selection as applied to what he called "the favoured races." In short, the idea is to help things along by consciously attempting to improve the breeding stock. Schools are meant to tag the unfit – with poor grades, remedial placement, and other punishments – clearly enough that their peers will accept them as inferior and effectively bar them from the reproductive sweepstakes. That's what all those little humiliations from first grade onward were intended to do: wash the dirt down the drain.

6) The *propaedeutic* function.

The societal system implied by these rules will require an elite group of caretakers. To that end, a small fraction of the kids will quietly be taught how to manage this continuing project, how to watch over and control a population deliberately dumbed down and declawed in order that government might proceed unchallenged and corporations might never want for obedient labour."

In 1924, the great H.L. Mencken wrote for *The American Mercury,* that the aim of public education is not: to fill the young of the species with knowledge and awaken their intelligence. . . . Nothing could be further from the truth. The aim.. . is simply to reduce as many individuals as possible to the same safe level, to breed and train a standardized citizenry, to put down dissent and originality. That is its aim in the United States . . . and that is its aim everywhere else."[19]

In 1959, a well-read book-length essay, *The Child the Parent and the State*, by James Bryant Conant, mentions in passing that the modern schools we attend were the result of a "revolution" engineered between 1905 and 1930. There are no real details but those years coincide with the inception of a few think-tank social engineering institutions which we will discuss in later chapters.

The reality is, no matter what angle of social engineering for a cultural revolution in the 20th century we discuss, we will and must always bring the effects back to how these saturated the schools. Remember, imprisoning the children is the primary goal of the opposition.

As we make our way through the discussions in every chapter, we will see how a social and emotional vacuum was created for the 'schools' to fill. The scientific and industrial revolutions added the horrors of behaviourism and the industrial organization structures of factories and assembly line concepts to the schools.

As mentioned, a few select and thoroughly suspicious social

---

[19]   http://www.quebecoislibre.org/08/080915-11.htm p.1

engineering think tanks came into being and garnered unheard of power over populations, social structures and governments with all of their schemes for social control launched in? The schools. The facts are inarguable. In the end the family, the parent, has been removed from the raising of the child. There is a term referring to the power that the 'schools' have usurped. *In loco parentis.* In the place of the parent.

From an article on mind control by Jeffrey Steinberg comes a telling passage attributed to a piece written by Lord Bertrand Russell, one of the founders of the Tavistock Institute, wraps it up for the 20th century;

"Russell had been working on the concept of the scientific dictatorship for decades. In his 1931 book, *The Scientific Outlook,* he had devoted a chapter to ``**Education in a Scientific Society.**" Here, he was equally blunt about his oligarchical totalitarian vision. Drawing the parallel to the two levels of education provided by the Jesuits, Russell asserted: "In like manner, the scientific rulers will provide one kind of education for ordinary men and women, and another for those who are to become holders of scientific power. Ordinary men and women will be expected to be docile, industrious, punctual, thoughtless, and contented. Of these qualities probably contentment will be considered the most important. In order to produce it, all the researches of psycho-analysis, behaviourism, and biochemistry will be brought into play.... All the boys and girls will learn from an early age to be what is called `co-operative,' i.e., to do exactly what everybody is doing. Initiative will be *discouraged* in these children, and insubordination, without being punished, will be scientifically trained out of them.[20]

For the children chosen to be among the scientific ruling class, education was to be quite different. "Except for the one matter of loyalty to

---

[20]   Steinberg, J. 2000. From Cybernetics to ittleton: Techniques in Mind Control. http://www.schillerinstitute.org/new_viol/cybmindcontrol_js0400..html p.1

the world State and to their own order," Russell explained, "members of the governing class will be encouraged to be adventurous and full of initiative. It will be recognized that it is their business to improve scientific technique, and to keep the manual workers contented by means of continual new amusements."[21]

Sadly, the school system has been mined ever deeper from the year 2000, when George W. Bush took over the White House. There was his No Child Left Behind plan, in which schools were paid according to the number of minutes a child was in school. Children began to forget what the playground looked like as elementary school struggled to meet criminal standards of conformity. Time at the drinking fountain was considered to be time lost. In fact, the application of constant, relentless pressure from internal and external sources with no time for recreation is a tremendously effective mind-control technique.

Some of the subject matter that is clearly completely inappropriate and actually provably and legally abusive will be visited in other chapters. The new wave of Common Core, against which legions of educators who simply can no longer sleep at night are fighting, brings the punishment down to the very toes of the children.

And I want to note that in 2009, the Council on Foreign Relations made direct attempts to usurp the functioning of the schools. Here's what their report said:

"The lack of preparedness poses threats on five national security fronts: economic growth and competitiveness, physical safety, intellectual property, U.S. global awareness, and U.S. unity and cohesion, says the report. Too many young people are not employable in an increasingly high-skilled and global economy, and **too many are not qualified to join the military** because they are physically unfit, have criminal records, or have

---

[21] *Ibid.*

an inadequate level of education.

Human capital will determine power in the current century, and the failure to produce that capital will undermine America's security," the report states. "Large, undereducated swaths of the population damage the ability of the United States to physically defend itself, protect its secure information, conduct diplomacy, and grow its economy."[22]

Security? Physically defend itself? Too many are not qualified to join the military? Human capital? Could this be because if we step away from the brainwashing apparati for a moment, we may decide not to be part of the killing machine?

Yet, any subject that truly develops critical thinking and independent, imaginative skills is being diluted and removed from the state curriculum...

There is so much to say. It will all be said under the various headings. Primary to remember is, Plato. Calvin. Spinosa. Fichte. Mann, Inglis....Let them **NOT IMAGINE. I Mage In.**

I Mage In. What power, what human co-creative power then, lies in the imagination? Facts, history, are devised, written, rewritten and rewritten by the plantation managers on behalf of the Predator. Let them imagine, and they can free themselves. I Mage In. The Predator knows this all too well.

One of the ways our innate human nature works for and against us is in what John Lash calls the concept of neotony. In other words, we are born with very unfinished systems – brain, emotions, senses and so on -- and so it is imperative to the Predator to get us away from our families, from our mothers especially, so that what goes in is what THEY want to go

---

[22]   CFR: US Educational Reform and National Security.
http://www.cfr.org/united-states/us-education-reform-national-security/p27618

in and it is all damaging. Neoteny allows us to be submitted to massive behavioural programming when we are the most vulnerable. You may see this reminder in each chapter, as well go along, because it is absolutely critical that we realize this. [23]

There has been nothing more important for the enemy than disconnecting the human imagination; I Mage In. I am the Magician and what I manifest, I bring 'in,' I incarnate. This is the open secret. That and the knowledge of the sacred word, which is not yes, it is No. Stopping the madness really is as easy as remembering the sacred word, imagining something better and different, and allowing the critical mass principle to work. It has been proved over and over again that once a certain number of living beings 'know' something, suddenly they *all* do. This is why raising the consciousness of our plight is so important; more important than waging war against the enemy. Turn your attention from their distractions. Turn off your television set if you do nothing else.

We can raise consciousness, put down the toys they stuck in our hands, walk away, refuse to join their military, join a home school community, or support artistically driven schools, such as Waldorf schools, and so forth. Rudolf Steiner developed the Waldorf school in 1919 specifically as an antidote to compulsory state schooling. Form a co-op of parents and develop a home-school or unschooling group. Just be cognizant of who is involved and vet everyone for safety as many of the psy-ops run on us over the last hundred years have poisoned us individually, seeking to turn us on our own children.

NB: If you currently reside in a country which outlaws homeschooling, such as Germany, please find ways to create and/or support alternative pedagogies and curricula. It is not enough to transplant the state formula into a smaller school for it is the formula itself which is to blame.

---

[23] Lash, John. Perspectives on the War on Terror, Environmental Distaster, and GlobalManipulationhttp://www.metahistory.org/gnostique/telestics/GnosticLens.php p.1

One has only to reassure the 'state' that goals are being met. The rest can be approached as creatively, as organically, and as imaginatively as can be conceived. There are no limits to the human imagination, there are no limits to what a child can learn through the arts, there are no limits to the capacity of the human memory. These are simply muscles that needs to be exercised.

Further Reading

Dillon, Ariel. Education in Plato's Republic
http://www.scu.edu/ethics/publications/submitted/dillon/education_plato_re
public.html

Plato, *The Republic.*

http://johntaylorgatto.com/

Underground History of American Education by John Taylor Gatto online
to read: *http://johntaylorgatto.com/chapters/index.htm*

Source of English text: Johann Gottlieb Fichte, **Address to the German
Nation**,ed.,George Armstrong Kelly. New York and Evanston: Harper &
Row Publishers, 1968, pp. 92-129. Source of original German text: J. G.
Fichte, Gesamtausgabe Werkeband 10[Complete Works Volume 10].
Stuttgart - Bad Cannstatt: F. Frommann, 1988-2000, pp.183-212.

Other books by Gatto:
Weapons of Mass Instruction
Dumbing Us Down
On The Scientific Management of Children: A Short Angry History

And so forth.

**Council on Foreign Relations US Education Reform and National
Security**
http://www.cfr.org/united-states/us-education-reform-national-
security/p27618

Sheldon Richman, **Separating Schools and State, How to Liberate American Families.** Future of Freedom Foundation 1994

Prof. Alexander Inglis's, *Principles of Secondary Education* 1918

James Bryant Conan, *The Child the Parent and the State,* 1959

Homeschooling http://en.wikipedia.org/wiki/Homeschooling (every state has a large group with a multitude of smaller, local groups)

Unschooling http://www.naturalchild.org/guest/earl_stevens.html

What is Waldorf Education?
http://www.whywaldorfworks.org/02_W_Education/
AWSNA American Waldorf Schools of North America awsna.org
Waldorf or Steiner schools in every country around the world as the fastest growing new educational paradigm on the planet. (Be aware, that Waldorf/Steiner strongly discourages the use of or exposure to the media until the age of 12. Be aware, also, that I, as a Waldorf/Steiner teacher with three children came to it late and had to backpedal with my children because I was unlearning the brainwashing with which I had grown up. You can do this, too).

Chapter Two

"The unexamined belief is not worth holding."

Give me a baby and I can make any kind of man. This statement is attributed to Dr. John B. Watson, pioneer researcher in human behaviour at Johns Hopkins University. Before we proceed with the investigative strand of this chapter, I am going to point out that much the same sentiment was expressed by Ignatius Loyola, the founder of the Jesuits, master social manipulators and power-mongers. There is a bit of a debate as to the exact wording. I wonder how much that really matters as they are all horrifying in exactly the same measure. I think it is useful to put them all here:

"Give me the child, and I will mould the man." [24]

"Give me the child for seven years, and I will give you the man."

"Give me the child until he is seven and I care not who has him thereafter."

"Give me the child till the age of seven and I will show you the man."

If one understands, as we will discuss, that the child is very much 'not born' in most of the fundamental ways but rather lives very much in symbiotic etheric contact with the mother until about the age of seven then we understand that the child is actually that vulnerable and we meet these statements in true comprehension. Obviously, the Jesuits

---

[24] It is of interest to the author that not only has this maxim been ascribed to Loyola and to Dr. John Watson, the behaviourist, but something eerily similar has been ascribed to V.I. Lenin: Give me four years to teach the children and the seed I have sown will never be uprooted. -- Vladimir Ilyich Lenin - See more at: http://thepeoplescube.com/lenin/lenin-s-own-20-monster-quotes-t185.html#sthash.43xhs4Zx.dpuf

understood this perfectly well. That first seven years is almost all.

With that in mind, let us also be aware that the 20th century gave birth to another link in the belief chain that binds us: the science of behaviourism. One of the chief purveyors of this line of scientific inquiry was Dr. John B. Watson. Simply put he 'discovered' that he could teach babies 'fear' by conditioning. Watson observed that newborn babies had no fear of the dark – they had no innate fear of animals, etc. However, he also discovered that could easily *make them* fear anything.

Before we shake hands with Dr. Watson, however, it is useful to note that the science of behaviourism stands on pillars of probably genuinely clean and ethical scientific research which came just prior. As with all things, in the wrong hands, bad things happen. There is always someone ready to use information to gain control over the human beings on this planet. That requires a discussion, however brief, of primary psychopathy. That will come later. It also begs another mention of the broad idea of black magic, the darkness out of which manipulation can operate: maybe? Consider the following,

"The ultimate danger...is civil disobedience: people massively refusing to cooperate, and the government not being able to enforce its political decisions anymore, — with its own agents refusing to enforce its edicts against people, and people being ready to fight back against anyone trying to enforce them. That's why governments will actively campaign to prevent their opponents from coordinating an overthrow: constant propaganda through media and education control, harassment of potential high-profile dissenters, denial of working conditions, hefty fines and imprisonment for those who do not cooperate with the system (which begins with paying taxes), etc. Measures of this kind are necessary to keep the government exploitation going..." [25] Behaviourism and its mechanisms, refined to a dark and powerful art, would become the essential tools of the

---

[25] Government is the Rule of Black Magic. p.1 http://vortexcourage.me/2014/09/28/government-is-the-rule-of-black-magic-part-one/

few seeking to control the many.

To be fair, and to continue with the original discussion, we must include another fellow and his minions here. That will be Dr. Franz Boas, inventor of 'modern anthropology,' most of which is an additional exercise in manipulation of our minds and energies with fabricated constructs.[26] It is a shame because there is a reasonable and rich human study there. Unfortunately anthropology started with a lie that served a political agenda and still, all too often does.

Regardless, in our sites first is poor old Julius Von Sachs. This is a scientist who collated and tested and re-announced the age-old wisdom that plants react to stimuli and manoeuvre themselves within their environment in order to take advantage of conditions for their optimum well-being. No doubt, had we approached a farmer 2,000 years ago, and asked, he could have told us this, too. Life adjusts itself to its environment in order to reap maximum benefit and thrive. This is its nature. The inverse can also be stated: if possible, life avoids that which causes it to weaken or even fail. It is this simple but primary paradigm that allowed the behaviourists and their masters to attempt to take over the world and all life upon it. They simply conducted *in situ* experiments in places where we were mandated to be, such as our 'schools,' our hospitals, our universities – which are largely a playground constructed to keep us as far away from enlightenment as possible, and our legal and political systems. Full spectrum dominance.

Nevertheless, Dr. Julius Von Sachs fleshed out this idea and classified the phenomena under the heading of 'tropisms.' [27] What made this

---

[26] For example, see this: Roberto J. Gonzalez. *Towards mercenary anthropology? The new US Army counterinsurgency manual FM 3–24 and the military-anthropology complex* Anthropology Today, Volume 23, Issue 3, p 14-19 June 2007 Examples such as this abound.

[27] Julius Von Sachs, 1832-1897. http://embryo.asu.edu/pages/julius-von-sachs-

identification truly important was the following: in the historical development of botany, plants were conceptualized in a very rigid way in terms of science until the beginning of the last century. This matters because the characterization of all life and what constitutes life matters. In fact, the push to define 'life' has been an unstoppable steamroller with the goals of characterization, location and control. Had plants not mattered as much as they do, and the life they contain, there would be no Monsanto.

Aristotle postulated the theory that plants were 'fixed' to a certain spot and had no sensitivity (but then Aristotle also devised and codified the system of hierarchy, an unnatural system of thinking in the world that scleroticizes and suffocates the life in life). That is how old the notion is. According to Aristotle, whether or not something is alive depends on whether it moves by some innate principle of will. Therefore, there is always speculation as to what is a plant and what is an animal. What is life; what is alive? This is a big deal when the Predator wants to convince us that some things are acceptable when we know, in our deepest intuition, they are not. The mimicry of life is one of its primary goals.

By the way, a **tropism** is a biological phenomenon, indicating growth or turning movement of a biological organism, usually a plant, in response to an environmental stimulus. In tropisms, this response is dependent on the direction of the stimulus. (Feel free to blow the dry dust off the technical definition). And, from the Encyclopedia Britannica: "Julius Von Sachs...was...a German botanist whose experimental study of nutrition, tropism, and transpiration of water greatly advanced the knowledge of plant physiology, and the cause of experimental biology in general, during the second half of the 19th century."[28]

Sachs' research data led, by proxy, to the development of a stable of insects, known as 'durable machines,' collected and researched by Sachs' protegee, Jacques Loeb. Loeb, "constructed a stable of creatures he called

---

1832-1897 p.1

[28]   http://www.britannica.com/EBchecked/topic/515271/Julius-von-Sachs

"durable machines" in his laboratory at the University of Chicago: two-headed marine worms, metamorphosed slime moulds, hydras with mouth and anus reversed, and artificially propagated sea urchins. (For this last, he was known as the instigator of a new virgin birth in the lab and was nominated for the Nobel Prize.) Both men inspired awe in their day, one as a wizard, the other as a prophet, and both brought assembly-line-like methods to biological processes. But it is Loeb's self-proclaimed "technology of living substance" that provides an understanding of the birth of human engineering in America."[29]

For the purposes of discussion in this chapter, Loeb is part of a trail that leads next to one, John Watson and his contemporary, Ivan Pavlov. Loeb, as a student, conducted brain function experiments on animals that led to the conclusion that animals would adapt without the luxury of possessing intact brains. Pavlov, as we tend to be aware, moved squarely into the realm of experimentation with the behaviour of animal subjects, most notably the dog.

"Tropisms always began on the outside of the creature they affected, manifesting themselves through the involuntary workings of the response mechanism as a shifting, a twitching, a pulling, or a turning. Such machinelike creatures had no 'inner' contents: no will, no strivings, no conscience of their own." (Loeb)[30] Perhaps it is this 'thinking' or erroneous definition of life that allows the Predator to conduct massive experiments in manipulation of large human populations without ever considering whether or not it should be done. The definition of life is convenient for such.

As stated, the very definition of life is what was at stake. It's one thing to conduct an experiment on a chair. It is quite another to conduct the same experiment on a child. Those lines were blurred, then erased, as a matter of both convenience and power. It may well be, since many of the

[29] New York Times. http://www.nytimes.com/2006/02/12/books/chapters/0212-1st-lemov.html?pagewanted=print&_r=0 p.1

[30] *Ibid*

practitioners of these sciences and modes of operating one upon the other in this world, are or were primary psychopaths, that the application of behavioural methods to human beings and the 'successful' outcomes indicated that there was no will, no conscience, and no striving. That conclusion certainly would ease the path of horrific manipulation.

Unlike the pseudo-science of psychiatric analysis, for which no true scientific investigation was ever conducted or provided, there were an ocean of behavioural experiments conducted from the beginning of the 20th century onward. That a person's behaviour can be modified and controlled is not really open to debate. It is, however, horrifying in many ways that such great lengths were gone to to establish this and its subsequent crowd control uses. There were some very key, "who the hell do you people think you are?" moments in and around the 20th century. This was certainly one of them.

Despite them being contemporaries, one must mention Ivan Pavlov before one moves on to John Watson because Watson often cited Pavlov's work in his own research. Pavlov did not really come first. While Ivan Pavlov was not a psychologist, and reportedly disliked the field of psychology altogether, his work had a major influence on the field, particularly on the development of behaviourism. His discovery and research on reflexes influenced the infant behaviourist movement.[31] Other researchers utilized Pavlov's work in the study of conditioning as a form of learning. His research also demonstrated techniques of studying reactions to the environment in an objective, scientific method. This was tropism applied to animals and, ipso facto, to human beings.

The most obvious example of Pavlovian training can be seen at each and every American middle and secondary school, as children jump up and move to the ringing of a bell, in the very same manner as Pavlov's dog and for the very same reason. Even if half a dozen or more specific class subjects taught by separate teachers were absolutely necessary, which

[31]   http://www.britannica.com/EBchecked/topic/447349/Ivan-Petrovich-Pavlov

54

they are not, in terms of learning and calm concentration, moving teachers rather than crowds of children is what makes more sense. Hence the ringing bell and the stampeding chaos is, in fact, a training in compliance for the captive children. "...the purpose of state schooling was *not intellectual training but the conditioning of children* "to obedience, subordination, and collective life." Thus, *memorization outranked thinking*... whole ideas were broken into fragmented "subjects" and school days were divided into fixed periods "so that self-motivation to learn would be muted by ceaseless interruptions."...signalled by the ringing of the Pavlovian bell.[32] Is this sonotropism; movement or growth in response to sound? Yes. Most importantly, this is Classic Conditioning.[33] Furthermore, the changing of classes once every forty minutes and landing with a different mix of students trains children to have little tolerance for a stable group, or sameness. They are indeed trained to have shorter and shorter attention spans.

Finally, we arrive at the infamous Dr. Watson. As noted, his experiments were conducted at Johns Hopkins University in Baltimore, Maryland, on living human babies. The simplest way to make a baby fear something, he found, was to make a loud, sudden noise behind them when they were engaging with whatever the good doctor wanted them to fear; for example, petting a rabbit. Where once the baby delighted in the warm, soft fur of a gentle bunny rabbit, now the baby shrieked in terror when the rabbit was brought before him or her. Success...I guess. Bear in mind, this was done in the name of science, and *that* god dictated all in the 20th century. Nothing remained sacred or imperturbable. No ambient human quality, precious capacity or sacred power was left undamaged. Make no mistake, science is just another religion with a specific set of belief systems and, unless you understand the math or the other pertinent science well

[32] Richman, S. *Separating School and State:How to Liberate American Families.* Ch.3, p.1. http://www.sntp.net/education/school_state_3.htm
[33] Pavlov's Dogs. http://www.simplypsychology.org/pavlov.html p.1

enough to verify findings, you are simply placing your belief in the 20th century god. Simple.

Through these experiments, Watson formulated a pivotal theory that was one of the foundations of 20th century social and cultural engineering – he claimed that the primary motivator for human beings is fear. Ipso facto, if you want a human being to do or not do something, scare them. [34]

Sound familiar? This is Dread, 'D' number 3 of our 3Ds. We do not come into this world embracing fear. It is **taught** to us. Subsequently, our Dr. Watson postulated that, because he could make a baby fear anything he wanted it to fear, human beings were controllable. Behaviour is predictable. They respond according to various tropism paradigms. Therefore, people are controllable. True enough. Good news for those who wanted nothing more than to be in control.

In the end, the behaviour game was dominated in the 20th century by one figure: B.F. Skinner. Skinner postulated that all behaviour was controllable (as they all did) and that there was no free will: everything humans did therefore must be a reflex or reaction to stimulus. This is the conclusion we speculated about previously. This does not conform to that aforementioned definition of life...movement based on intrinsic will. And so, on the verge of being utterly objectified, we were pushed over that cliff. According to Skinner's paradigms we aren't even truly alive. Interestingly, the top echelon of psychopaths who seek to rule this world are constantly trying to destroy the collective will of the people so someone understands it does exist, the will, even if we are being convinced it does not.

Burrhus Frederic Skinner was an American psychologist, behaviourist, author and inventor of apparati for human experimentation. He taught with some notoriety at Harvard University until 1974. Good consequences, bad consequences...outcomes were all a matter of

---

[34]   Cherry, Kendra. The Little Albert Experiment: A Closer Look.
        http://psychology.about.com/od/classicpsychologystudies/a/little-albert-experiment.htm p.1

56

reinforcement. This is the moment it seems that the idea of things that are true and false at the same time came to the fore. Yes, we find that proper behaviour elicits a positive outcome and vice versa but it is not because we are an agent whose free will is an illusion. These things don't go together; the foundation is deeply flawed. The shaky foundation did much, though, to convince the population that what was being done to them and around them was okay. It also served as a 'get out of jail free' card for the abusers. That was critical. [35]

As an author, Skinner produced a novel in 1948 called *Walden Two*, that explained his philosophy very simply. It is a supposed utopian novel, which I imagine depends on what one's definition of utopia is, presenting the idea of applied behaviour analysis. **The characters reject free will and the proposition that behaviour has anything to do with a spirit or a soul. Systematically altering environmental variables produces an engineered sociocultural system.** Skinner's work was, at first, quite controversial. His operant principles, behaviour modification..the creation of sterile, neutral terms for an absolute invasion of sovereignty. Skinner referred to these principles as 'healing.' Healing of what and to whom? Healing meaning 'no independent or creative behaviour will be tolerated.' Healing meaning Imagination is a disease.

These behavioural science paradigms that became entrenched were a ghoulish foundation for the psychiatric operators at the Tavistock Institute later on. The behaviour modification paradigm worked well for the Frankfurt School, as well.

Another major player in 20th century behaviourism was Hobart Mowrer. His speciality was Operant Conditioning. "The principles of operant conditioning have taught us to recognize how certain coping techniques can reward, and therefore continue anxiety disorders. Two

[35] McLeod, Saul. *Free Will and Determinism in Psychology.*
http://www.simplypsychology.org/freewill-determinism.html

similar coping strategies for dealing with anxiety symptoms are called *avoidance* and *escape*...

...As the name implies, *avoidance* refers to behaviours that attempt to prevent exposure to a fear-provoking stimulus. *Escape* means to quickly exit a fear-provoking situation. These coping strategies are considered **maladaptive** (as opposed to the so-called 'normal' fight or flight response?) because they ultimately serve to maintain the disorder and decrease functioning. Operant conditioning enables us to understand the powerful impact of these two coping strategies. Both coping strategies are highly reinforcing because they remove or diminish the unpleasant symptoms. Unfortunately, they do nothing to prevent the symptoms from re-occurring again and again in the future."[36]

It is also true that this system was used to direct the behaviour of individuals and populations through the 'development and maintenance of phobias.' One would hope that this paradigm of operant conditioning would be applied solely to alleviating recipes for anxiety. However, the reverse is also true. They can and have very much been applied to creating anxiety and trauma.

"In 1947, O. Hobart Mowrer proposed his two-factor theory of avoidance learning to explain **the development and maintenance of phobias**. Mowrer's two-factor theory combined the learning principles of classical (Pavlovian) and operant conditioning. Based upon the principles of classical conditioning, it was assumed that phobias develop as a result of a paired association between a neutral stimulus and feared stimulus. (Thank you Dr. Watson for creating so effectively feared stimuli and teaching us how to populate our consciousness with them). However, classical learning theory could not explain the continuation of avoidance

---

[36]   Matthew D. Jacofsky, Psy.D., Melanie T. Santos, Psy.D., Sony Khemlani-Patel, Ph.D. & Fugen Neziroglu, Ph.D. of the Bio Behavioral Institute, edited by C.E. Zupanick, Psy.D. and Mark Dombeck, Ph.D. *Operant Conditioning and Avoidance Learning*

58

and escape behaviours. These behaviours often led to further distress and interference in a person's life such as: 1) the avoidance of pleasurable activities; 2) the inability to engage in daily activities and responsibilities; and 3) the inability to maintain interpersonal relationships.

"The second stage of Mowrer's model attempted to explain why people felt so compelled to avoid anxiety-provoking stimuli; or failing that, escape from the stimuli. The answer comes from Skinner's theory of operant conditioning and the environmental rewards produced by these coping strategies. Mowrer proposed that the escape from anxiety-provoking stimuli resulted in the removal of unpleasant emotions. Thus, avoidance becomes a reward and increases the behaviour of avoidance. For example, an individual with social anxiety will feel a significant decrease in anxiety once he or she decides to avoid attending a large social event. This avoidance results in the removal of the unpleasant anxiety symptoms thereby reinforcing avoidance behaviour. As such, it becomes the person's preferred method of coping with future social events. Similarly, suppose this same person attempted to go to a party, despite his/her reservations, and experienced a panic attack while there. If this person immediately exited the party, the panic will subside, and the behaviour of escape will be rewarded by the swift reduction in panic symptoms. Avoidance and escape are called negative reinforcement.[37] The removal of unpleasant symptoms leads to an increase in that behaviour."

So, now we verified scientifically that when one's hand is burned in a fire, so to speak, one removes the hand and hopefully does not re-insert it. However, techniques were developed to tie this basic human response into a psychotic, trauma and anxiety-ridden pretzel in order to

---

37 Operant Conditioning and Avoidance Learning Matthew D. Jacofsky, Psy.D., Melanie T. Santos, Psy.D., Sony Khemlani-Patel, Ph.D. & Fugen Neziroglu, Ph.D. of the Bio Behavioral Institute, edited by C.E. Zupanick, Psy.D. and Mark Dombeck, Ph.D.

achieve some desired response. On a more sinister level, the response was not a one-off but rather an emotional environment or personality, something with which a human being has to then cope.

It is all well and good to be confronted with a pathology and then analyse it. It is another thing altogether to use it to destroy people and populations. This was part of the background to the Korean War, as so many other things were. Much work was done in the realm of mind control using this simple paradigm/technique.[38] It was a terrible moment in the history of the 20th century, a moment when the hurtle down the well-greased slope toward the complete demoralization of behaviour via behaviourism began. The twisted definition of life, the conclusion that humanity has no intrinsic will or conscience and therefore does not even meet the criteria of 'life,' granted permission to manipulate us, who must, after all, be soul-less, (if there is a soul). Thus was prepared the road to Hell. It is, of course, the fertile field which produced the 3Ds of which we have spoken.

Speaking strictly about making us obey, which is the point, a fairly recent and often used example of how we as a whole have been bent toward obedience to those in certain positions of authority is the following:

"...the Milgram Experiment ties in nicely with this concept. If you are unfamiliar with this experiment, in 1961, on the heels of certain Nazi war crimes trials, a psychologist named Stanley Milgram conducted this experiment across a range of 40 individuals to test their response to authoritative pressure. They were directed by the experimenter to deliver what they believed to be real electric shocks to another participant (actually an actor). The results shocked everyone. Only 1.2% of individuals were predicted to administer the highest voltage (450 volts); 26 of the 40 participants (65%)—some with clearly conflicted consciences—delivered

---

[38] Exerpt. The Search for the Manchurian Candidate: The CIA and Mind Control, by John Marks ©, New York: Times Books, 1979. Chapter 8.
http://www.conspiracyarchive.com/NWO/Manchurian_Can8.htm

this lethal electric shock. The only duress placed on the subjects was verbal cueing from a man in a white lab coat! You can imagine the disastrous results derived from the combination of conscience-lacking psychopaths as the authorities in executive power circles and the masses of people obeying such "authority" blindly in such large proportions." [39]

So. Answer? Sachs. Loeb. Pavlov. Watson. Skinner. Mowrer. Questions? Who stole our confidence in our own souls, free will and competence? Who stole our natural personality and integrated human psyche, created a void where it had comfortably resided, and replaced it with torment at one level or another? There are others who helped, I assure you. We will soon meet them.

These things never went away. We were, at the ring of a dog's dinner bell, taught to 'not see' them. In the vacuum created, many things just as bad for us as dog's dinner were inserted. If anything, the programming gets worse, more fine-tuned, easier to apply with hellish results for humanity.

It's been about not only discovering how to manipulate humans based on what's inherently human but about creating explanations – manufacturing so-called sciences and their theories – that might justify the recreation of human society (human resources) to benefit the elite. Scratch that. I no longer refer to them as the elite for the only thing 'special' about them is what they lack. I do not refer to them as the Illuminati for they are not enlightened. I refer to them, singly and collectively, as The Predator. We have moved from behaviourists to cybernetician.

The 20th century behaviourists demonstrated that it is possible to describe laws of human behaviour, despite Franz Boas' hysterically insistent postulate that there was no such thing as a basic human nature. There are laws of human nature from which it is possible to derive general

[39]   McLeod, Saul. *The Milgram Experiment.* http://www.simplypsychology.org/milgram.html. p.1

principles of behaviour and a tool-kit to go with it called behavioural engineering. The blueprint requires that general laws of human behaviour be identified specific to desired actions and then social rules, such as those of political correctness, be set in place with appropriate punishments for breaking those rules.

From the rules, they say, an orderly society is manifested. This order is seldom if ever used as an explanation to justify the rules to follow — what matters is acceptance. Engineered consent. People to follow the orders in an ordered society are indispensable. **Behaviourists** discovered how we can be controlled. Cyberneticians are interested in the rules: what they are, what they can be, how to change them, what blueprints to use to elicit different behaviour, and so forth. Cyberneticians pay close attention to the potential of a situation, various forms of feedback, what works and what doesn't. Behaviour Engineering.[40]

Next Question: Who stole our self-respect and reverence for ourselves as rightful and deserving co-creators of the universe, sacred children of Sophia? Via an Infection, seemingly introduced to our individual and group bodies via behavioural engineering, and which has crossed so many boundaries, joining and separating and reuniting, enslavement has taken up residence. It is an Infection which has hidden our power from us, temporarily.

Doing just as much damage to perception, the environment and a natural social fabric, was the advent of the 20th century phenomenon of 'anthropology.' It is difficult to know quite where to place the early anthropologists because their profession was used deeply in behaviourist circles, in psychiatric circles, and in social and cultural engineering circles. It seems, after some thought, best to bring them up right away. The founding anthropologists, much like the social and behavioural laboratories which masquerade as schools, will come back over and over again. There

---

[40] The Macy Conferences. http://www.fornits.com/phpbb/index.php?topic=32643.0

are a few in the cast of characters who will, as well. Anthropology produced tools and programs used by all malevolent entities and the subsequent mind-control programs were run in schools. They are embedded one inside the other.

What we know as anthropology today was formulated and codified by Franz Boas and his followers, who included the famous Margaret Mead.[41] Franz Boas, often called the grandfather of modern anthropology, probably ranks with Karl Marx and Sigmund Freud as one of the most influential thinkers of the modern age. Note, I aid 'influential,' not beneficial. It is a pair of 20th century handcuffs we put on when we assume that influence is good. It is, after all, just manipulation of a sort. A Columbia University professor from 1899 to 1942, the students he trained dominated the discipline until recently. Boas has been accused in recent decades of both shading his data to support conclusions he wished to see and of creating little tableaus of 'scientific enquiry,' such as Margaret Mead's early studies, which have proved to be thoroughly fraudulent.

Cultural anthropology is, indeed and probably quite obviously, behaviourism. It is purely the study of various cultures (external influences) and how that directs behaviour in human beings. On the one hand, Boas insisted that there were no differences in human beings based on race. This was in response to the idea of cranial characteristics; the suggestion that different races had different cranial capacities and so forth. Thankfully, we don't need to settle this debate in this piece. It's somewhat beside the point. It simply has to be noted that this was one of the driving forces behind Boas' work.

"Boas was a foreign transplant. He arrived in America in 1886 already imbued with radical ideas, and like so many radical immigrants, hating America even before his feet left the gangplank.[32] He became one of

---

[41]   http://en.wikipedia.org/wiki/Franz_Boas p.1

[32] *Margaret Mead and the Heretic* by Derek Freeman, published by Penguin Press.

63

a rising generation of young scholars, many of them Jewish immigrants like himself, who were hostile to America's Anglo-Saxon establishment and who were bent on subverting its values. Once he had established himself at Columbia University, Boas began his political campaign by nurturing a following of admiring students, many of them women, who would go on to become apostles of his new approach to social analysis which would do so much to subvert traditional social values and sexual morality."[42]

He also took on the notion of adolescence and what might be responsible for creating what he saw as a miserable human being in the teenage years. Franz Boas, his disciples, and other like-minded academics launched a full-scale intellectual war against the notion of cultural hierarchy, the idea that cultures could be graded or ranked on a scale of comparison. They questioned all standards of classification, they denied that there was any intrinsic difference between the races, they revived the debate about nature and nurture. Unlike the behaviourists and cyberneticians, **the early anthropologists denied that there was any such thing as universal "human nature"**. It was, in short, a supporting role assault on Western standards and values. This is where a political agenda inserted itself into 20th century social science. These statements are what is often referred to as a truth sandwich. We can happily agree for such a long way through the thought process and then, suddenly, we bite into the lie or the issue. Maybe if we put a little 'mustard' on it, and wash it down with a cola, the lie in the middle of the truth sandwich goes down mostly unnoticed.

In this case, it is the conclusion that there is no such thing as 'human nature.' We have not got, according to Boas, anything fundamental that characterizes us as brothers and sisters on the planet. This is incredibly interesting in light of the fact that Boas was emphatic that there are no biological differences among the races. Hence there would have to be, by

---

[42]   http://www.mcadamreport.org/The%20McAdam%20Report%28513%29-04-19-05.pdf p. 19

definition, our biology in common if nothing else. What we have, solely, are out differences. If we truly bought that paradigm, we would basically have to postulate that there are hundreds of different homonid species on earth because we have nothing basic in common. Incoherent nonsense, yet fundamental to this anthropology. The name itself is even incoherent based on the territory the field took over. Anthropos...humanity. 'Ology...' Biology? Sociology? Psychology? What exactly is it? I think it is closest to call it an 'Apology.' Especially when honing in on the specific cultural anthropology. Humanity's Apology. Apology for humanity? In fact, adding 'osophy' as in 'Sophia,' comes much closer to our true and actual history. No culture has any need for Apologists.

It may be that this is where the idea of nature versus nurture (Boas came down on the side of nurture), would come into play. If nurture is all, then we have only the biological machine at birth. But there must be a seed of some sort, raw human material which can be shaped by this 'nurturing,' one way or the other. It is incoherent to state that there is no such thing as human nature even if we can only say that what we have in common is the ability to be nurtured. If we accept Skinner's ideas that 'all behaviour is controllable and that there was no free will: everything humans did therefore must be a reflex or reaction to stimulus,' we cannot accept that there is no such thing as human nature. We could say, if we wanted to do so, that human nature is, in fact, to come into this world without fear (John Watson), and to be completely shape-able and controllable via outside training forces (a la Pavlov) and to be nurturable (Boas). There must be, therefore, something intrinsically human, some capacity and potential, that we all share. However it is that we can be made to dance to the tune of the Predator, it is because we have a very identifiable, predictable and trusting human nature. Indeed, it is most available for abuse until the age of seven. (Which does not mean we are safe thereafter).

And, we must insist on including the study of epigenetics from now on in any evaluation of humans on this planet. We can be changed by outside environmental scenarios at a DNA level within two generations. This has been proved. Hence, 'nature' does indeed play as unequivocal a role in our formation as does 'nurture' and that means we have a baseline human nature. It is also a matter of how vulnerable we are when we arrive, more baseline human nature, and how important that is to Us and to Them.

It seems that Boas formed a construct – was presented with or wanted to present a conclusion – and then shaped and twisted data to support it. "Anthropologist David Thomas, curator of anthropology at the American Museum of Natural History in New York, tells the *Times* "once we anthropologists said race doesn't exist, we have ignored it it since then," but now, the reappraisal of Boas` work "really does have far-reaching ramifications." [43]

You can say that again. There is a race we do not ignore, we single it out for scape-goating when in fact **no race** deserves this. It is the Anglo-Saxon race. I cannot even type the word, 'white race,' here even if it the absolute truth without feeling as if the entirety of heaven will fall down and smite me. That is the kind of brainwashing we have endured in the last 115 years. (One gets the same feeling of impending doom when one mentions the destruction of the sacred masculine). No one race is more or less evil, more or less culpable, more or less astonishing than another and that includes the *white* race. Not only has a giant of modern social science—and a pillar of modern liberalism—tumbled from his pedestal (Boas), but the dogma that man is merely a blank slate, on which state bureaucrats and social engineers may scribble whatever ideologies they please, has toppled with him. If that dogma really can be killed, then much of the tyranny and chaos it has helped create will die with it.

Yet Boas was not the worst offender when it came to twisting

---

[43]   http://www.vdare.com/articles/franz-boas-liberal-icon-scientific-fraud p.1

data to support politically desired conclusions. He was simply the original offender. His student Margaret Mead has been shown to have outright fabricated much of her data on Samoan sex life in the 1920s, and the claims about the lack of genetic influence on IQ of several other scientists trained or influenced by Boas have also been challenged by later research. It was Franz Boas who suggested that the young Margaret Mead should go to Samoa. Boas suggested to Mead that the difficult phase of adolescent sexual adjustment might be peculiar to Western culture and that a truly liberated people, such as the Samoans, might not behave in so repressed a fashion as Western youth. He impressed upon her that this would be a very important contribution to social science.[44]

It should come as no surprise that the impressionable young Mead "discovered" exactly what her influential mentor sent her to find. The fruit of Mead's 1925-1926 south sea voyage was *Coming of Age in Samoa*, which was published in 1928. Millions of copies have since been sold in dozens of languages. It is easily one of the most influential books in the social sciences ever written; it made Margaret Mead the most famous anthropologist on the planet.

Mead has been thoroughly debunked, not the least of which efforts came in the form of the book, *Margaret Mead and Samoa: The Making and Unmaking of an Anthropological Myth*,[45] by anthropologist Derek Freeman. In fact, Margaret Mead was a working member of the darker groups at the Tavistock Institute and wrote for the Journal of the Frankfurt School. Her husband, Gregory Bateson, was a primary instrumental force in the MK Ultra mind control programs. As part of the Freudo-Marxist agenda meant to destroy western culture, the idea of the carefree, liberally sexual, happy South Sea islander was created. This was meant to shore up the idea that western Christian values led to

---

[44] See 1983. *Margaret Mead and Samoa: The making and unmaking of an anthropological myth.* Cambridge: Harvard University Press for more information.

[45] Ibid.

unhappiness. In fact, there may be truth to that statement. However, this is another truth sandwich. The goal of the program was to destroy the family by setting all against all.

Scientists engaged in the process of conditioning are also called "social engineers" or "new-science social scientists" and they play an integral part in what we see, hear and read. The "old school" social engineers were Kurt K. Lewin, Professor Hadley Cantril, Margaret Mead, Professor Derwin Cartwright and Professor Lipssitt who, together with John Rawlings Reese, made up the backbone of new-science scientists at Tavistock Institute." They eliminated traditional Judeo-Christian morality in favour of relative morality, which is, by the way, the second tenet of the Church of Satan. Moral relativism. Any kind of relativism, really, should ring alarm bells.[46]

"A nation," he heard himself say, "consists of its laws. A nation does not consist of its situation at a given time. If an individual's morals are situational, that individual is without morals. If a nation's laws are situational, that nation has no laws, and soon isn't a nation." –William Gibson, Spook Country [47]

Franz Boas, his disciples, and other like-minded academics launched a full-scale intellectual war against the notion of cultural hierarchy, the idea that cultures could be graded or ranked on a scale of comparison. Again, a truth sandwich. It is the notion of hierarchy that is so deeply destructive. Hierarchy itself is unnatural to human beings, another unsung common behavioural paradigm. They questioned all standards of classification, they denied that there was any intrinsic difference between the races, they revived the debate about nature and nurture. They denied that there was any such thing as "human nature". Boas adopted a value-

---

[46] Weeks, Dr. Byron T. Tavistock, the Best-Kept Secret in America http://www.american-buddha.com/lit.tavistocksecretweeks.htm

[47] Gibson, W. Spook Country. See: http://en.wikipedia.org/wiki/Spook_Country

68

free approach to anthropology. The emphasis here should be in the strict definition: humans without value.

Some background: in 1883 Boas had made a field trip to Baffinland where he became enamoured with the Eskimo way of life. He revealed his alienation from the modern world when he wrote in his diary: "I often ask myself what advantages our "good society" possesses over the "savages". The more I see of their customs, the more I realize that we have no right to look down upon them." Fair enough.

"When Boas completed his study of the Kwakintl Indians of Vancouver Island he wrote a glowing and detailed account of their culture. In keeping with his concealed subversive political agenda, he kept from his readers the fact that these "noble" savages also had a long tradition of slavery. Boas didn't want his readers to question his **"value-free"** approach to anthropology, especially then, when it had been only eighteen years since 600,000 European-Americans had died in a struggle over the worthiness of slavery in America." [48]

Whether she learned it at Boas' knee or brought it with her, Mead was a cultural relativist. Although she rejected western culture as a yardstick for other cultures, she did not adopt a posture of one culture being different than another. Rather, she insisted that in some ways other cultures were superior to her own. (Is *that* value-free? Isn't *that* hierarchical?) It is just at this point that Mead becomes suspect. Scientific neutrality should have been the order of the day unless one was looking to find something pre-decided. Despite much evidence to the contrary, she reported the Samoans as admirable behavioural models like Rousseau's unrepressed noble savages. She wrote of the Samoans: in paraphrase, they laugh at stories of romantic love, scoff at infidelity...believe explicitly that one love will quickly cure another...adultery does not necessarily mean a broken marriage...divorce is a simple, informal matter...Samoans welcome casual

[48]   Clough, T. 2001 http://www.weirdrepublic.com/episode12.htm p.1

homosexual practices...In such a setting, there is no room for guilt." [49]

Mead's tale of sexual liberation boldly challenged Western moral values and perceptions of perversion. She believed, one wonders if Boas convinced her to believe, that Americans were far too constrained by conventional morality; they were, in her opinion, repressed, guilt ridden and unhappy. Ultimately her book was not so much about Samoa as it was about what was wrong with western moral norms. Her ode to free love, however manufactured, places her squarely in the forefront of what became The Sexual Revolution.

Mead's cultural relativism negated western moral precepts by making them out to be less valid than the Samoan tribe because they were the cause of unhealthy repression. If, as she claimed, humans had no hereditary human nature, if our emotional selves were infinitely elastic, then why not shed the confining garments of our prudish culture and go completely native? That changed the way people in America raised their children.

"Sadly for America and the Samoans, it was all rubbish. The 'gullible' young Mead breezed into Samoa in 1925 without any knowledge of the language. She picked up what she could in one short course. She did not live with the Samoans, but stayed in the home of a Navy pharmacist. She spent much of her time working on an unrelated project and she quit the island after only nine months. What she took away with her is revealed, upon closer examination, to be little more than an adolescent prank lovingly bundled up inside Mead's own cultural relativist illusions." [50]

Years later, Samoan students studying at American colleges would denounce Mead for grotesquely distorting the truth about their culture. Anthropologist Derek Freeman, who completed over six years of

---

[49]   (Mead, M. *Coming of Age in Samoa: A Psychological Study of Primitive Youth for Western Civilization. 1928*).

[50]   Clough, T. 2001 http://www.weirdrepublic.com/episode12.htm p.1

field work on Samoa, concluded that *Coming of Age in Samoa* stands as **the worst example of "self-deception in the history of the behavioural sciences."** [51] Freeman clearly documented that almost everything Mead said about Samoan behaviour was dead wrong.

Mead claimed that the free-loving Samoans were never jealous or anxious in sexual matters. Repression and guilt are, in fact, widespread in Samoa and bridal virginity is highly valued. While Mead had asserted that Samoans took adultery lightly, the Samoan legal code in force at the time of her visit made adultery a crime punishable by fine and/or prison. In former times it had been punishable by death. Suicides were regularly reported in the local Samoan newspapers, but Mead proclaimed the absence of suicide among the Samoans to be a sign of their robust mental health. Mead wrote that rape was alien to the Samoans, but Freeman demonstrated that the rate of commission was several times higher in Samoa than in the United States. In fact, "among the highest in the world." [52] For his part, Boas was uncritically enthusiastic in his acceptance of whatever his students brought him that flattered his political prejudices. On many campuses Margaret Mead's *Coming of Age in Samoa* is still to be found in classrooms. If you are a student who is being indoctrinated with this nonsense, then you are a victim of educational malpractice. Demand a tuition refund.

There is much to be said about Mead and her husband and their efforts to thwart humanity in the 20th century. They will reappear in other chapters. For the moment, it is enough to become clear about for what the sciences that fall under the umbrella of behaviourism are responsible. As part of the three-pronged approach which formed at the beginning of the 20th century, all of which were meant to enslave people of free will, behaviourism certainly was the most experimentally-based. Through this

[51]   Holmberg, E. 2009. Sexual Fluidity: How You Too Can Become Gay or Bisexual.
[52]   The McAdam Report, No. 513, 04/19/05 p.19

we were taught to fear for no real reason, just because it was possible. We were taught that humans had no real life or free will, that we have no basic human nature, nothing we share. At least these postulates were floated to excuse the crimes of the Predator. None of these things are true on any level. It is critical to stop believing them.

One of the ways our innate human nature works for and against us is in what author John Lamb Lash calls the concept of neotony. In other words, we are born with very unfinished systems – brain, emotions, senses and so on -- and so it is imperitive to the Predator to get us away from our families, from our mothers especially, so that what goes in is what THEY want to go in and it is all damaging. Neoteny allows us to be submitted to massive behaviourial programming when we are the most vulnerable. [53] You may see this reminder in each chapter, as we go along, because it is absolutely critical that we realize and remember this.

It is now, and with great repugnance for the actuality, that the subject of primary psychopathy should be brought, however swiftly. A certain percentage of human beings are born with the absolute lack of conscience and no ability to empathize or feel and show compassion. It cannot be taught to them. It simply does not exist. This is the true Authoritarian Pathology. The greatest crime is that we have been taught to admire these creatures. In fact, they cannot be helped to develop any of these capacities for which we humans are known. There has been, in the last century, a tremendous amount of research done on the phenomenon of psychopathy. In fact, trying to help them actually makes them worse. The best thing, then, is to try very hard to eliminate them from positions of authority; positions from which they can either control of hurt other human beings. It is a biological anomoly and, since they do not feel emotion, we have no reason to believe that keeping them from positions of influence

---

[53]   http://dictionary.reference.com/browse/neoteny Many technical arguments beyond the scope of this essay indicate that *neoteny* has been a dominant theme of human evolution.

will 'hurt their feelings' in some way.

There is also such a creature as a secondary psychopath. While this result is even sadder than the first prognosis is the same. Where judgement must be used is in what I regard to be a third category: these are borderline people. They exhibit some clearly psychopathic tendencies such as utter self-absorption and little ability to empathize. However, the can also topple off the other side of the fence and exhibit genuinely human behaviour.

Our corporations, leadership positions, governments, judiciary...filled to the brim with psychopaths. We have been trained to call it 'leadership,' and 'the ability to make the hard decisions,' but, in fact, it is nothing more than a machine-like, unstoppable avarice. They are locusts – vampires with exceptional acting skills and more than a little bit of black magic behind them at the top levels. It could be argued that some of these people, due to their machine-like intellect and lack of moral constraints, have come up with some of the most powerful inventions of the modern age. However, these inventions have been put to terrible use by other psychopaths. Bill Gates is a great example. One understands the global changes due to the microprocessor but when one understands the other facets of the mind-control agenda, such as eugenics, one understands that someone like Bill Gates, a man who is a huge supporter of eugenics, is a monster with a very shiny image. Once the 'blood to dust" revolution is sorted out properly, the mask is ripped away.

Who are we now and what can we do? There is understanding our earth, Sophia, and our absolute right to be here. We are the positive energy, the symbiotic co-creator and Sophia is a Being, not a pet, nor a pile of rocks. There is the acknowledgement of the negative energy that amounts to an infection. Infections must be isolated from the general, susceptible populations and treated/healed. I imagine that is possible because for us and for Sophia, everything is possible. There is the recognition of our task, which was our task prior to the infection and remains so...a reservation of our sovereignty synthesized with a deep empathy for our entire environment. We have the responsibility and the destiny to advance, to metamorphose, to incarnate to higher and higher levels. We have the duty and the capacity to assist Sophia.

Morris Berman, a cultural historian, called it 'participating consciousness.' Owen Barfield conducted deep work on a similar subject, 'original participation.' John Lamb Lash has written extensively on the true nature of our planet and our being in *Not in His Image: Gnostic Vision, Sacred Ecology, and the Future of Belief* [54] and other books. Knowing is the answer. Re-member. Re-cognize. Don't allow the shaming mechanism set up to embarrass you or stop you from knowing what you know. Also, remember that the New Age movement is an invention of The Predator. The answers primarily do not lie there either. We will touch on the subject of the New Age and how the traits of Aquarius, as in the dawning of the Age of Aquarius, are being used against us. The traits of Pisces were certainly used against us. It seems too easy, yet here we are. It falls under the idea of 'critical mass.' Just enough of us have to realize our situation and then we will *all* realize our situation. It is all about the morphic field and how much is enough to initiate a change.

---

[54]   Lash, John L. *Not in His Image: Gnostic Vision, Sacred Ecology, and the Future of Belief* 2006 *Chelsea Green Publishing Co*

The term **participating consciousness** was co-introduced in *The Reenchantment of the World* to describe an ancient mode of human thinking that does not separate the perceiver from the world he or she perceives. Berman says that this original world view has been replaced during the past 400 years with the modern paradigm called Cartesian, Newtonian, or scientific, which depends on an isolated observer, proposing that we can understand the world only by distancing ourselves from it. That was Barfield's individuation. This alternative anthropology finds philosophical substantiation in the work of Owen Barfield, who postulated a phase of 'original participation,' in which human beings were able...indeed unable to avoid...completely living into their environment. Individuation was necessary and arrived in a complete form; we utterly severed ourselves from the environment. He said it was our task now to synthesize those two ways of being. Barfield maintained it was absolutely necessary and to be expected but the next step must be taken. Synthesis. We must be both part of and sovereign.[55]

Max Weber, early 20th-century German sociologist, was concerned with the "disenchantment" he associated with the rise of modernity, capitalism, and scientific consciousness. Berman traces the history of this disenchantment. He argues that the modern consciousness is destructive to both the human psyche and the planetary environment. Berman challenges the supremacy of the modern world view and argues for some new form of the older holistic tradition, which he describes as follows:

"Participating consciousness" involves merger, or an entering into one's environment, and demonstrates a psychic unity, or ability to 'live into' everything, that has long since passed from the scene. Alchemy, as it

[55]   Barfield, Owen. Saving the Appearances, A Study in Idolatry. 1988

turns out, was the last great coherent expression of participating consciousness in the West. *Alchemy is,* not was. We lose sight of that when we are too busy watching The Simpson's reruns. [56]

Author and philosopher John Lamb Lash, has provided an entire re-membering environment, as well. His 'metahistory" is a path beyond the contrived scripts of history and culture, toward a world free from enslavement to historical lies and unexamined beliefs. Humanity is a species endangered by its beliefs, and most of all, its fracturing and fractured dichotomy, the religious illusion of superiority juxtaposed against the idea that we are the bacteria, the scum, the invader of the earth and she would be better off without us. Pick your poison. Neither is true.

"To go beyond history is not solely a human prerogative, for the path ahead is not ours alone, but the way of all sentient beings. Closely aligned with deep ecology, and going deeper, this site develops open source spirituality that can reflect the innate sanity of humankind. It explores the question of what is a true planetary view, a way to live bonded intimately to the earth and coevolving with the non-human world. From and reprinted with the express permission of John Lamb Lash:57

The Way Beyond Belief

Orientation to Metahistory

One aim of Metahistory.org is to encourage and support belief-change. Socrates said,

"The unexamined life is not worth living." Rephrased in metahistorical

[56] *Max Weber, Sociological Writings.* Edited by Wolf Heydebrand, published in 1994 by Continuum. https://www.marxists.org/reference/subject/philosophy/works/ge/weber.htm
[57] Lash, John L http://www.metahistory.org/

terms, "The unexamined belief is not worth holding."

Easy enough to say, perhaps, but how many of the beliefs that you hold have you really examined?

Are the beliefs you hold innate to you, based on your own experience and judgment, or acquired from others without choice or examination on your part? You have the right to believe whatever you like, but is what you believe truly right for you, or is it someone else's idea of what you ought to believe?

Belief, by definition, depends on suspension of critical judgement. The power of beliefs rests mainly in the fact that they cannot be judged, rationally refuted, or critically disproven—or proven. They are "unfalsifiable," to use Carl Popper's term. Beliefs may be patently absurd and ridiculous on face value, but those who adopt them are empowered..."

Additionally, another impulse has been born over the last ten years and it is coming from South Africa. It is called Contributionism and it is presented under the name, Ubuntu. Granted the setting for the genesis of this movement appears to be South Africa. However, it applies everywhere and Ubuntu Movements are springing up all over the world. The general principles are sound but very foreign to the world we live in in the early 21st century. This Ubuntu manifestation also calls itself Contributionism. What is different? The state educates for the benefit of the state, which it then purports to distribute to the community. The introduction of money and capitalism short-circuited that route, assuming it was ever intended to be that way. It appears to be the mission of this Ubuntu Movement to localize the work and the sharing of rsources and so forth.

With all the wealth and natural resources existant in the world today, it has been proved repeatedly that each human being alive could and should have all that they could wish for. However, the idea here is that the system cannot be fixed and one should not waste any time in the attempt. One should simply decide what one wants instead and start over.

In fact, human beings have rights...simply because we are human beings...that are inalienable. The land, the earth, the water, the air, and any commodity (non-living) belong to the people of the earth: every single one of us. This is the starting place. We don't have to purchase them or steal them or conquer those who have them because they already belong to us. This is something we have been trained to forget for a very, very long time.

Interestingly, this group reminds us that it is not just the air we breathe that belongs to us but the airwaves themselves. No one owns those, they are a naturally occuring phenomenon of which everything is made. Since the atmosphere and the airwaves belong to each human being then so does what we call the 'sky.' These things do not belong to any small collection of people under any guise whjo claim to have dominion over them. corporation who has unlawfully claimed exclusive rights over it. These things which make up the very fabric of our environment have been stolen and we can and should reclaim them. Money should be eliminated as the artificial construct that it is and the enslavement tool that it is. Food and all of the resources which allow warmth or transportation should and can be simply given to the people free of charge. That which goes into making these things, including the labour, belongs to the people, after all.[58]

Obviously, this sort of newly developing social and living philosophy has at its core the foundations of human nature, true Natural Law, and so is good for all people everywhere. Each culture would find at the baseline of Contributionism nothing to really interfere with its own folksoul. This is simply a declaration of a return to Sophia and each other.

---

[58] http://www.ubuntuparty.org.za/

It is worth considering.

79

Further Reading

1. (http://www.mhhe.com/cls/psy/ch14/encount.mhtml)

2. Thomas Clough, http://www.weirdrepublic.com/episode12.htm

3. (Francis, Sam. http://www.vdare.com/articles/franz-boas-liberal-icon-scientific-fraud   Francis died   in 2005)

Lash, John Lamb *Not in His Image: Gnostic Vision, Sacred Ecology, and the Future of Belief*

Tellinger, Michael. *UBUNTU Contributionism - A Blueprint For Human Prosperity*

Lemov, Rebecca. Excerpted from *World as Laboratory* Very highly recommended reading.

Matthew D. Jacofsky, Psy.D., Melanie T. Santos, Psy.D., Sony Khemlani-Patel, Ph.D. & Fugen Neziroglu, Ph.D. of the Bio Behavioral Institute, edited by C.E. Zupanick, Psy.D. and Mark Dombeck, Ph.D. *Operant Conditioning and Avoidance Learning*

archive.today *Margaret Mead Hoax*

Freeman, Derek. *Margaret Mead and Samoa: The Making and Unmaking of an Anthropological Myth*

Lobaczewski, Andrew M. *Political Ponerology: A Science on the Nature of Evil Adjusted for Political Purposes.*

Berman, Morris. *The Re-enchantment of the World.*

Barfield, Owen. *Saving the Appearances: A Study in Idolatry.*
 Public Domain

80

Lash, John Lamb *Not in His Image: Gnostic Vision, Sacred Ecology, and the Future of Belief*

Tellinger, Michael. *UBUNTU Contributionism - A Blueprint For Human Prosperity*

Cleckley, Hervey, MD *The Mask of Sanity: An Attempt to Clarify Some Issues About the So-Called Psychopathic Personality.* http://www.cassiopaea.com/cassiopaea/sanity.pdf

Chapter Three

From Blood to Dust

One of the most successful literary agents in New York City, when confronted with the actuality of my book *The Sun Thief* and its topic, said to me, too many people would have to know this was going on for it to be possible (the relentless dumping of poisonous aerosols into our atmosphere). This was a man of some creative mind and intelligence and yet like most modern Americans, and other citizens of the world, he has completely lost the plot. It was a disturbing and depressing moment. There is only one word to keep in your pocket, one paradigm, one giant iron link in the chain that binds us: compartmentalization. It is time to make friends with this concept if one has not already. The only real obstacle may be being too young to remember things being any different but I doubt it.

This is part of the 'rationalization' of our waking life, our spiritual life, our material life. A 'ration' is a part of a whole, a fraction, a fracture. Our understanding of that word in everyday parlance is skewed. We think it means 'logical,' when it most certainly does not. It means 'in parts,' and to rationalize is to break into pieces. We have been utterly and completely rationalized and, to add the usual salt in the wound, we have been trained to thank our masters for the injury. Indeed, consider the other common definition of rationalization. We also use it to describe forcing the reality or truth of a situation into some strangled moral pretzel so we don't have to do the upright thing. We are absolutely amazing in our capacity to stare Wrong right in the face and call it Right. It is astonishing. Yes, we live in a rational world, unfortunately, thanks largely to the Industrial folks. Rational is actually incoherent; it doesn't stick together, and is incomprehensible. So let's get that straightened out right now. We must return to our wholeness and health.

People who believe what they are taught by schools and via mass media will often have an inverted idea of white and black, of who is being exploited and who is exploiting, of what are the principles of creation, and what are the principles of destruction. The less awake people will indeed invert black and white on a broad area of issues, wherever the official propaganda is working its magic. More alert people will be confused into seeing a blurry self-contradictory gray everywhere. This is the pitfall of relativity, the opposite of stable Natural Law.[59] The less personal the subject, the greater the likelihood of deception, inverting the long-range moral vision of sleep-walking human beings, and cultivating a convenient moral blindness in others. In the end, the living area is absurd and schizophrenic.

The fertile soil for the unchecked growth of all of these social monstrosities is the modern school. Once again, we return to one Horace Mann and his ambitious work for the great railroads and coal interests in New England in the mid-19th century. Despite his being hailed as an education reformer, Mann was merely an ambitious politician and an attorney for the railroads. It was this concentrated power centralization responsible for bringing, as we noted in Chapter One, compulsory schooling to the United States. The romantic tale of Mann striving to bring the very best and most enlightened method of education to the people is just that – a fairy tale. The old fairy tales contain critical archetypes.

---

[59] http://files.meetup.com/1332202/Natural-Law-Sovereignty-And-Survival.pdf or http://web.archive.org/web/20080212071300/http://etext.lib.virginia.edu/toc/modeng/public/Hob2Ele.html

This fairytale, however, is what we call a Lie. The railroad magnates, like the industrialists and bankers, like the rulers and governments humiliated by defeats on the battlefield, wanted a compliant and placid citizenry, one that would not impede their plans.

From the railroad magnates, we moved to the industrialists: from blood to dust in a very real way. Henry Ford, for example, was pivotal in rationalizing (shattering) our 20th century, to our profound detriment. And, as we travel this path, it would be good to have a look at this from the US Bureau of Education circular, 1872: Inculcating knowledge teaches workers to be able to perceive and calculate their grievances making them more redoubtable foes in labour struggles.[60]

Taylorism, also known as Scientific Management, came into being when Bethlehem Steel hired Frederick Taylor to increase efficiency at the factories. It began in the 1880s. Industrialists quickly realized that Taylorism came with an unexpected but welcome side effect: it disempowered any worker who had the ability to challenge management. The colonial economist Adam Smith had stated clearly that, in his estimation, the division of labour would create a social catastrophe. Regardless, Taylor set about to fracture, divide, shatter labour into the smallest possible pieces.

For Taylor, this sought-after efficiency meant: mechanized tasks, tasks broken down as far as humanly possible, and measurable production targets. It might be that one's job suddenly was only to turn a screw to the right as a piece of machinery came by. A simple three-second task that could be repeated several thousand times a day. In fact, workers under this regime were/are expected to be moving in this repetitive fashion 57

---

[60]   http://www.basicincome.com/bp/files/The_Underground_History.pdf p.99

out of every 60 seconds. Due to the barely tolerable simplicity of their 'specialized' task, this was actually quantifiable. Thus, they were made into 'specialist tools.'

In the beginning, Taylor himself called the system 'process management,' which department is still alive and well in most corporate structures. (As an aside, George W. Bush used the same calculating criteria in No Child Left Behind. It may also surprise the reader to know that the mighty and radical education reformer, John Taylor Gatto, was the rebellious grandson of this particular Taylor). As the decades went by, the debilitating scientific management initiative simply spread and diverged and, not surprisingly, became more specialized itself as we encountered operations management, operations research, industrial engineering, manufacturing engineering, logistics, business process management, lean manufacturing and so on. "In political and sociological terms, Taylorism can be seen as the division of labour push to its logical extreme (I might substitute the word rational here), with a consequent de-skilling of the worker and dehumanisation of the workers and the workplace." [61]

However, there was more to this system than efficiency. The proud legacy of 19th century machinists and machine shops was highly skilled, self-empowered labour. Machinists were, therefore, able to challenge management since they were not easily replaced. Management found this to be unacceptable. In adopting a system of narrow specialization of tasks, industry quickly de-skilled its labour force and made every worker very, very expendable. Jobs reduced to their basic elements allowed

---

[61]   Thoughts and Theories of Scientific Management.
www.appreciatingsystems.com/)

companies to exercise demonic levels of control. No one had the know-how to take on a complete project any longer – there were no longer the 'craftsmen.' In the United States, the machinists were able to hold small guild-like caches of self-respect and autonomy until the 1980s.

In fact, Henry Ford said something akin to: I'm too smart to have these *rational* principles imposed on me but the workers are too stupid to know what to do without them. Once ensconced in industry, these sorts of mindless repetitive tasks eliminated the natural use of the **imaginative** side of the brain, those human impulses ground to a halt and the left brain, the **rational** side, became our dictator. Our hemispheres, which should be working equally and communicating with each other, do not and this has been artificially imposed upon us. We are not 'like this' at birth, just as we are not 'fearful.' That side of us is deliberately being shut down, turned off, assassinated. The Imagination is dangerous to the Predator.

When Henry Ford invented the sister apparatus to Taylorism, the assembly line, for the first time, the machine – the assembly line itself – controlled the workers. This was a catastrophic moment for humanity. Indeed, the Ford system operated under a hierarchical system on all levels. So tasks were fractured and reduced and broken into parts, the speed of the assembly line called the shots, and there was an upper level management scrutinizing production quotas. This system found its way into our schools because it was so profoundly successful in dis-empowering the human being and, because as the behaviourists have tried to teach us, we are but machines. [62]

Fordism and rationalism create much more than worker dissatisfaction, a generic, somewhat cleaned-up term. These are

---

[62]   http://history1900s.about.com/od/1910s/a/Ford--Assembly-Line.htm

86

dis-empowered people, less likely to participate in anything, their health and mental well-being terribly impaired -- the irrational consequences of the rational. Rather than return to a healthy, holistic, human way of creating and working, the industrialists discovered that if their companies provided some avenue for the worker to talk about how miserable they were, they would at least continue to function. Thus, the idea that deeply unhappy workers were simply defective human machines and not dignified human beings supremely aware that they were living in a concentration camp of some sort, reinforced the illusion of helplessness. So Taylorism weakens workers in the workplace and everywhere else to boot. This is to be desired by the industrialists, who make up a significant operating portion of the Predator.

Billions of us and a handful of them and yet Taylorism combined with Fordism is so effective a soul-killer that we submit. An entity that drives every ounce of energy toward profit regardless of the social damage is a **psychopathic** entity. We submit to the psychopath because they train us to do so from as young as they can get hold of us.

Indeed, Taylorism quickly became the darling of the fledgling fascist regimes that marked the early to mid-20th century. Mussolini set up an entity to promote Taylorism. Lenin actually wrote, in paraphrase, we must introduce Russia to the study and the teaching of the Taylor System and its implementation. This system is perfect for the introduction of a fascist state, a state that requires the complete submission of a cowed population. It is an all but forgotten fact that the introduction of Taylorism by the Bolsheviks caused a major rebellion within Russia in 1921, called The Kronstadt Rebellion. Workers **imagined** a mutually-owned working system. Taylorism took that away from them. They saw the beast for what it was.[63]

The industrialists then set out to master the inner world of the worker when it became patently clear that the worker on a specialized assembly line tended to work at the slowest rate that went unpunished. (Ah, the small but ever-present rebellious quirks of the human soul.) Rest breaks had already been introduced by Taylor, thus the mandated fifteen minute break twice in an eight hour shift with which we are all mostly familiar. This can-opener inserted into the human psyche was helped along by something called The Hawthorne Experiments. These massively important experiments were conducted between 1924 and 1932 at The Hawthorne Works, a division of Western Electric, near Chicago. Simply put, as we have noted earlier, allowing workers to talk about their feelings defused their will to rebel. (Paging Dr. Freud!) The workers had one place to feel as if they mattered, they existed, they were not invisible as they lived and died on a hamster wheel. The wheel didn't change, in the meantime. The wheel still provided maximum profits for industry and later for corporations.

Additionally, the scientists running these experiments selected some simple changes (ie, changing the lighting in the workplace) just to see if this small bit of empowerment soothed the tortured psyches of the workers. It did indeed help. Interestingly enough, it was the lighting level at an electric plant that was selected to allow the workers some control over. Quite the placebo; quite the metaphor. We'll let you turn the overhead lights up or down as a substitute for having some real control in an electrical plant.

In reality, the workers had almost no more power than they had before. The company, however, could make a very big show about how much it cared about its employees and worker

---

[63] Beissinger, Mark R. Scientific Management, Socialist Discipline and Soviet Power. 1988 p.40

satisfaction. And, importantly, production rose. They backed off ever so slightly in order to squeeze that little bit extra out of the employee and called it humanitarian. In fact, it is now referred to as The Hawthorne Effect. The production did rise as a result of the workers having some interest shown in them. And from here, the study of Industrial Relations developed: what do we need to do to increase production now that the actual work itself has been reduced to its smallest component. It has everything to do with profits and nothing to do with humanity. The common theme here is that industry, whether large or small, engineer their way out of humane and empowering treatment of their workers.

The way this backfires slightly is that employees start caring about each other and each other's opinions and so there is some strength in that very human tendency to care. Even that, though, does little to increase an individual's true power and to enliven the work space and the imaginative, creative hemisphere of the brain. It is simply a very human gesture of helping each other through an absolutely horrifying situation but it does not change the fact of the hamster wheel.

The Hawthorne Experiment may seem, at first glance, to be a social engineering technique on a fairly small scale although it certainly has been adopted as a method of appeasing deeply dissatisfied workers globally. In fact, the same strategy makes up the process of political elections and party systems. There is more than enough data to strongly suggest that all elections are controlled and a selection of candidates are offered, any of which will be fine with the controlling entity. It is the suggestion or illusion of choice or control over one's destiny or environment that has kept us all from overturning political structures as they exist. This manufactured consent or tolerance by the masses is a very real outcome of social studies like The Hawthorne Experiments, perhaps even a direct result of that particular study. I believe the tolerance is at an end.

And, finally, for various reasons – only one of which is the control of the individual worker – the Rockefeller Foundation, Blood to Dust writ large, gave out 50 million dollars for the pursuit of the formation of the social sciences around the globe. between 1922 and 1929. Their stated goal? To establish a better organization in society at large. The first question: who decided that society needed to be altered, for what purpose, and who decides what society metamorphoses into? This project, like all the universal social engineering and cultural revolution projects of the 20th century, has no moral or ethical basis. The very first casualty is the free and sovereign individual. Indeed, these are glaring examples of psychopaths happily at work, beavering away at the rest of us...the herds...as if we were toy milk cows to move around on the kitchen table

One answer to this question, in a manner of speaking, is to note that this social effort was put forward as a way to deflect public anger at the Rockefellers for their glaringly unscrupulous business practices. It was a public relations ploy. Interestingly, and in keeping with the psychopathic mindset, the Rockefellers set out to change society such that society did not mind their machinations rather than adjust themselves to the general moral and ethical norms already in place. The height of success, in the end, was to create a society that actually admired their psychopathic, immoral and unethical practices. One sees then the Industrial or Corporate Magnate lionized on the front cover of Time Magazine and so forth rather than behind bars where his or her actions should surely have landed them. This brainwashing, as stated, began in 1922. The offshoot, The Yale Institute of Human Relations, came into being in 1929, with an initial investment of 7 million dollars, again from the Rockefeller charities. All of the money given to the Yale Institute combined with the moneys given by the government, made this the largest social science project ever created. The arrival of this institute, and all of the moneys poured into it, occurred just a couple of months before the Crash of 1929.

To briefly reiterate, recall that Taylorism itself, demanded complete and thorough efficiency of time and action and space. Tasks were broken down as far as they could go such that each worker had simple, repetitive tasks unplugged from context or capability. Mr. Ford then added the assembly line in which parts were conveyed from point A to Point B, each to be addressed in some way by a worker en route. The Hawthorne Experiments addressed the phenomenon of workers barely meeting basic mandatory goals as they became desperately unhappy in their robotic existence by allowing them to both address small environmental changes and by establishing the idea of what can only be seen as therapists/priests in the workplace, allowing the workers to express their depth of unhappiness in a safe and private way. These things kept the workers on the treadmill. And, as always, leaders in industry realized that it might actually be cost-efficient if those who ended up on their payrolls could be trained from as young an age as possible to not only accept being a cog in the great wheel but to find it desirable and a mark of success. (The irrational consequence of this further push for rationality was, of course, the mid-life crisis, when people realized just how much of their precious life had been tossed into the garbage, used by the industrialists like toilet paper). Goodness knows, the Rockefellers were on the case, determined to find ways to change every aspect of society to work in their favour!

Hence we have the introduction of something called The Gary Plan as we travel back to the schools as training ground and laboratory. From our friend John Taylor Gatto:

"...east of Chicago, in the synthetic U.S. Steel company town of Gary, Indiana, Superintendent William A. Wirt, a former student of John Dewey's at the University of Chicago, was busy testing a radical school innovation called the Gary Plan soon to be sprung on the national scene. Wirt had supposedly invented a new organizational scheme in which school subjects were *departmentalized*; this required movement of students from room to room on a regular basis so that all building spaces were in constant use. Bells would ring and just as with Pavlov's salivating dog, children would shift out of their seats and lurch toward yet another class.

In this way children could be exposed to many non-academic socialization experiences and much scientifically engineered physical activity, and it would be a bonus value from the same investment, a curriculum apart from so-called basic subjects which by this time were being looked upon as an actual menace to long-range social goals. Wirt called his system the "work-study-play" school, but outside of Gary it was referred to simply as "the Gary Plan." Its noteworthy economical feature, rigorously scheduling a student body twice as large as before into the same space and time, earned it the informal name "platoon school." (The Underground History of American Education. JT Gatto).

In 1973, I found myself in one of these warehouses. This was a year that was supposed to see schools change to adjust to the baby boom and a swell in the ranks of children my age, which, at that time was Grade 9. My high school (secondary school) housed 4,000 students. Four thousand. We operated on a college-style schedule of classes either Monday, Wednesday, and Friday or Tuesday and Thursday. I can confirm that no one knew what any child was doing at any time, certainly no one in the administration. There were simply too many of us. Mostly, we felt invisible and it was a wretched experience for the majority. The experiment was revealed to be a dismal failure after a few years and other schools were built to reduce the population of the one behemoth. It had been a test, an experiment on seeing how many students one could warehouse under exact conditions, and had little to do with schooling much less education.

Back to Mr. Gatto:

"While the prototype was being established and tested on children of the new industrial proletariat in Gary, the plan itself was merchandised from news stand, pulpit, and lecture circuit, lauded in administrative circles, and soundly praised by first pedagogical couple John and Evelyn Dewey in their 1915 book, *Schools of Tomorrow.* The first inkling Gary might be a deliberate stepchild of the scientific management movement occurred in a February 1911 article by Wirt for *The American School Board Journal,* "Scientific Management of School Plants." But a more thorough and forceful exposition of its provenance was presented in the *Elementary School Teacher* by John Franklin Bobbit in a 1912 piece titled "Elimination of Waste in Education."

Interestingly, professor of sociology Herbert Marcuse was sent back to Germany after WWII to 'de-nazify' Germany. He was one of the leading lights of the Frankfurt School and the primary driver behind the student uprisings all over the world in the 1960s. Much was done to industrialize both Germany and France along the US model at the same time Marcuse addressed the fascist state of Germany. People will argue that Germany and France had their own industrial revolution but this is somewhat different. Industrial capitalism joined hands with Freudo-Marxism and not for the first or last time that century. It would be the campaign to fracture and compartmentalize and Taylorize those societies, as well.

The assembly line nature of schools, the offspring of the impossible situation in the workplace, still exists and is deeply entrenched no matter how very harmful it is to our children; the fracturing of tasks, and so forth, creates alienation, low self esteem, dissatisfaction, and people who are least likely to vote or participate. A fragmented environment which includes no path for expression of your own capacities diminishes individuals in every way. The school setting, already regimented beyond tolerance and compulsory, to boot, was and is now set up to fracture...or rationalize... every part of what it is to be human into pieces. These pieces cease communicating with each other, the Whole is lost. This helps no one but the corporatist, the industrialist, the Predator. *From blood to dust.*

Also, remember, we are able to characterize our situation as 3D. Debility. Dependency. Dread. Which of the 3Ds is outlined here? All, probably. Debility because we have so many of our capacities taken away from us. Dependency because we have no knowledge of the whole, the context, and unity anymore. We think we haven't a leg to stand on against our masters because we are no longer craftsmen, artisans, farmers and whole people. We think we must be handed food and health and habitat because we don't know from what parts of the magical heavens these things come. We are becoming like the apes in the opening sequence of 2001:A Space Odyssey, hurling sticks at a contraption that fell from the sky. And dread, because we believe we are at their mercy and in constant danger of disappearing entirely. If we have no place on the hamster wheel, do we even exist?

Participatory Economics (Michael Albert), Social Threefolding (Rudolf Steiner), and Contributionism (The Ubuntu Movement of Michael Tellinger) are just three of the remedies which have been fermenting and gaining ground very much as guerilla movements around the world. We spoke of Michael Tellinger in the previous chapter.

Social Threefolding is a daughter movement from Anthroposophy, a philosophical study created by Rudolf Steiner around the turn of the 20th century. A small definition follows:

Social threefolding is a theory that suggests increasing the independence of society's three primary realms (economy, politics, and culture) in such a way that those three realms can mutually correct each other in an ongoing process. The movement aims for democracy in political life, freedom in cultural life (art, science, religion, education, the media), and uncoerced associative cooperation in economic life.[64] It originated out of the philosophy of Anthroposophy founded by Rudolf Steiner. Steiner held that it is socially destructive when one of the three spheres attempts to dominate the others; for example, theocracy means a cultural impulse dominates economy and politics; traditional types of capitalism mean economic life dominates the polity and culture; and state socialism means government dominates culture and economy. A more specific example: Arthur Salter, 1st Baron Salter has suggested that governments frequently fail when they begin to

---

[64] social-ecology.org/2009/01/rudolf-steiner's-threefold-commonwealth-and-alternative-economic-thought/

give "discretionary, particularly preferential privileges to competitive industry."

Steiner said the three social spheres had very gradually, over thousands of years, been growing independent of each other, and would naturally tend to continue to do so. Consciously effecting stages of this independence thus works in accordance with society's natural evolution, and gradually leads society beyond the three forms of domination mentioned.

Many institutions have striven to realize a relative independence of the three spheres within their own structures; the Waldorf schools deserve special mention in this regard.

Another application has been the creation of various socially responsible banks and foundations. Though many concrete reform proposals to advance a "threefold social order" at various scales have been advanced, Steiner emphasized that the specifics of how this could best be done are contingent on the particular situation. The RSF Social Finance in San Francisco is a great example in the United States. They specialize in socially responsible investing.

There are these sorts of financial institutions springing up globally should one be of the mindset to stay with a monetary system. As I have indicated, we really won't be talking about money here unless we have to. There are other things going on that need our attention.

Participatory Economics (Michael Albert) is similar to what Tellinger proposes and what RSF is doing. However, it still involves money and so for me is less attractive than Ubuntu. We must shake off the money chains.[65]

It is a good moment here to review this statement: too many people would have to know about this. It isn't possible. (chemical spraying). For those who have spent time in the military, it is deeply understood how far compartmentalization can go. For the rest of us, the deep shattering and fracturing of our attention should be evident now. Need to know, hierarchy (which is a way not to allow moral men to rise but to keep moral men down), and reduced focus have been beaten into all of us. A handful of people can direct the activities of millions without anyone really knowing the full story of why and how and who and what is going on. It is a simple matter.

https://www.princeton.edu/~achaney/tmve/wiki100k/docs/Participatory_economic
s.html

Recommended Reading

Tellinger, Michael. *UBUNTU Contributionism - A Blueprint For Human Prosperity*

Cheminade, J. *FDR and Jean Monnet, The Battle Against British Imperial Methods* *http://schillerinstitute.org/fid_97-01/002-3_monnet.html*

Participatory Economics *https://www.princeton.edu/~achaney/tmve/wiki100k/docs/Participatory_economics.html*

Threefold Social Order *http://www.douglassocialcredit.com/resources/resources/Wachsmuth%20Threefold%20for%20Website.pdf*

Gatto, J.T. *http://ethosworld.com/library/John-Taylor-Gatto-underground-history-of-american-education-1-9.9.pdf*

Gatto, J.T. *The Cult of Scientific Management* *https://www.johntaylorgatto.com/chapters/9j.htm*

Chapter Four

The Cryptocracy

It is exceptionally difficult to know which of the two most destructive centres of social engineering for cultural revolution to introduce first. They began, were at work, and remain side-by-side. Both exist and are operating at full-bore capacity today. One was and is the operative arm of the war machine, the banks, and the propagandists. The other operates on the never-surrendered goal of a Freudo-Marxist world. They are each global and they use each other's systems to enhance their own despite the fact that they may seem to be at philosophical odds with each other. In the end, it is likely that each believes it will best the other. For the moment, they walk in lock-step. They are indeed the left and right arms of the Predator.

As with the subject for the following chapter, The Frankfurt School, it is easiest and most sensible to capture the gestures of each via the leading personalities and practitioners who operated within the confines of these toxic stables. Each debilitating stream turned loose on the world has its own progenitor, who in turn, either issued marching orders to the 'corps' of gathered followers and disciples. Thanks to Taylorism and Fordism and the Hawthorne Experiments, many who work for the cause don't have any idea to what they are actually contributing. Thanks to compulsory Prussian-style schooling, they are trained to desire being part of a group 'doing the right thing' for 'the right person or entity.' Thanks to what was learned via Behaviourism, methods of subtle but nearly irresistible coercion are in place, and reinforced every minute of every day. There are a few key parts left to explore before we take our pieces and glue them back together to form a Whole Picture.

Perhaps it is easiest to begin with The Tavistock Institute, still headquartered in London. It traces its genesis to the British East India Company's Opium Wars and so, is the older of the two. The term "psychiatry" was first used in 1808 by Johann Christian Reil, and it means "doctoring of the *soul*."[66] The primary schools of psychiatry were established in the early 1800s in Leipzig and Berlin.

Wilhelm Wundt established the first psychological laboratory at Leipzig University in 1879. Some of his most famous students were Ivan Pavlov, William James (the "Father of American Psychology"), and G. Stanley Hall (the mentor of John Dewey, the "Father of Progressive Education"). Pavlov is part of the cultural fabric, largely because of his stimulus-response experiments with dogs. In Clarence Karier's *Scientists of the Mind*, one reads concerning James that "we pass from a culture with God at its centre to a culture with man at its centre." [67]

William James was also noted for his description of reality as a mass of confusion and Hall founded "genetic psychology." Hall and James fused in the form of John Dewey, an educational psychologist, who co-authored the *Humanist Manifesto* in 1933. Dewey, John B. Watson and other leading psychologists in the early 20th century were interested in the behaviour of people as machines. They didn't believe that man had a soul.

Thus it was not surprising that at the 6th International Congress of Philosophy, which took place at Harvard University in 1926, it was stated that the ***soul or consciousness now is of very***

---

[66] http://www.thetruthseeker.co.uk/?p=8242 p.1

[67] Keerns, Martin. Part II: *Dumbed-Down Word Monkeys Who Think that Keeping Up with the Joneses and Not Being the Stupidest Guy or Gal in the Room is All That Really Matters.* p. 276 (Karier, Clarence, *Science of the Mind.*)

little importance.

Do yourself a favour. Re-read this last sentence. Let it sink in.

What does all this have to do with Tavistock? In 1920, the Tavistock Institute of Medical Psychology (TIMP) was founded. It was involved in psychotherapy, and psychiatrists at the Tavistock Clinic wanted to apply their findings to the general public in the form of certain social service programs.

Some of the names which act as bridges between the Frankfurt School and the Tavi, as it is known when knocking about London, are Sigmund Freud, Franz Boas, Margaret Mead, Herbert Marcuse, Theodore Adorno, Aldous Huxley, HG Wells, Bertrand Russell, Cecil Rhodes, the Fabian Socialists...there are many.

Funding was initially provided by the British royal family, but soon included the Rothschilds (related to Lord Northcliffe by marriage, as well as to the Goldsmiths, from whence many modern royal spouses come) and the Rockefellers. Wellington House would grow into the Tavistock Institute in 1921 after the propaganda "victories" of the First World War and the Federal Reserve banking system (created in 1913) had been secured.

Three elements combine to make the Institute unusual, if not unique: it has the independence of being entirely self-financing at this point, with no subsidies from the government or other sources; the action research orientation places it between, but not in, the worlds of academia and consultancy; and its range of disciplines include anthropology, economics, organizational behaviour, political science, psychoanalysis, psychology and sociology. One can purchase the research volumes produced by said Institute for a cool $24,000 or more per book. Therefore, the research manuals are accessible but only by a very select few.

At the base, the Tavistock is a War Machine. It is the developer and distributor of Traumatology (Dread). It wrote the 'shock and awe' textbook.

Here are some of the now well-known terms that can thank The Tavi for creating: Dual Reality, Engineered Consent, Double Speak, Group Think, Double Bind, False Identity, Split Personality, Mass Mind Control, Group Dynamics, Propaganda, Think Tank. The list is long.[68] The flavour of these buzz words is a sound indicator of what they really represent so, if you feel somewhat uncomfortable as you take these in, listen to your intuition. Just stop for a moment and entertain the notion of a 'buzz word,' then think Pavlov once again.

As with everything else here, an exhaustive investigation of The Tavistock would likely exceed a thousand pages. Dwelling on any of the subsidiaries at length would lead to overload. Any additional investigation the reader decides to take, and hopefully will take at some point, will easily yield more information than one can stomach. The broader strokes are necessary to help make doors between the chapters...the compartments...the fractions in the plan and the engineering. This is our goal.

Dr. John Rawlings Rees is put forth as the founder of The Tavistock Institute. That is actually debatable. John Rawlings Rees OBE MD RAMC (25 June 1890 – 11 April 1969) was a wartime and civilian psychiatrist.[69] He was a member of the group of key figures at the original Tavistock Clinic and became its medical director in 1934. In research, this idea that Rees was the founder is a bit like a sore thumb. Maybe, but there is so much that comes before. However, the Tavistock is known for the study

[68] http://ionamiller.weebly.com/psywar-central.html p.1
[69] Summarizing the work of Dr. John Coleman, http://educate-yourself.org/cn/tavistockarticlesindex04jun04.shtml p.1

termed Traumatology and much of that is due to the Hegelian 'problem, reaction, solution' formula already in place. That is create the problem, coerce the reaction (which is predictable) and then ride to the rescue with the solution. We see it every day to the detriment of so many. Diseases require vaccines or pills. Cause riots then send in the police. Enact 'colour revolutions' so leadership can be replaced. Stage the problem, engender the programmed reaction, provide the desired solution. It is all around us and we have become so used to it, we can't even see it any more. Bring down the World Trade Center so we can create the terror within and lock down the United States in a fascist police state. And, be so slick about it, that the population says thank you, sir, may I have another....never realizing they are placing the bars in the windows of their own prison. One may wonder, then how do we tell a false flag from a real emergency? (Hint: there are only false flags.)

Dr. Rees developed the "Tavistock Method," which induces and controls stress via what Rees called "psychologically controlled environments" in order to make people give up firmly held beliefs under "peer pressure."[70] What a lovely entry for the old resume or CV.

Rees' Tavistock Method was based on work done by British psychoanalyst Wilfrid Bion regarding the roles of individuals within groups. This design was later shifted in a series of conferences (1957-1965) led by A. Kenneth Rice, chairman of Tavistock's Centre for the Applied Social Research. The shift was to the dynamics of leadership and authority relations in groups.

In 1930, TIMP had been involved with the second biennial Conference on Mental Health, where psychiatrist J.R. Lord advocated control of not only nature, but human nature, as well as

---

[70]   Ibid.

of the necessity to disarm the mind. So, there is a 'human nature,' something we all share and the mind, or Imagination, needs to be made powerless. Why would any non-psychopath see the amazing human mind as in need of neutralizing?

Rees went even further than this on June 18, 1940, at the annual meeting of the National Council for Mental Hygiene of the United Kingdom. In his speech on "Strategic Planning for Mental Health,"[71] he issued a proclamation congratulating himself and his fellows for the following, specifically: : infiltration and permeation of every educational activity in national life; a useful attack on a number of professions, including teaching, pastoral interests, politics, law and medicine. The aims were clear. Politics, industry and public life should be within their sphere of influence. They would become a fifth column into the area of mental health, unrealized until the deed was done. Ah, the good old Tavi.

Whereas the entry of Great Britain and the the United States into WWI was driven by the greed for money, land and blood of the British Crown, the Rothschilds and the Rockefellers, much was learned about how human beings respond to trauma which like most has most definitely been used against us. This knowledge was gained as a result of artificially constructed Great Wars. That says it all.

One of the most prolific researchers on the Tavistock Institute, Dr. John Coleman, has written exhaustively on its evolution. From the evidence in his book, *The Tavistock Institute of Human Relations, Britain's Control of the United States*, we can surmise that Tavistock was formed to be a propaganda creating and disseminating organization in London in the run-up to WWI. In fact, Arnold Toynbee referred to it as that black hole of disinformation -- a lie factory.[72] However much surface evidence

---

[71]   http://www.cchr.org.uk/psychiatric-drugs/undermining-morals/ p.1

104

there is that the Tavistock appeared as a tangent to WWI, in fact, it
was in 1821, operations that were to shape the destinies of
Germany, Russia, Britain and the United States were transferred to
what became the Tavistock Institute. The fact is, the collective
attributes of the Tavi were focused on breaking down stiff
resistance to WWI, but the Tavi was already an entity. There is
always stiff resistance to war such that a method of overriding this
was wanted. Human beings as such don't really enjoy killing each
other.

That project was given initially to Lords Rothermere and
Northcliffe and their mandate was to produce an organization
capable of manipulating British public opinion and directing that
manufactured opinion down the desired pathway to support for a
declaration of war. Arnold Toynbee was selected as 'Director of
Future Studies.'[73] Two Americans, Walter Lippmann and Edward
Bernays were appointed to handle the manipulation of American
public opinion in preparation for the entry of the United States into
WWI, *and to brief and direct President Woodrow Wilson.*[74]

From a somewhat crude beginning prior to Wellington
House, grew an organization that was to shape the destiny of
Germany, Britain and more especially the United States in a
manner that became a supremely sophisticated organization meant
to manipulate and create public opinion, what is commonly termed,
"mass brainwashing." This is accomplished via several main lines,
not the least of which are trauma and advertising. Television
programming is just what it says it is: programming. Off-shoots of
this group have gone on to overthrow cultures in much of the

---

[72] Summarizing Dr. John Coleman.
http://www.whale.to/b/coleman_b.html

[73] Ibid.
[74] Ibid.

world.

However, let us begin at the 'beginning' for purposes of our discussion, with Lord Rothermere and Lord Northcliffe. Together they represented the major newspaper outlets of their day and, with the use of such to whip England into an anti-German frenzy based on utter lies, we see the first example of the modern use of both propaganda and the media to sway entire populations to turn on each other. The Associated Newspapers (AP) dynasty was formed in 1896 when Alfred Harmsworth and his brother Harold formed the *Daily Mail*. The newspaper was meant for the phenomenon of a new middle class. Alfred later became Lord Northcliffe and Harold the first Viscount Rothermere. When Lord Northcliffe died without an heir, Lord Rothermere assumed control of the business empire which later passed to his descendants.

Harold Sidney Harmsworth, 1st Viscount Rothermere, was a highly successful British newspaper proprietor. Rothermere owned the *Daily Mail*, the *Mail on Sunday* and the *London Evening Standard*. Alfred Charles William Harmsworth, 1st Viscount Northcliffe, was also a British newspaper and publishing magnate. As the original owner of the *Daily Mail* and the *Daily Mirror,* he exercised vast influence over British popular opinion. These two are often referred to as two of the 'Great Press Barons.'

. Nevertheless, these men were ordered to vilify and demonize the Germans, starting at the top, and soon Kaiser Wilhelm was depicted as a child-eating zombie roaming the nightmares of his people. Eventually, a British citizenry with absolutely no quarrel with an unsuspecting German citizenry was hell-bent on ripping them all limb-from-limb. What an intoxicating ride that must have been for the psychopaths at the top. A World War promised to be, and was, a blood bath, a blood sacrifice of perhaps unprecedented proportions...at least in written history. It has to be said that the mission, the implementation and the results of the force behind the Tavi is black indeed. Greed, power-mongering, blood sacrifice as an end in itself in some real ways – the are expressions of evil.

One of the most interesting discoveries, which deserves some discussion later, is the fact that The Tavistock Institute made it its business to launch an attack upon the female, the Mother, the Sacred Feminine, and the Frankfurt School focused on bringing down the male, or the Father figure, or the Sacred Masculine. As we have noted, these are uneasily competitive partners, the Tavistock Institute and the Frankfurt School, each co-opting the other's work, each assuming inevitable supremacy. On one level, the destruction of the nuclear family is illustrated in bold letters here, to be replaced by the military and the 'school,' both of which together constituted the stranglehold of the government or even the Predator. On another level, a deeply disturbing one, these machines are after the Divine Feminine and the Divine Masculine. Ultimately, it is Sophia, our living earth being who is the target.

Mind you, once the study of trauma was under way, Traumatology became a tool used to manipulate groups of people by traumatizing them in various ways. [75] Dread is one of the 3Ds in the 3D world we inhabit. And, everything is kept in chaos, in flux, in crisis such that groups can be manipulated on a moment's notice. We are all ready to go over the top in every way at all times because we are all in a deeply traumatized.

This began with Wellington House, as we've said, which some referred to as a World War I propaganda factory. It was run by a group obsessed with the psychology of the masses far more than the individual, although the institute became expert in all

[75]   Norman, Gillian. *"Mind Wars."* http://www.rense.com/mindwarstalk.html
     p.1

forms of manipulation. Theirs was a psychology shaped by war loosed upon the world. Later, John Rawlings Rees studied shell shock and located the human breaking point. The military Operation Research was then turned on the public, secretly. Tavi became a full-fledged *Cryptocracy, or Shadow Government.*

Traumatology was/is retrogressive psychology to shock doctrine, which created crisis strategy or post-traumatic culture. By now this must seem very similar to the studies of John B. Watson in teaching fear. That's because it is. The Tavistock readily embraced all of the research findings of the behaviourists as well as the new anthropologists and the untested theories of the psychoanalysts. At the time, there was ample experimental data behind behaviourism, almost entirely manipulated field research behind the new field of anthropology, and no – as in zero -- scientific testing behind the theories of Freud and his disciples. A scientific trio has been built and used in which houses (paradigms) were definitely built upon the sand, should anyone anywhere ever care to inspect the construction. This foundational flaw has never been corrected because the set-up was too useful as established.

Rees had use of a behavioural psychiatry shaped on war, one that is still shaped on war and trauma. Keeping the world in chaos just at the breaking point is tremendously effective for the purpose of social and cultural engineering. All one has to do is look around at the constant false flag operations, pointless wars and conflicts, and things that go boom in the night to understand what is happening based on this information. There is a group practising social engineering for cultural revolution – devising a society they want, without our consent – and using emotional (and physical) abuse at a level almost beyond comprehension to get what they want. John Rees MD created Psychological Shock Troops to control society.

For example, in a key document written by one, Colonel J R Rees, October, 1940, *Strategic Planning for Mental Health,*[76] the subject was of making plans for winning the war and for establishing work for mental health firmly for the future. This fascinating paper sets out the beginnings of a covert plan to make mankind healthy and stating that only psychiatrists are equipped to make mankind healthy.

Key quotes culled from the text discuss infiltration of social organisations; our attack on the professions; long term plan of propaganda; personality tests for Members of Parliament; keeping [this] council's true work hidden with no mention of the so-called mental hygiene they supported; experimentation with films and the media; what exactly constituted the right propaganda, and so forth.

This document formulates a hidden and subversive plan to implement Mental Hygiene on British people and by extension all society. By Mental Hygiene they mean to re-educate, re-frame, force people into their new way of thinking. Those given the new mind-set are deemed hygienic or in a clean state of mental health.

As we have noted, Rees was deeply involved with the Tavistock Institute and in 1948 was President of the World Federation of Mental Health. Tavistock is a key root of mind control and psychiatric subversion as also developed by the Frankfurt School which researched ways of destroying western cultures by means of psychological attack on families and society. Rees is known to have performed drug experiments on prisoners.

For example, during the Second World War, Tavistock

---

[76] Pdf available here: http://www.cpexposed.com/documents/cp-historical-mind-control-documentation-colonel-john-rawlings-rees

was part of Great Britain's Psychological Warfare Department. On May 7, 1944, Dr. Rees of Tavistock and the British War Ministry injected Nazi prisoner Rudolf Hess with the narcotic Evipan. According to Lt. Col. Eugene Bird in *Prisoner No. 7*: Rudolf Hess, (in the chapter titled "A Secret Drug"),[77] Rees examined Hess dozens of times. Rees and his associates caused Hess's memory to fail using chemicals. What exactly was the point of experimenting in this way on Hess in particular?

In 1945, Rockefeller Foundation medical director Alan Gregg toured various institutions that had been involved in war medicine to see if any group would commit to undertake the kind of social psychiatry that had been developed by the Army during wartime (e.g., cultural psychiatry for the analysis of the enemy mentality), and see if it could be relevant for the civilian society (on April 11, 1933, Rockefeller Foundation president Max Mason assured trustees that in their program that the Social Sciences would concern themselves with the rationalization of social control and the control of human behaviour).[78]

"Following Rees' breaking point model, Tavistock took the healing genius of Freud and Jung (Freudianism, by the way is an assumption with no science to back it up. Jung, who broke away from Freud, plumbed the depths of archetypes and the true subconscious), and aimed it like a water cannon loaded with mass psychology."[79]

Against the masses. We stumble across more buzz words, a Tavistock speciality: Group Dynamics, Group-Oriented Personality, Group Process, and Group Relations. The therapeutic state actually became toxic rather quickly. It may well have been

---

[77]   https://www.thetruthseeker.co.uk/?p=8242 p.1

[78]   Cuddy, Dr. Dennis. http://www.newswithviews.com/Cuddy/dennis122.htm p.1

[79]   Miller, Iona. http://tavistockagenda.weebly.com/introduction.html p.1

born that way.

Another Tavistock pillar, Edward Bernays, (Freud's nephew), developer of the 'field' of propaganda and architect behind the coup staged on the United States by the Federal Reserve wrote two critical treatises early on, *Crystallizing Public Opinion* in 1923 and *Propaganda* in 1928. *Propaganda* is available as a pdf online.[80] While in New York City, Bernays invented public relations, opinion polls (which were used to shove the Federal Reserve down our throats), and consumerism.

Some of the other important players, names we are mostly familiar with, associated with The Tavi were Aldous Huxley, father of the LSD experiments; Margaret Mead whose anthropological studies were proved time and again to be complete frauds, who wrote on Child Development and Stress and who also, coincidentally, wrote for the Journal of the Frankfurt School; and Mead's husband, Gregory Bateson, who coined the term 'Double Bind,' and who was in the forefront of the MK Ultra mind control program.

The Tavi motto? Keep them undisciplined, uneducated, disorganized, confused, distracted, and disengaged. Only a thorough understanding of behaviourism and mass psychology forged into traumatology could accomplish all of those things all the time. Keep them drugged, they said, give them what we make them think they want. Tavi is the master of:

1. Destabilization
2. Social Turbulence
3. Series Shocks
4. Superficiality
5. Segmentation

---

[80]   Please see Further Reading at the end of this chapter.

6. Dissonance

7. Suggestibility

8. Superstition

9. Sensitivity

10. Dissociation

11. Spectacle (aka, Bread and Circuses)

12. Sensate Society

and last but certainly not least – Social Slavery.

All of this was developed and accomplished because industrialists wanted to go to war and make enormous amounts money, which they still do today, in case it has escaped anyone's attention that we are and have been for many decades, in a constant state of war. There is always a villain created for us to bring down. *The scenarios is always the same. Always.*

When the Tavistock Institute came to the United States, as inevitably these vampiric organizations do, they came by way of the University of Michigan, Kurt Lewin, MIT, the CIA and Operation Paperclip.

Kurt Lewin created The National Training Laboratories, known as the **NTL Institute**, an American non-profit behavioural psychology centre, in 1947. NTL became a major influence in modern corporate training programs, and in particular developed the T-Group methodology that remains in place today. A note on T-Groups. The concept of encounter as "a meeting of two, eye to eye, face to face," was articulated by JL Moreno in Vienna in 1914-15, in his "Einladung zu Einer Begegnung"[81] ("Invitation to an Encounter"), maturing into his psychodrama therapy. It was

---

[81]   http://agso.uni-graz.at/mitterndorf/moreno_werk/031_einladung_zu_einer_begegnung.htm

pioneered in the mid-1940s by Moreno's protege Kurt Lewin and his colleagues as a method of learning about human behavior in what became The National Training Laboratories (now NTL Institute of Behavioural Science) that was created by the Office of Naval Research (a hive of Operation Paperclip scientists) and the National Education Association in Bethel, Maine in 1947. First conceived as a research technique with a goal to change the standards, attitudes and behaviour of individuals, the T-group evolved into educational and treatment schemes for non-psychiatric patient people.[82] The T-Groups are the sensitivity training groups, the human resources training group, or the encounter group – using role play and in what people refer to as 'touchy-feely' groups so popular beginning in the 1970s.

NTL began publishing *The Journal of Applied Behavioural Science* in 1965 and it remains a renowned publication contributing a body of knowledge to the field that increases our understanding of change processes and outcomes. The NTL Institute continues to work in the field of organizational development. The original centre in Bethel, Maine continues to operate, but the organization has moved its headquarters to Silver Spring, Maryland. Bethel, Maine, by the way, is also home to one of the major apologists for Chemtrailing and Geoengineering, at Colby College.

Most people are already familiar with Massachusetts Institute of Technology in Boston, Columbia University in New York City, as well as The New School for Social Research there and Yale University in New Haven. The University of Michigan as a site seems a bit out-of-the-way and appears to have to do with the study of Human Relations. Since this is a mid-western centre of

---

82   Miller, Iona. From T-Groups to Six Sigma: Subversion in Personal Development and Leadership Training. 2015 http://ionamiller.weebly.com/t-groups-paranoia.html

industry in the US, U Michigan makes some sense. Research yielded an interesting article as an example. The title is as follows: *Human Relations written by* Louise E. Parker and Richard H. Price, *The Effects of Managerial Support and Managerial Perceived Control on Workers' Sense of Control over Decision Making.* (Hawthorne Experiments, anyone?)[83]

I don't know if that title bothers you, but it sure bothers me. The manager's job is to provide the **perception** to the workers that they have any control at all. Not the actual empowerment – the appearance of empowerment. It's all a game, a hologram, a waste of individual sovereign rights, th Deluxe version of the Hamster Cage. It is also one of those things I describe as a poor imitation of something real, something human, something en-*live*ned. This is the speciality of the Predator, an entity with no real enlivening powers or capacities but an entity which wants more than anything to be a co-creator. It is not possible. The 'fruits' of the Predator are always wax fruit, smoke and mirrors, just so much sand through the fingers of the receptive hand, no matter how many pats on the back It gives Itself. (The hoopla over Transhumanism is one of the very best examples of this culture of death attempting to mimic life and calling it immortality, which isn't even to be desired. Who would want to be trapped on the material plane, unable to evolve, ascend or advance? There is a sinister agenda lurking below the sinister agenda in this case).

From a mass psychology and a toxic therapy, we come to the 'Invisible College' of Cultural Psychiatry. The Tavistock's Dr. William Sargant wrote *The Battle for the Mind, The Physiology*

---

83   Parker,L. and Price, R. *Human Relations:The Effects of Managerial Support and Managerial Perceived Control on Workers' Sense of Control over Decision Making. http://hum.sagepub.com*

of Conversion, which might otherwise be termed 'brainwashing.'

William Sargant is a key figure who changed the face of psychiatry - for the worse. Sargant's ideas on mental and behavioural 'patterns' were to influence the notorious CIA-funded Canadian psychopath Dr. Ewan Cameron, who will not be addressed in this volume, leading to malpractice disguised as treatment for schizophrenia. 'Therapy' consisted of wiping the mind of its experiences. Loss of memory of this type and depth makes one wonder, if one has a cosmology that includes reincarnation, if the act of doing this is strictly in the conscious? The etheric sheath is the one just outside the physical body and, as such, is the seat of the memory. The water in the body carries memory, as well, though, and any shock would damage the water in one's body. It is something like 75% or more of who we are. Much of the practices covered in this discussion can be easily classified as spiritual crimes of the highest order.[84]

In *'Battle for the Mind,'* Sargant announced that prolonged, intense emotional stress did indeed cause a complete collapse of the brain and memory, at least temporarily, and allowed behaviours to be implanted. Brainwashing, indeed. Sargant acknowledged that inducing suggestibility is a *brainwashing technique, noting that these were means of indoctrinating people religiously and politically.* Perhaps my characterization of the esoteric memory is too deep to be reached but the water inside one's body is certainly very vulnerable. (Hence the danger from such things as microwaves, which boil us at the cellular level at very low exposures.)

At any rate, this procedure was none other than a form of experimental electro-shock therapy (ECT). Using Sargant's

---

[84]   On the book, *The Battle for the Mind, The Physiology of Coversion.* http://vserver1.cscs.lsa.umich.edu/~crshalizi/reviews/battle-for-the-mind/ p.1

methods, Cameron transformed the dynamics of political and religious conversion - as described by Sargant in '*Battle for the Mind*' - by employing in the medical situation what Sargant calls physiological conversion. Sargant really did provide knowledge underpinnings, making clear that physiological brain disturbances induced from the outside were required. The study of physiology is, of course, a foundation of medical science - not that Sargant says much about the actualities of physiological conversion, leaving others to describe outcomes. He didn't need to go into details; secrecy was of the essence, just as secrecy explains the pretence brainwashing was treatment. Aided by being able to publish his theories and his impressions in professional journals (as well as in '*Battle for the Mind*') and by the absence of any objections, Sargant achieved his aim of turning brainwashing into therapy. The reason schizophrenics were given an inordinate amount of ECT, compared with depressives, is because Sargant's brainwashing became accepted medical practice.[85]

As well as being a practising psychiatrist, William Sargant was a Minister of Religion for the Congregationalist Church. The subtitle of '*Battle for the Mind*' - '*A Physiology of Conversion and Brain-Washing*' - gives a clue to the fact that this book combines Sargent's two great interests, psychiatry and religion. In tandem with Cameron, his intention is to restate in medical terms the fruits of a careful study of the methods of evangelical, and even of African religions, in order that psychiatrists might take over and develop the 'science' of brainwashing. Occasionally, he says as much.

In his opinion, "if a simple medical means of breaking up chronic obsessions is ever discovered, one of the final weapons

---

[85]   On the book, *The Battle for the Mind, The Physiology of Coversion.* http://vserver1.cscs.lsa.umich.edu/~crshalizi/reviews/battle-for-the-mind/ p.1

will have been forged for the armoury of the *religious and political conversion practitioners*." (Emphasis added.) Away from Sargant, the term employed was 'depatterning' rather than the populist 'brainwashing,' but the euphemism was no more scientific. What mattered in those days was authority and not science. Sargant depended on it. We are not speaking here of 'depatterning' the violently insane, for example, but the normal everyday citizen. Who gave these people permission to do this on an unwitting population? This absolutely and fundamentally constitutes medical experimentation without informed consent. The men, both Sargant and Slater, indicated that the methods they developed were still in use as of 1951 because they work but any theory behind them is irrelevant.

In wartime Britain, Sargant was an influential authority, at the forefront when it came to advising on the best ways to deal with battle trauma. He helped to get ECT machines humming across the land, ostensibly to treat shell shock, and he was keen on psycho-surgery, too. It is possible some of the reality behind the words was experimentation, as a hidden agenda of which he approved motivated the militarily inclined Sargant - that the West should develop mind control before the Russians and Chinese did. Who needed Joseph Mengele with this man around?

It is clear from the book that a lot of the reality was, in Sargant's eyes, treatment for mental distress. He suggests that cures occur with the physical physiological techniques, including ECT. In fact, the roots of this particular appreciation came not from religion but from Pavlov. Sargant acknowledges that *inducing suggestibility* (marketing and advertising) is a brainwashing technique. Unfortunately for the world, this is a seminal work for the understanding of the history of psychiatric theory and practice.

Eric Trist was another founding member of the

Tavistock Institute and chairman from 1956 - 1966. He spent his last years in the preparation of *The Social Engagement of Social Science*[86] – Tavistock's work on mass brainwashing, delineating in detail a theory of social turbulence, based upon the theories of Hegel. (Crisis, Reaction, Solution).

Trist postulated that the administering of a series of traumatizing shocks upon a society would destabilize it, lowering the overall character of the society's reasoning. Trist suggested that by late 1963 the world had moved into a condition of "permanent social turbulence" that would serve to usher in a new condition of society, a new paradigm, and a new possibility for remaking the face of the planet. Traumatology. Permanent Social Turbulence. Are we not living it?

Back in the mid-1970s, Eric Trist and Fred Emery, two leading Tavistock brainwashers and experts on the effects of mass media, forecast that, by the end of the century, the United States were likely to become just such a fascist police state. The two developed a theory of social turbulence, by which a society is delivered a series of shocks--administered as shared, mass phenomena--energy shortages, economic and financial collapse, and *terrorist* attacks. If the shocks were to come close upon each other, and if they were delivered with increasing intensity, then it were possible to drive the entire society, into a state of mass psychosis, Trist and Emery said. They said that individuals would become disassociated, as they tried to flee from the terror of the shocking, emerging reality; people would withdraw into a state of denial, retreating into popular entertainments and diversions, while being prone to outbursts of rage.

That rage could easily be steered, said the two brainwashers, by those who had access and control over the means

[86] Pdf. http://www.moderntimesworkplace.com/archives/ericsess/ericsess.html 3 volumes.

of mass communication, most notably television. Then we can have scenarios such as we have had in Egypt, in Libya, almost in Syria, all over the Middle East, Yugoslavia and the Ukraine. Constant turmoil, terror, complete emotional exhaustion of the population of the planet, and total control by just a few. All that would be needed would be a panel or administration of authoritarian psychopaths in legislation or judiciary or executive office either willing to take these orders for a population or issue the orders themselves. We have had that mix in the United States for some time.

It was the view of Trist and Emery, in two works widely circulated among the networks of brainwashers and social psychiatrists associated with Tavistock, and among the psychological-warfare operatives of the U.S. and Britain, that the process of watching television was itself a brainwashing mechanism.[87] They cited their own studies, that regardless of content, habituated television viewing shuts down the cognitive powers of the mind, and has a narcotic-like effect on the central nervous system, making the habituated viewer an easy subject for suggestion and manipulation; in addition, they found that such effectively brainwashed "zombies" would hysterically deny that there was anything wrong with them, or, even, that such manipulation of what they "thought" were possible. However, we will save that discussion for the chapter on entertainment and the media.

The Tavistock plays a pivotal role in shaping political, social, educational, and economic 'opinions', especially in the United States. It is in the United States where mass deception about child development, child empowerment and "crowd control" media

---

[87] Emery, F. *Latent Content of Television Viewing.*http://www.moderntimesworkplace.com/archives/ericsess/sessvol1/Emeryp574.opd.pdf

propaganda is most profoundly universal due to highly unconstitutional wrongful authority by the federal government.

Meanwhile, sixty odd years ago, the journal *Human Relations* was founded jointly by the Tavistock Institute, the University of Michigan and the Institution for Social Research (the old Frankfurt School). Briefly, at the centre of this circle in the US stands the CIA but please let us not forget all the other black ops organizations. Tavistock provided most of the detailed programs for establishing the Office of Naval Intelligence, (ONI). This wing of intelligence dwarfs the CIA in size and scope. The U.S. Government gave billion dollar contracts to Tavistock. Tavistock's strategic planners provide most of the long-range plans used in the defence establishment. Once again, the Tavistock Institute, and Chatham House from whence it operates, are located in London. England. This is one of the realities that simply must dawn on a population that believes it is separated from the British crown.

From the CIA, money pours out to Foundations, Associations, Institutes and Funds of all sorts. From these, money is delivered to news services, journalists, universities, magazines, conferences, charitable groups, and education associations. The Tavi is a $6 billion dollar globe-squeezing octopus comprised of Foundations – 10 Institutions, 400 plus subsidiaries, 3000 plus study groups and think tanks...all aimed at dismantling ideals, creating trauma and war, conditioning, engineering consent, and manipulating human beings on a level that is nothing short of global spiritual rape.

From its on opening statement at its website:

...the **Tavistock Institute** *is an independent not-for-profit organization which seeks to combine research in the social sciences with professional practice. Problems of institution-building and organizational design and change are being tackled*

in all sectors - government, industry and commerce, health and welfare, education, etc. - nationally and internationally, and clients range from multinationals to small community groups. A growth area has been the use of a developmental approach to evaluation of new and experimental programmes, particularly in health, education and community development. This has also produced new training events alongside the regular programme of group relations conferences. The Institute owns and edits the monthly journal Human Relations(published by Plenum Press) which is now in its 48th year, and has recently launched (in conjunction with Sage Publications) a new journal Evaluation. (The Journal of Human Relations was ostensibly published by the University of Michigan. Editor's note).*

Three elements combine to make the Institute unusual, if not unique: it has the independence of being entirely self-financing, with no subsidies from the government or other sources; **the action research orientation places it between, but not in, the worlds of academia and consultancy; and its range of disciplines include anthropology, economics, organizational behavior, political science, psychoanalysis, psychology and sociology.** (emphasis added).

So reads the opening paragraphs of the Tavistock Institute home page.[88]

Tavistock joined the Research Centre for Group Dynamics (RCGD) at the University of Michigan to publish the international journal, as we noted earlier, relating theory to practice. The first volume contained articles such as "*Overcoming*

---

[88]   *http://www.tavinstitute.org/ further investigations, http://netteandme.blogspot.co.uk/2014_10_01_archive.html* and

Resistance to Change," and "*A Comparison of the Aims of the Hitler Youth and the Boy Scouts of America.*" The Tavistock Institute would use Lewin's techniques to arrange "therapeutic communities." [89]

Lewin received his Ph.D. from Berlin University in 1914, and in 1932 came to the U.S. During the Second World War, he worked for the U.S. Office of Strategic Services (which would become the CIA) in psychological warfare. He founded the RCGD in 1946 followed by a research arm of the National Education Association. He then began the NTL.   Over the next two decades, the NTL would spread its operations to various countries around the world. And in its Issues in (Human Relations) Training (1962), its sensitivity training is referred to as "brainwashing." Recently, NTL has conducted programs relevant to Tavistock such as "*NTL and Tavistock: Two Traditions of Group Work,*" "*Tavistock Program: Re-Thinking and Planning for Organizational Change,*" and "*The Tavistock--Task Working Conference.*"

The year after Tavistock and the RCGD began publishing Human Relations, that journal (Vol. II, No. 3, 1949), published "*Some Principles of Mass Persuasion*" by Dorwin Cartwright who helped establish the Institute for Social Research at the University of Michigan. In this article, it is explained that bending the will of the people through mass media is a simple and completely conceivable process. Cognitive structure is actually modified by mass media and a person can be induced to do something he or she would not ordinarily do.

Finally, an offshoot of the Tavistock Institute, AK Rice Institute for the Study of Social Systems claimed as its mission: to understand covert processes affecting leadership/authority in

---

[89]   Cuddy, Dr. Dennis. Tavistock. http://www.newswithviews.com/Cuddy/dennis122.htm
        p.1

groups using the Tavistock group relations tradition of open systems. For all intents and purposes, the Rice Institute is the Tavistock Institute in America. It is known as the Social Research Institute.

Since I entered politics, I have chiefly had men's views confided to me privately. Some of the biggest men in the United States, in the Field of commerce and manufacture, are afraid of something. They know that there is a power somewhere so organized, so subtle, so watchful, so interlocked, so complete, so pervasive, that they better not speak above their breath when they speak in condemnation of it.
(President) Woodrow Wilson, The New Freedom (1913)[90] Public Domain (December 28, 1856 – February 3, 1924)

There is still so much to say. The purpose here though is to create an understanding of the massive global hijacking that has occurred so that we can understand that the modern paradigm is a false paradigm. The aim is to take all the fractured pieces and put them together so that we can understand our context and heal.

Nota Bene

Behaviourism

"In 1964, Fred Emery, who would be a senior member of Tavistock, wrote "Theories of Social Turbulence" which he explained more fully in *Futures We are In* (1975). According to this theory, individuals or societies faced with a series of crises will attempt to reduce the tension by adaptation and eventually

---

[90]   Wilson, W. *The New Freedom.* https://www.gutenberg.org/files/14811/14811-h/14811-h.htm p.1

123

psychological retreat as if anaesthetized (similar to Pavlov's 'protective inhibition response'). This can lead to social disintegration, which Emery called 'segmentation.' " [91]

Education

In 1970, the Association for Supervision and Curriculum Development (ASCD) of the NEA published *To Nurture Humaneness: Committment for the '70s,* in which Sidney Jourard (Fellow at the Tavistock Clinic and former president of the Association for Humanist Psychology) delivered the bad news: we are in a time of revolt and the end result will either be fascism or pluralistic. Corporations go hand-in-hand with fascist government.

In the 1990s, the Tavistock Institute not only began a new journal titled *Evaluation* in 1995, but the Institute and the European Commission also worked on a feasibility study to research the effect of using "Smart Cards" in competence accreditation.[92] The study was carried out in the U.S. and parts of Europe. The project involved assessing and validating students' skills, with information placed on personal skills Smart Cards which control employment. The implication, of course, is that without this one will not be employed.

From Blood to Dust

Relevant to this, in October 1997 the Tavistock Institute (and Manchester University) completed a final report for the European Commission, and described in a report summary that

[91] Cuddy, Dr. Dennis. Tavistock. http://www.newswithviews.com/Cuddy/dennis122.htm p.1
[92] Ibid.

124

there will be "partnerships between government, industry, and representatives of worker organizations." The report summary also described "the relevancy of Goals 2000, SCANS (U.S. Department of Labor Secretary's Commission on Achieving Necessary Skills) typology with its profound implications for the curriculum and training changes that this will require," valid skills standards and portable credentials "benchmarked to international standards such as those promulgated by the International Standards Organization (ISO)." The report summary went on to say that "there is increasing attention being focused on developing global skill standards and accreditation agreements." Smart Cards.

Just as an aside, I want to bring up an off-shoot of the Tavistock Agenda, called the **Cerebral Inhibition Meeting**. [93] The Macy Cybernetics Conferences were preceded by the Cerebral Inhibition Meeting, organized by Frank Fremont-Smith in May, 1942. This was an invitation only meeting attended by: Gregory Bateson, Lawrence K. Frank, Margaret Mead, Warren McCulloch, Arturo Rosenbleuth, and Lawrence Kubie, among others. We will be looking into that. There were two topics at this conference: Hypnotism, introduced by Milton Erikson and Conditioned Reflex, introduced by Howard Liddell. *Cerebral Inhibition.* (Still think Mead is an innocent and enterprising anthropologist?) These meetings gave birth to Cybernetics. There is a critically important article to be gleaned from all of this written about her husband, Gregory Batesone published a critically important article called, **"Gregory Bateson and the OSS: World War II and Bateson's Assessment of Applied Anthropology** by Dr. David H. Price.**94**

[93]

    http://www.fornits.com/phpbb/index.php?PHPSESSID=cba3678 098f6ce80cfd201397c518b39&topic=32643.msg391743#msg391743

[94]   **"Gregory Bateson and the OSS: World War II and Bateson's Assessment of**

Welcome to the Tavistock emotionally, physically and psychologically attained feudal fascist state of the future, under the power elite's planned World Freudo-Marxist Government. Wait 'til you meet the other arm, The Frankfurt Institute.

What can you do right now, this minute, to turn the ship around? In the case of this entity:

• Turn off your television. Get it out of the house, if you can. This is Job One.

• Stop going to movies until you have educated yourself about their programming.

• Stop reading popular magazines and newspapers of any kind. None of it is true, they are all actors, bought and paid for, or threatened. At best they are hypnotized.

• Find and watch alternative news sources on the internet for all your news, bearing in mind that the
Predator is absolutely furious about the lack of ability to plug all the information holes on the internet and is constantly infiltrating.

• Remember the phenomenon of a 'truth sandwich.' Look for the Big Lie under the mayonnaise and pickles.

• Learn about the 'Colour Revolutions' and how they work. F. William Engdahl is a good source.

• Re-train your mind to *really know* that all history is a very recent construct. It is made up for the most part to suit the Predator's Agenda.

• Make yourself part of a group of people on the trail to the truth

Applied Anthropology by Dr David H. Price, USA
http://www.currentconcerns.ch/index.php?id=1110

127

Recommended Reading

Clarence Karier *Scientists of the Mind*

John Dewey *Humanist Manifesto*

Colonel J R Rees, *October, 1940, Strategic Planning for Mental Health.*

Edward Bernays *Crystallizing Public Opinion in 1923 and Propaganda in 1928*

Dr. William Sargant *The Battle for the Mind, The Physiology of Conversion*

Eric Trist *The Social Engagement of Social Science*

Eric Trist
http://www.moderntimesworkplace.com/archives/ericsess/sessvol3/Tristp517.opd.pdf

The Alan Gregg Papers
http://profiles.nlm.nih.gov/ps/retrieve/Narrative/FS/p-nid/212

McFate, Dr. Montgomery. Anthropology and Counter-Insurgency: The Strange Story of their Curious Relationship.
http://www.au.af.mil/au/awc/awcgate/milreview/mcfate.pdf

Chapter Five

What the Inmates Prescribed...Pathocracy

A pathocracy has been loosely described as a system of government created by a small pathological group that takes control over a society of normal people. We could easily call our social environment either a crypto-pathocracy or a patho-cryptocracy. Both are true. It all depends on whether one regards secrecy as the leading factor or the psychopathy of those keeping the secrets. The pathocracy is not our natural cultural environment. Our cultural environment is under violent attack by the pathocracy.

Our folk souls, expressed collectively as our cultures, are the tangible parts of our incarnated souls and mustn't be politicized or used to separate us unduly. They are the beautifully embroidered costumes in which we have chosen to dress our Universal Human. This, along with the human child, are what is truly under the most vicious attack by means of social engineering. The pathocracy is the Predator. This brings us from one arm, The Tavistock Institute, to the other arm; The Frankfurt School.[95] The Frankfurt School has absolutely nothing to do with the German people, folk soul, or culture. It is a thing apart, conceived of and run by psychopaths but geographically situated initially in Frankfurt largely for darker esoteric reasons. Let us never, ever mix these things up again for all our sakes. Many, many destructive entities have been birthed in Germany precisely because Germany is the seat of so much that is deeply artistic, philosophical, powerful and profound. The Predator feeds on the

[95]   http://en.wikipedia.org/wiki/Frankfurt_School

destruction of these impulses, like a vampire. The Predator dresses itself up in what cultural costumery it can steal and stands downwind so we, the prey, are unlikely to smell it until it has us in its slavering jaws.

In order to dig down to the the origins of this group, this 'think-tank', if you will, of The Frankfurt School (more accurately known as the Institute for Social Research), one has to have a brief look at both the unfolding of the Bolshevik Revolution which failed so miserably in Russia and, to a somewhat lesser degree, the workings of The Fabian Society in England.[96]

To the best of our rather confined-at-the-moment knowledge, we can speak of two kinds of revolution. One is blatant *political* **revolution**, which could be characterized as the gaining of power through violence and the use of terror. The Russian Revolution is a good illustration of a blatantly political (armed) takeover with a Marxist base. Another is the coup d'etat in the United States which began with the election of Woodrow Wilson, who took his orders from Chatham House-The Tavistock Institute. This continued with the engineered 'example' assassination of John F. Kennedy and eventually segued into a true political (read: violent/terror-based) coup-d'etat on the heels of 9/11. This is where Americans find themselves today...as an occupied nation, every bit as much as any other occupied nation on the planet.

The other is *cultural* **revolution** in which one chips away from within, via social engineering. It matters only how quickly or slowly, the basis of civilized society in the country one wants to subdue –its culture, way of life, beliefs, morality, values, etc. Even when it is 'quick,' it is still a long-term plan. The United States is also a prime example of a long-term socially-engineered

---

[96]   http://en.wikipedia.org/wiki/Fabian_Society

cultural revolution with a Freudo-Marxist base. In fact, it might be worth saying that there appear to be two sometimes cooperative, sometimes opposing forces at work in the United States, as I noted previously. Each thinks it will emerge triumphant in the end but fascism and Freudo-Marxism, despite being birthed by the same set of circumstances, cannot co-exists. Neither should exist, at all. The brutal machine of 20th century social engineering allowed the 9/11 coup d'etat to take place.

At the beginning of the 19th century Joseph de Maistre, French defender of the monarchy, leader of the counter-enlightenment, writer, philosopher and so forth, characterized cultural revolution.[97] To some it seemed that conquest itself, war and the like, were a thing of the past. A nation could be killed from within, such as with the use of the social engineering techniques devised by the Freudo-Marxists. Once again, successful Marxism itself is the modern underlying foundation of the slow-boil cultural death. Used as the basis for a sudden political revolution, however, it tends to fail.

All Marxism is a shadow; it's a critique; it's a sort of feeding on the road-kill carcass of something which exists with you or before you. Essentially, the recipe is as follows: tear it apart, turn it around, re-engineer it and come to a conclusion on the basis of a negation. So the negation of that which exists before is the key to this type of thinking. (Negation, opposite, shadow...remember photography here). This is the inversion tactic we see everywhere today when we are not so thoroughly overwhelmed with situations and data and loud noises that we can actually see the outlines of a

---

[97] "Modernity and the theologico-political problem in the thought of Joseph de Maistre and Fyodor Dostoyevsky: A comprehensive comparison" https://www.ruor.uottawa.ca/bitstream/10393/24358/1/Racu_Alexandru_2013_thesis.pdf p.67

thing. The true problem is that this inversion, this critiquing, is the *entire point* – the communist dialectic – the dialectic being the only point. It is struggle for the sake of struggle. Without struggle there is no reason for existence. How well this philosophy of perpetual conflict goes with the application of Traumatology via The Tavişţock Institute.

Ruthless criticism of all that exists: by this Marx meant all the elements of *Western* culture. These ideas of Marx matched those brought into play by the Freemasons at the same time. It will suffice to remember that the essential thing is to isolate men from their families and hence cause them to lose their moral compass.

After Marx issued the *Communist Manifesto*[98] in 1848, Marxism as such concentrated on political and economic action. Its attack on Western culture moved on to Plan B. In the 1920s, followers returned to the script set out in 1848. After the October Revolution in Russia, Lenin sought to export revolution to Central and Western Europe in order to save it in Russia. "This problem was that of *the imperative need for the extension of the revolution on an international scale.* And for the Russian revolution this problem was posed amidst the special circumstances of the imperialist war, a war that had led to the destruction of the Russian state and the establishment of the dictatorship of the Soviets after October 1917." [99]

Indeed, revolution almost failed in Russia, but was yanked from the jaws of obscurity by American industrial and British banking support. Marxism failed in Hungary, too, where Bela Kun in 1919 was not able to maintain a Communist regime.[100]

[98] Marx, K. Communist Manifesto. 1848
https://www.marxists.org/archive/marx/works/download/pdf/Manifesto.pdf
[99] The 1918 Treaty of Brest-Litovsk: Curbing the Revolution. Part One. p.1
https://libcom.org/book/export/html/45641

132

The Hungarian Georg Lukacs,[101] whose name will emerge again in
relation to The Frankfurt Group, tried hard to push a cultural
revolution down Hungarian throats but was stopped when outraged
citizens objected to the early sexualization of children. This
technique appears again and again as an instrument of profound
destruction. That appears again and again to be the line they
cannot cross, thankfully. It is happening today in Germany, in
England, and coming soon to the United States.

To be sure, revolution failed in Germany, where the
Spartacus League, founded in 1916, organized an uprising in Berlin
in 1919, which was fiercely suppressed. It failed in Italy, where
Communist parties and unions were subjected to a crushing defeat
by the ex-Bolshevik, Mussolini.

Reflection led to conclusions regarding strategy
especially via a meeting (Communist International) organized at
the end of 1922, on Lenin's initiative, at the Marx-Engels Institute
in Moscow.[102] It's aim was to solidify the concept of cultural
revolution as opposed to outright violent political revolution and
the basis of its further dissemination. Dialectic: tear it down, turn it
around, try it out. The attack, in whatever form, would be
relentless.

Participants in the first Comintern meeting were Karl
Radek, Lenin's representative; Felix Dzherzhinsky, representative
of the *Soviet Bolshevik* global network; Willi Munzenberg; and
Georg Lukacs. (It is important to clearly delineate the difference

---

[100] http://en.wikipedia.org/wiki/Hungarian_Soviet_Republic

[101] Georg Lukacs, Stanford Encyclopedia of Philosophy.
http://plato.stanford.edu/entries/lukacs/

[102] https://www.marxists.org/history/international/comintern/

133

between a mercenary political overlay and a Folk Soul, for it is no more the Russian people themselves who are violent and ruthless or communistic than it is the Americans themselves who are the warmongers of the world. We are talking about the strategies of upper-echelon government gangs and thugs for whom no one voted. It is the ugly yoke laid upon our collective shoulders).

Let us consider the two most influential members at this meeting: Willi Munzenberg and Georg Lukacs. Willi Munzenberg played an important role in the creation of the Comintern. He was a German Communist leader in the inter-war period who brought a sense of organization to the proposed cultural revolution.

Georg Lukacs was of a Jewish family from Hungary, an aristocrat, son of one of the Hapsburg Empire's leading bankers. He was the People's Commissar for Culture and Education in Bela Kun's Communist government in Hungary. He developed the subject "Revolution and Eros,"[103] in other words, to use the sex instinct as an instrument of destruction. This meant trying to awaken a completely inappropriate and cataclysmic sexual impulse in very young children, as well. Modern historians link the shortness of the Budapest experiment to Lukacs' orders mandating 'sex education in the schools, easy access to contraception, and the loosening of the divorce laws' – all of which repulsed Hungary's Catholic population. Since young children never really heal completely from that sort of fracturing of the psyche, this is destruction writ large. As mentioned previously, this tactic backfired and destroyed the Hungarian attempt.

Lukacs' role in what was to come was decisive and demonic. He brought his ideas to the cultural revolution in the

---

[103] The Frankfurt School and the War on the West.
http://billmuehlenberg.com/2009/05/11/the-frankfurt-school-and-the-war-on-the-west/
p.1

134

United States, which then spread like a disease around the world. This cultural rape benefited from Lukacs' connection to German artists and intellectual movements at hand in the neighbourhood of the founding of The Frankfurt School. The Bolshevik Revolution had not been brought about by spontaneous mass demonstrations, he knew quite well, but by the disintegration of Tsarism, the corruption of the ruling class, and by **the erosion of that class's faith in itself and its will to hold to power.** This would be the bottom line for all future attempts: the erosion of trust and faith of the individual in him or herself while being stuffed into a pathologically individualistic straight-jacket. *I don't trust myself at all but I am all I have.* Quite the paralysing predicament.

Lukacs determined that any political movement capable of bringing Bolshevism to the West would have to be 'demonic,' it would have to 'possess the religious power which is capable of filling the entire soul...''[104] According to an eyewitness, during meetings of the Hungarian Soviet leadership in 1919 to draw up lists for the firing squad, Lukacs would often dare the world to judge him. Psychopathy. Vultures hovering over road-kill.

Cultural revolution strategy was the best bet in producing the conditions for the longed-for Communist revolution. The obstacle? Western civilization itself. Of all the pillars of western civilization the two which would prove to be the strongest and the ones that most needed elimination were the idea of God and the human institution of the family. The FS via Lukacs called for a complete redefinition of the soul. This focus was in tandem with the goal of redefining the soul as set out by the initiators of psycho-analysis. In fact, it is the human soul which

---

[104] http://new.euro-med.dk/20140106-world-communism-of-the-pharisees-nearly-succeeds-satans-one-world-governance-by-stinking-pervesity-school-of-frankfurt.php

has been under direct attack from the onset.

Lukacs identified the main difference between Russia and the West as the cultural matrix which highlighted the uniqueness and sanctity of the individual. Western ideology maintained that the individual, through the use of reason, could discover Divine Will in a one-to-one relationship. This implied that the individual could change the universe in pursuit of the Good. As long as the individual held that belief, some idea he or she could solve society's ills, then society would never reach the state of abject hopelessness necessary for a socialist revolution. This has been the basis of the all-out attack on the American middle class, as well, as a foundational and functioning social unit. The US is the only country in the world which has had a true middle class, now all but destroyed. (As of the time of this writing, 2014, there are 65 million Americans living on social welfare). Nonetheless, the US would have to do. Russia had been, in their estimation, much too much of a collective cohesive soul, for success. Perhaps, the land of the individual would surrender itself, young and raucous and inexperienced as it was, not in one fierce blast but over time, gradually, yielding to the patient, relentless, drip of water decade after decade after decade. Indeed, it was the very qualities which seemed to make it vulnerable that, in the end, would also be its greatest strengths and no transformation of the world could take place without destroying the American will. The United States was destined to be the gesture of transformation into sovereign individuality. All nations have a mission. All missions had to be short-circuited.

No matter the technique, Willi Munzenbürg[105] called for

105

http://en.wikipedia.org/wi

sheer destruction as the goal. The intellectuals would be organized and used to make western civilization stink. All values were to be corrupted, a dictatorship was to be imposed.

The second point of attack culled from this meeting: exploit the ideas of Sigmund Freud in a Marxist way, for Bolshevik purposes. Hence the Frankfurt school members became Freudo-Marxists, two would-be destroyers of the human soul entwined in a double-headed death dance. Freud, of course, was concerned, obsessed even, with the sexual act.

"The start of the conceptual debasement of man's sexual instincts had been begun by Sigmund Freud...sex, the most explosive aspect of the human psyche, was to be unleashed. An amalgam of neo-Freudianism and neo-Marxism were to destroy the fragile defences of Western Civilisation's immune system."[106]

It seems evident that the nature of the sexual act was and, now is, completely misunderstood. This was associated with a lower (meaning more basic and, if you will, closer to the earth, whirling at a slower speed and frequency. It does not mean dirty or filthy.) chakra. All chakras are powerful, all have a divine purpose, none is necessarily more powerful than another as each has its own purpose. It is true that the lower chakras are more easily injured. It is also true that not rising above the third chakras means being locked into a lower consciousness. This is the reason they are targeted and sex is an avenue. An easy avenue. Sex, the easiest aspect of the human experience to exploit, was about to be

---

ki/Willi_M%C3%BCnzenberg Willi Munzenberg(sic)

[106]   Arnaud de Lassus, The Genesis of the Cultural Revolution, The Frankfurt School
    http://www.apropos.org.uk/documents/FrankfurtSchoolApropos21A4
    offprint_001.pdf Ralph de Toledano, op.cit. P. 24.

debased and our inner spirit was about to be chained to that chakra. It is hoped that this will prevent our full incarnation as divine spiritual beings.

To everything there is a season. It is easiest to injure this chakra when we are children. Catastrophic injury is as easy as waking up that chakra before it is time. (Hello, sex education for kindergartners). It is also a tried and true method of mind control to use the moment of sexual release as a moment of 'programming.' However, that is a bit beyond the intended scope of this book. However, the following is one of an avalanche of modern examples: from a recent newspaper article in the United Kingdom, based on a very sexually explicit book being given to five-year-olds we summarize, teachers are being asked to explain that there are different levels of pornography, and not all pornography is bad. This trend is becoming global, with teachers being forced into roles as sexual offenders in a real way and parents unable to effectively object. One of the main directives of The Frankfurt School was the drive a Marxist take on Freud's Pansexualism into the world at large.[107]

Prior to the rise of Hitler and the arrival in the United States of the erstwhile Frankfurt School, an Institute for Marxism was founded in Frankfurt in 1923. Given the anti-Bolshevik sentiment attendant with the world wars, the FFS quickly adopted a more neutral and wholesome label: "The Institute for Social Research," while finding a home at the University of Frankfurt. Eventually, it was referred to as the Frankfurt School.

107

Sergio Salvatore, S and Zittoun, T. Ed. Cultural Psychology and Psychoanalysis: Pathways to Synthesis p.61

138

The choice of Frankfurt was natural. It was and has always been one of the prime centres of influence in Germany and in Europe. It is the seat of several financial dynasties as well as prominent Illuminati. Frankfurt was also the German city that had the highest percentage of Jews in the population of any German town as well as an unusually high number of middle-class sympathizers with socialism and communism. This 'School' (designed to put flesh on their revolutionary program) was started at the University of Frankfurt in the Institut für Sozialforschung. To begin with school and institute were indistinguishable. In 1923 the Institute was officially established, and funded by Felix Weil (1898-1975). Weil was born in Argentina and at the age of nine was sent to attend school in Germany. He attended the universities in Tübingen and Frankfurt, where he graduated with a doctoral degree in political science. While at these universities he became increasingly interested in socialism and Marxism. According to the intellectual historian Martin Jay, the topic of his dissertation was 'the practical problems of implementing socialism.'[108]

Carl Grünberg, the Institute's director from 1923-1929, was an avowed Marxist, although the Institute did not have any official party affiliations. But in 1930 Max Horkheimer assumed control and he believed that Marx's theory should be the basis of the Institute's research. When Hitler came to power, the Institut was closed and its members fled to the United States and migrated to major US universities—Columbia, Princeton, Brandeis, and California at Berkeley.

[108]   Jay, M. Creation of the Institut für Sozialforschung, 1973.
https://www.marxists.org/subject/frankfurt-school/

However, the Frankfurt School rejected revolutionary Marxism and instead used and advocated "gradualism", a step-by-step long-term plan to change the character of the West through stealth and infiltration, which could be achieved via the incorporation of Freud's pseudo-scientific technique. It was a matter of the chances for success rather than some revulsion at sudden political upheaval. History had demonstrated that Marxism did not have the social dynamite to make that happen although several of its members had been unapologetically involved in those prior. An unfortunate hybrid has developed between post-war secular/capitalist concerns and Marxism. If the fetid balance between the two wavers even a little the resulting infection is fascism.

At the same time, the phenomenon of The Fabian Society joined the revolutionary wave. In 1905, American Fabians established the *Rand School of Social Science* in New York City and incorporated the *Intercollegiate Socialist Society* to promote socialism among college students. A founding member was American Fabian John Dewey, considered the 'father' of progressive education, and an atheist, socialist, and evolutionist.

In 1921 the Fabian Rand School changed its name to *The League for Industrial Democracy* and established a network of 125 chapters with the aim of de-Christianising America. Dewey became president of it in 1941. Dewey also co-founded the New School for Social Research (NSSR) in 1919, which is a Fabian-socialist institution that is the American equivalent to the London School of Economics and Political Science. This school was funded by the Rockefeller Foundation and the Carnegie Corporation.[109]

---

[109] Marxism and the Planned Corruption of America.
http://www.crossroad.to/Quotes/brainwashing/2009/frankfurt-dewey.htm p.1

(We should pause for a moment here and acknowledge that we keep seeing the date, 1919. The attempted Hungarian Marxist revolution, the founding of the New School in New York, and so many other negative initiatives. However, it was also the year Rudolf Steiner established the first Waldorf school in Germany as an antidote for the Compulsive Pavlovian model in use.)

Some of the original members and important personalities at the Frankfurt School were: Erich Fromm (1900-80); Theodor Adorno (1903-69), media mogul and author of the book *The Authoritarian Personality;* Karl Korsch (1886-1961); Wilhem Reich (1897-1957); Friedrich Pollock (1894-1970); Walter Benjamin (1892-1940); and Herbert Marcuse (1898-1979), who was accepted as a member of the Institute in 1932. It is important to note that Herbert Marcuse's arrival strengthened the group of those within the Institute who had adopted a dialectical Marxism. Strategically placed members meant that the struggle would be spread everywhere like a virus, finding hosts upon which to feed in every conceivable niche of human life. The debate was all.

Even fifty years ago many of the 'values' that face us via the media and elsewhere would, among ordinary and apolitical people, been regarded as abhorrent, a nightmare, impossible for sane people. Now these values are the norm and to speak out against them at all is to attack choice at best and even commit "thought crimes."[110] That we can even consider the idea of a 'thought crime,' is both ludicrous and dehumanizing. Our thoughts are our own; our imagination the emperor of such. However, the ideas of thought crimes and thought police does speak to the

---

[110] It was Lenin's Minister of Education who coined the term Political Correctness and Lenin himself who invented the word racism.

ultimate target of these 'revolutions,' and that, we mustn't forget is the very powerful human imagination, which resides in our thoughts and our heart-mind. Regulations tangent to our very thoughts suggest someone or something else 'owns' them. Our imaginations are the true prisoners but only because we do not realize the chains are an ingrained hologram and not made of iron links. Our imaginations are the true prisoners because we dare not use them for fear of being tagged politically incorrect. It has gone that far.

The Frankfurt School grew up in Germany in a very yeasty, volatile time, just prior to Hitler's rise, in the belly of a stunned, confused, and yes, victimized nation. The ground was fertile because Marxism feeds on crisis; crisis as a way of life and development, and this was a group of very disappointed post-Russian Revolution Marxists. Some of the crises were, in fact, created by both the FS (Frankfurt School) and the Tavi (Tavistock Institute). Creating trauma and crisis was the business of The Tavistock Institute, as we now know, and they had already practised with a world war scenario on the same populations. Certainly the stunned post-WWI German population was the direct result of the creation of such by pre-WWI Tavistock 'social engineers.' Like the Tavistock Institute and their policy of 'all trauma, all the time,' the FS created conflict if there wasn't any handy. Conflict without rest is the perfect medium and the perfect canvas for a human takeover. (I believe this is also how one elicits a confession from a political prisoner).

For the highly motivated Frankfurt School group, the opportunity for dialectic, the constant agitation of one crisis against another was meat for the table. It is the struggle that counts rather than the outcome so there must be struggle, no matter what. Endless critique; endless vistas of struggle; endless debate and so forth. The FS set out to critique all of Marxism, transform it and set it upon modern western society, which it would also critique unto death. The addition of Herbert Marcuse as the 'leader' of the now stereotypical student demonstration fine-tuned that point. Once again, a protest, which I believe is actually a process test of selected aspects of social engineering is called a 'demonstration.' Demonstration = Process Test? I often wonder, based on what we have learned regarding the cultural engineering successfully conducted in America, if protester simply stands for 'process tester.' This isn't far-fetched if one realizes what a television 'program' actually is. Programming, indeed.

One of the truly interesting and unintentional by-products of the tenets of Bolshevism reworked by the FS is actually fascism, as was briefly mentioned above. Mussolini was a reformed Bolshevik, for example, and discovered very early that the recipe the FS had written toward engineering a society served quite well, if one was alert and opportunistic, to sway a population toward dictatorship. The reason will become apparent when we discuss a bit further on the goal of the destruction of the family, in particular the father-led family. The vacuum created is an irresistible invitation, a siren song even, to a dictator. In fact, it seems the FS has spent as much time staunching the flow of blood from that slightly misplaced incision – unleashing the fascist dragon upon the world – as it has in pushing its agenda according to its original timetable; the biggest irritation being that fascism invaded and occupied all the Freudo-Marxist room to maneuver.

The Frankfurt School is then, a bit contrary because there's a strong streak of pessimism and despair in it, combined with the absolute conviction that they, as a small group of intellectuals, could critique all of Marxism, set it right, and set it loose – properly – to create endless struggle and eliminate balance in the rest of the world. Why? Distraction. Endless occupation of our attention such that the elite could do whatever they wanted to do while we were busy. This arrogant pessimism will come up again as it is important.

Pessimism, despair and arrogant optimism all in the same basket: the Frankfurt School's brand of Freudo-Marxism. Another very unusual facet is that very Germanic forms of Marxism such as those proffered by Adorno and others who were prominent in the school, linked to forms of Anglo-Saxon, American and **imperialist** thought. Why is this? The existence of fascist governments in central Europe at a certain time caused all of these FS types to seek refuge in the United States, for one thing. Hitler cast them out of Europe, closing down the Frankfurt School. Of course, having been shut down by Hitler is something of a badge of honour. For example, one of the first things Hitler did was close all the Waldorf schools. The point seems to have been silencing any voice that deviated from his own. It was the fascist in the guise of 'authoritarian father figure' stepping in where the Sacred Masculine and the father-led family had been cut down. Rationalized, again. Broken into small pieces.

It is prudent to note here and at other opportune times all of the moments we have introduced 'fathers' of something. The 'father' of behaviourism, the 'father' of anthropology, the 'father' of psychoanalysis, the 'father' of progressive education, and so forth, right on the heels of the push to destroy the father-led family and put something else in his place.

For another thing, the tentacles of the imperialist agency of the Tavistock Institute were already in the United States and the

144

industrialists had invited them to the banquet. The Tavi was originally funded by the British crown, the industrialists and the obscenely wealthy and powerful European banking families. Today, we are witnessing the uneasy sibling relationship between the imperialist forces and the Freudo-Marxist forces the world over. The fascists exist as the miniature poodle on the lap of the imperialists, everybody uses each other and assumes their own group will emerge triumphant.

Theodor Adorno,[111] an original member of the FS, must be introduced here and entertained at least briefly, because he conducted a monumental and completely unscientific work regarding what he called the Authoritarian Personality which is still touted as real social science even today. In reality, this study and the consequent book was a function of the inverse of science...take a theory and then go looking for facts to support it, even manufacturing them, rather than collecting facts and then formulating a theory to explain them. It (the book-study)[112] was commissioned, this study, by The American Jewish Committee, not by any university. No matter what, it was a major broadside into the American psyche. The FS members, upon entry to academic America, were confronted with an empirical culture. Germany had still been in a philosophical era, focused on philosophy rather than data. In the US, one goes out and gets numbers: sociological methods such as polls and petitions and such, however dubious, are used. So the FS, whose original group was fundamentally concerned with anti-semitism, became empirical. It was, in fact, a

[111] Theodor Adorno Biography. http://www.egs.edu/library/theodor-adorno/biography/

[112] Published in 1950 by Harper & Brothers NY. It was written by Adorno, along with Else Frenkel-Brunswik, Daniel J Levinson, R Nevitt Sanford, in collaboration with Betty Aron, Maria Hertz Levinson and William Morrow.

145

philosophy of anti-semitism looking for vindication long before there was any sort of empirical data.

When Theodor Adorno was at the University of California and the Frankfurt School had been closed down by a certain notorious government in Germany, he developed various psychological theories as a reaction to fascism, making a dubious connection between fascism and anti-semitism. One can be a fascist without being an anti-semite; one can be an anti-semite without being a fascist. (It is fascinating that these people operated in a truly reactionary way, as the FS appeared to begin with as a reaction to the disappointment over the failed Bolshevik Revolution, and subsequent empirical studies were conducted not only in a haphazard way but based upon truly fallacious reasoning).

The Authoritarianism Personality was actually the last of five volumes produced by Adorno. Erich Fromm developed a questionnaire[113] meant to identify the respondent as authoritarian, revolutionary, or ambivalent. The questionnaire was originally Freudian. Nine personality traits were identified. Some were: adherence to conventional values, the tendency to reject people who do not hold conventional values, the tendency to believe dangerous things happen in the world, and a supposedly exaggerated concern with sex. Several scales were actually developed from this questionnaire: E for ethnocentrism, PEC for political and economic conservatism, A-S for anti-semitism, and others.

He developed what he called the "F" scale. ("F" was F for Fascism.), a personality test which under a different name we still use quite widely. It's a test for the authoritarian personality, to

---

[113]   Fromm, E. 1969. Part 4.
https://www.marxists.org/archive/fromm/works/1969/human.htm

see how fascistic you are in relation to trigger words. The crime that was committed here...the moral and esoteric crime...was this: the sacred masculine has a quite natural place within the context of the family unit. There is no equals sign between father and fascist any more than there is necessarily an equal sign between fascist and anti-semite. As we have travelled the rocky social roads of the 20th century, many have decried the loss of the strong father figure in the lives of children. So let us locate the boundary once more between one thing and the other. Is there an equals sign between conservative and anti-semite? I have not found it to be so and this is an inverse case of prejudice. It is like trying to prove a negative. Additionally, some of Adorno's conclusions about relationships between children and parents and anti-semitism were ludicrous in every sense of the word. Yet, generations of students have been taught that his conclusions were sound. This is always and eternally the point: students are programmed with this faulty data and sent out into the world to live, survive, procreate, love, laugh and so forth and they never quite realize that the reason happiness or meaning eludes them is because they are operating under a pernicious and destructively subversive paradigm.

Some history: The first of the two authoritarian projects was launched in January 1943, by a team of three social psychologists at the University of California at Berkeley, Else Frenkel-Brunswick...Daniel J. Levison, and R. Nevitt Sanford. What started out as a modest $500 grant to study the roots of anti-Semitism, would soon mushroom into the biggest mass social-profiling project ever undertaken in America, up until that time. It also gave rise to the development of questionnaires, polls, use of statistics, and so forth that have dictated social movements for a century no matter how flawed or easily skewed these forms of information gathering proved to be.

In May 1944, the American Jewish Committee
established a Department of Scientific Research, which was headed
by Frankfurt School director Max Horkheimer. Horkheimer
established a project, called Studies in Prejudice, with generous
funding from the AJC and other agencies, including the
Rockefeller foundations. The Studies in Prejudice offered
employment to a number of Frankfurt School members who, for
various reasons, were not coopted directly into the war effort (for
example, Herbert Marcuse and Franz Neumann were brought into
the Research and Analysis Section of the Office of Strategic
Services, or OSS, the forerunner to today's Central Intelligence
Agency). Hedda Massing, Marie Jahoda, Morris Janowitz, and
Theodor W. Adorno all worked on the Studies, and, under
Horkheimer's direction, they all formally reconstituted the
International Institute of Social Research, the transplanted
incarnation of the original **Frankfurt School** of Weimar Germany.

The most significant of the five Studies in Prejudice,
produced for the AJC during 1944-50, was **The Authoritarian
Personality** (New York: Harper, 1950). Authors Adorno, Frenkel-
Brunswik, Levinson, and Sanford assembled a large research team
from the Berkeley Public Opinion Study and the International
Institute of Social Research, to conduct thousands of interviews of
Americans, to profile their allegedly deep-seated tendencies toward
authoritarianism, prejudice, and anti-Semitism. Dr. William
Morrow, the leading protégé of Dr. Kurt Lewin, who was one key,
bridge figure between the **Frankfurt School and the Tavistock
Institute,** was a research director for the Authoritarian Personality
project.

148

The study was an exercise in self-fulfilling prophecy and Marxist/Freudian self-delusion. Long before the first survey questionnaire was drafted, Horkheimer and Adorno had written exhaustively about the "authoritarian" character of the American nuclear family, about the "problem" of the American people's belief in a transcendent monotheistic God, and about the underlying fascist character of all forms of American patriotism. They falsified the survey data, in advance, by devising a series of scales, purporting to measure the American population's tendency toward anti-Semitism, ethnocentricity, anti-democratic ideology, and, ultimately, fascism.

An authoritarian figure in today's parlance is someone like Dick Cheney, who is in all probability a primary psychopath. Again there is no equals sign between this and the strong father figure. Had Cheney been a woman, meaning not a father figure, with the same characteristics he still would have been exactly the same dangerous authoritarian figure. By way of understanding, I recommend the book, *Political Ponerology: A science on the Nature of Evil Adjusted for Political Purposes* by Andrew Lobaczewski.[114] In it, a thought was put forward that powerful people perpetrate evil in a systematic way. There is a tendency to rationalize evil as standard human behaviour, in the face of the idea that there is no real standard and hence the development of political correctness, and in the face of evidence to the contrary on an individual level. These judgements may have been rendered to suit particular agendas by the few and too hastily as a response by the many.

Ponerology and "successful" psychopathology (i.e. not the

---

[114]   Essays on this book.
   http://www.cassiopaea.org/cass/political_ponerology_lobaczewski.htm

"violent serial killer" type, but the Stalin, Pol Pot, Cheney, Rockefeller, Kissinger, Bill Clinton, or Donald Rumsfeld type) clinically explain how "pathocracies"—the system of government created by a small pathological minority that takes control over a society of non-psychopaths—are generated and dominated by those that possess an inborn error (psychopathy) prevalent in 4-6% of the population which is physiologically unable to feel normal human empathy.

They are emotionless, selfish, cold and calculating, and devoid of any moral or ethical standards, yet they are intelligent, charming, driven, focused, and therefore tend to achieve the highest positions of power by concealing their true nature under a 'mask of sanity.' This concept applies to all existing hierarchical power structures."

The uses of hierarchy, which are profoundly counter-intuitive to human nature on the one hand and designed to keep moral human beings down on the other, were/are intrinsic to the work of the Tavistock Institute. The development and use of canvassing strategies were/are a fundamental hallmark of the Frankfurt School (Institute of Social Research and its daughter-organizations). One of the prime initial drives of the FS was to identify the causes of anti-semitism, which they saw as dominant, mostly based on their own cultural environmental experiences. Their lunatic conclusion seemed to be that the children of father-led families, whom they dubbed 'authoritarian,' were prone to anti-semitism. By their logic then, the traditional father in a nuclear family would be prone to being a fascist. The logic of this argument is terrible yet so much of it has enabled the cultural and social revolutions of the 20th century. We have lost so much. We can regain it if we but understand what it is.

150

In fact, Theodor Adorno gave us within the confines of the tome *The Authoritarian Personality* this proposition: The only way to deal with anti-semitism was to destroy the nuclear family. Another postulate was that repressed hostility toward parents turned into anti-semitism. Positive feelings toward the family = negative feelings toward Jews. Obviously, there was a much deeper agenda here. First, people who were worried about whether or not their parents loved them and who were ambivalent about their sexuality were identified as the ideal liberal personality. In this case, it would mean more the ideal candidate for conversion to their philosophy.

The FS saw the typical nuclear family in America with the father in the lead as extremely dangerous (certainly an obstacle and, frankly, one might agree in that they would be dangerous to the cultural coup d'etat planned).[115] Determined that they were people accustomed to following orders – this is a desirable spot if one wants to be the one giving the orders. So, the attack was two-fold: identify and grow a mass of followers and identify and destroy the opposition. In fact, find the vulnerabilities of the opposition and use them. The goal was not the protection of the Jews from prejudice, but the creation of a definition of authoritarianism and anti-semitism which could be exploited to force the 'scientifically planned re-education' of Americans and Europeans away from the principles of Judeo-Christian civilization, which the FS despised.

They posited that when 'nature' is rejected, hatred develops (of the Jews specifically). The Jews, in their opinion, had every repressed negative amoral situation theoretically or

---

[115] As did V.I. Lenin who is attributed with saying this: Destroy the family, you destroy the country. -- Vladimir Ilyich Lenin - See more at: http://thepeoplescube.com/lenin/lenin-s-own-20-monster-quotes-t185.html#sthash.43xhs4Zx.dpuf

151

potentially experienced by any culture anywhere at any time projected onto them. Because America would demand data to back up this theory, they began the Authoritarian Personality Studies at University of California at Berkeley. Questionnaires were designed to tap people's attitudes about Jews, then to try to demonstrate that the attitudes were a pathology. Their results? People with a healthy nuclear family – with parents they looked up to and, importantly, some sort of religious handrail, tended to have negative feelings about Jews. How those things go together in reality is a mystery. However, according to their 'logic', the only way to deal with that was to break up the family. This seemed to be the answer to every problem extant to the FS. Break up the family.

Anxious feelings about parents, by the way, was interpreted as a sign of deep affection. The deeper agenda at work here is one that is much more closely aligned with the Prussian/Compulsory Education phenomenon. That is to create a vacuum where authority has stood such as it can be filled with whatever the Predator wants it filled with. In fact, as noted above, these tests indicated that the ideal liberal personality was 1) ambivalent about their sexuality and 2) unsure about whether their parents loved them or not. This was the ideal target.

Indeed, in the forward to the seminal Institute of Social Research (Frankfurt School) tome *The Authoritarian Personality*, written in 1950 and oft-quoted in sociological and academic circles, it is declared that in the studies conducted to come up with the conclusions within, respondent groups with a significant number of minorities were excluded.[116] That is the other pillar of

116   The Authoritarian Personality, Studies in Prejudice Series, Volume 1 T.W. Adorno, Else Frenkel-Brunswik, Daniel J. Levinson and R. Nevitt Sanford, Harper & Brothers, Copyright American Jewish Committee, 1950. online pdf.

152

political correctness, in fact. There can never, ever be anything that constitutes a majority because a majority can collect itself up and reject an idea or way of life. (In industrial life, there can never, ever be anything that constitutes a whole as that creates an empowered human being. The terms are different but the goal is the same). In schools, there can never ever be one teacher who brings the whole of a curriculum, there must be many, many teachers bringing slim fractions of the same.

At any rate, this book was ordered undertaken by The American Jewish Committee, not any university. It concludes by the very statements about how the study was conducted that racism is a uniquely white characteristic: which conclusion is genuine racism in action. The fact is any group can select study factors in or out to achieve the 'results' for which they are looking. Any group anywhere can play fast and loose with the facts, the ideology or end justifying the means. There is no rigorous science in evidence here. *This speaks to all questionnaires, statistics, polls, petitions and such and one should be aware that they have many uses but are only reflective of reality in that the data collected can be used to direct groups of people in certain directions.* Interestingly, the Jewish culture quite correctly understands and guards the necessity of a nuclear family to ensure the carrying forward of their culture. The destruction of the western nuclear family then is deeply suspect if the group calling for such in funded by a large Jewish special interest group.

Consider the assault on the father and the destruction of the Sacred Masculine and Feminine. Both are crimes against humanity; crimes of the highest order. The outright war declared against these two divine principles stems from Fabian socialist doctrine, Marxist doctrine, the skewed and unscientific fringe tenets of Freud's work, the work of Franz Boas and Margaret Mead, and the genocidal social engineering plans of the FS and the Tavi. The assault on the Sacred Masculine was one of the first steps in the destruction of western culture along with the forced capture of our children from the mid-1800s onward and the application of industrial and behavioural principles which severed a child from its family and placed it in what amounts to a concentration camp for indoctrination as well as withholding of that to which it has every right.

We must here revisit the introduction of sociological studies, questionnaires and such, devised to support the social proposition in question. As we have noted, these, along with petitions do much to reveal the weak points of each of our societies so that they can be manipulated on a grand scale. Plans are made: short-term and long-term, and out temperatures are taken so to speak along the way so that plans can be altered to continue to achieve the end result.

One of the best examples of this recently was the Ron Paul Campaign in the United States Presidential election of 2012. I, myself, was a very happy delegate for Dr. Paul from the sovereign state of Maine. Dr. Paul is a libertarian and constitutionalist who has never compromised his standards in any way.

Since Dr. Paul's political message is exceptionally dangerous the goal, and the status quo created from the results of the Hawthorne Experiments as mentioned in Chapter 3, the question is always asked: how is it he was allowed to conduct his libertarian campaigns across a nation so clearly thirsting to hear his old but new message regarding the US Constitution and the true American Folk Soul? He clearly won the Republican Nomination in 2012 although many, many strategies were used to bury those figures. I was a witness to some of them myself. So why was this campaign allowed? It was allowed as a way to take the cultural temperature of the American people. The Social Research Groups and their masters would like to know how well and truly they have been able to beat the notion of sovereignty out of the American citizenry. Then pressures can be applied in areas that seem to need more work. On one side, it was a grand sociological study on a national level. On the other side, it was also a cry for justice and help from a people enslaved. So where are the mass uprisings?

I propose that demonstrations such as those we lived through during the Vietnam War and collective demonstrations such as the Occupy Movements serve the same function. A protest is, in fact, a Process Test. These were developed and made to blossom by Herbert Marcuse of The Frankfurt School for various reasons but Process Test is one of them. Hence, the so-called reaction to injustice in the form of a protest movement is as concocted as the problem it addresses. In addition, this all serves to keep us occupied around a situation, in an endless hamster-wheel loop, while the Pathocracy goes on about its business unmolested.

Consider the following from an essay written by a retired Naval Commander regarding the Frankfurt School incursion into the ranks of military training: "The vehicle for this introduction was the idealistic Boomer elite, those young middle-class and well-to-do college students who became the vanguard of America's counter-culture revolution of the mid-1960s... These New Totalitarians are now in power as they have come to middle-age and control every public institution in our nation. But that is getting ahead of the story.

The cauldron for implementing this witches brew were the elites of the Boomer generation. They are the current 'foot soldiers' of the original Frankfurt School gurus. The counter-culture revolution of the 1960s was set in motion and guided intellectually by the 'cultural Marxists' of the Frankfurt School -- Herbert Marcuse, Eric Fromm, Theodor Adorno, Max Horkheimer, Wilhelm Reich, and others. Its influence is now felt in nearly every institution in the United States. The elite Boomers, throwbacks to the... idealist Transcendental generation of the mid-1800s, are the 'agents of change,' who have introduced 'cultural Marxism' into American life.

William S. Lind relates that 'cultural Marxism' is an ideology with deep roots. It did not begin with the counter-culture revolution in the mid-1960s. Its roots go back at least to the 1920s and the writings of the Italian Communist Antonio Gramsci. These roots, over time, spread to the writings of Herbert Marcuse.

Herbert Marcuse was one of the most prominent Frankfurt School promoters of Critical Theory's social revolution among college and university students in the 1960s. It is instructive to review what he has written on the subject:

"One can rightfully speak of a cultural revolution, since the protest is directed toward the whole cultural establishment, including the morality of existing society ...there is one thing we can say with complete assurance. The traditional idea of revolution and the traditional strategy of revolution have ended. These ideas are old-fashioned ...what we must undertake is a type of diffuse and dispersed disintegration of the system." This sentiment was first expressed by the early 20th century Italian Marxist, Antonio Gramsci.

Gramsci, a young communist who died in one of
Mussolini's prisons in 1937 at the age of 46, conjured up the notion
of a 'quiet' revolution that could be diffused throughout a culture --
over a period of time -- to destroy it from within. He was the first
to suggest that the application of psychology to break the
traditions, beliefs, morals, and will of a people could be
accomplished quietly and without the possibility of resistance. He
deduced that "The civilized world had been thoroughly saturated
with Christianity for 2,000 years..." and a culture based on this
religion could only be captured from within." [117]

The early 20th century played host to a seething,
steaming cauldron of incoherent, sadistic groups vying for control
of the planet and everything on it. Alas, when they combined all
their data and implemented strategies based on the same, the
human being was vulnerable in a way it may never have been
before. There are real questions as to why now, why at just this
time in history? We will get there. Let's just say for now that
timing is everything: humanity is on the verge of an explosion in
engaged capacity and ability for which the Imagination – I Mage In
– would very much endanger any Control System.

Many of these ideas have fed through into the doctrine
which is now called political correctness, but they've morphed and
changed over time: rigidity about the rules of the game, the auto-
pilot tendency to follow a leader without question, **undue** respect
for authority which was at one time dialectically related to the idea
that you want to exercise authority yourself — and now the idea of
a sovereign human being tends to be a foreign one and is always
located in an outside body of some kind, and this sort of thing.
Undue respect for authority is the reverence for earned wisdom

[117] Atkinson, Dr. Gerald. CDR USN (Ret.)What Is the Frankfurt School and Its Effect on America? p.1 http://www.wvwnews.net/story.php?id=8183

turned on its head, hence the dust-binning of our elderly. At our very core, though, we are well aware that something is very wrong. Our children especially know this.

Were these strategies developed for human good? No, that was never really the point, by all accounts. It was always about gaining control for the sake of gaining control. The struggle for the sake of the struggle and the carrion grab the spoils while the rest of us are busy arguing semantics. The problem with *all* Marxist theory is that it's counter-human, completely counter-intuitive and unnatural even when it sounds good. Our connection is to Sophia, the divine in nature; we have our being in that substructure. Spend as much time as one likes trying to draw us in the leftist vein (or any political vein) but we are not as that would portray us and we will always leak out the sides and under the door, so to speak.

Let us be clear. The one thing that remains is the determination to make things come out differently. This is what all of the 'institutes' are about, putting their collective and controlling will into subduing the masses and driving us through their tunnel. One of the reasons for the extraordinary rapacity of communist terror is, I think, a sense of disappointment as large as the universe itself that the Marxist recipe did not work, the soufflé fell on a cosmic level. And there's a strong element of secret and hidden and underhanded–and not so secret and concealed, in the regime change phase, that 'if humanity can't be captured in one way we'll fall on them in another'. Our body fits in the box, but you've removed our limbs in order to make us fit.

In speaking about the FS, we want to make sure we talk specifically about three major individuals: Georg Lukacs, Theodor Adorno, and Herbert Marcuse. We've spoken a but about Adorno but he truly belongs to the chapter on media. We have mentioned Lukacs as a founding member of the FS with a violent and sadistic history in Hungary.

It is important to understand just exactly what Lukacs gave birth to: Cultural Terrorism. This method was meant to identify and transform the sort of a society that could actually be made into a Marxist society. Cultural terrorism -- an attitude, a state of mind - not a set of values to be dogmatically followed. Cultural terrorism is an atomic bomb level state of the power of the individual. It is **extreme pathological individualism.** It is not the natural situation of a sovereign human being. Like everything else, the FS co-opted a natural human capacity and tortured it until it was a Frankenstein's version of what it had been. That is the Shadow that thinks it can create but cannot. It can mangle, torture, hack its victims into a different state of being but that is not creation, it is destruction.

Note the following from a piece called The Cultural Terrorist Manifesto: A terrorist who hijacks an airplane or plants a bomb in a crowded shopping centre apparently doesn't care who gets hurt as long as he (sic) achieves his aim. That innocent people are turned into bloody corpses or maimed for life is not his concern. The cultural terrorist is no different. The cultural terrorist, an assassin of the future, an executioner of morality. Cultural terrorism, an attitude, a state of mind - not a set of values to be dogmatically followed. Cultural terrorism is a celebration of the power of the individual.

Our aim is to pollute the minds of the public, to sow the seeds of insanity into society. Our victims are of all ages - everybody from the cradle to the grave. Man cannot bear too much reality and as a result of this the cultural terrorist is in the business of providing a reality attack. An over exposure of reality - the dirt behind the day dream. No subject is taboo, all must be exposed. No one is sacred. Everybody as well as everything should feel the wrath of the cultural terrorist. The object of cultural terrorism is to exploit situations and people in order to cause a reaction, preferably negative. Our aim is to make money in order to finance our war which we wage upon society, The money is required so that we can purchase the technology which will tear into the heart of all that is considered normal. We are the cancerous cell that would painfully destroy all that is in contact with it. We are working to erase the conforming instinct. To prevent humanity from ever acting with a common will.

The cultural terrorist's weapons are anything that enables him to inflict his views upon others...Confusion as a weapon / Confusion the key word.[118]

The point of every one of these independent social engineering entities, now acting as a many-armed beast is this: **To prevent humanity from ever acting with a common will.** Polluted minds, seeds of insanity, a reality attack on human beings of all ages. There are no boundaries or rules or taboos anymore. Hence, no one is safe from anything. And it is not the so-called terrrorists we should fear but those who purport to protect us from the terrorists. No one of any age is sacred. No part of any human is sacred. Money, war, blood sacrifice,darkness...these are the goals of the cultural terrorists, those who practice social engineering toward the cultural obliteration of all folk souls, beginning with those in the west.

---

[118]   media.hyperreal.org/zines/est/articles/ctm.html

And so, since Natural Law, which is universal, simple and inescapable, says the only true crime is theft, the cultural terror of the Freudo-Marxists is an absolute crime against natural law. It is the theft of our very humanity all the way down to the soul. Communism has infected and mutilated the world to a degree most people haven't even begun to understand. It is seen as a leftist movement, when in fact, it is profoundly far to the right. For a true communist, liberals are scum. Lenin recommended allowing the social democrats their time, in order to weaken the right, then the way would be opened on both sides for communism.

Once safely inside the US, speedy dissemination of the FS into the nation's universities became an urgent goal, in the same way Boas spread his politicized anthropology among the universities except that his strategy was to carefully and thoughtfully place teams within specific universities. The dissemination of cultural revolution was quick and occurred just after WWII thanks to the GI bill. Tens of thousands of potential professors and teachers were passed through the New School for Social Research because they were desperately needed, with very little effort put into vetting credentials.

Of the other top Institute figures, Herbert Marcuse is typical.[119] He started as a Communist, became a protegee of Martin Heidegger even as Heidegger was becoming a Nazi. Coming to America, he worked in the WWII office of Strategic Services (OSS), and later became the US State Department's top analyst of Soviet policy during the McCarthy era. In the 60s he became a guru of the Left and ended his days starting The Green Party in West Germany. He was also sent to Germany in 1950 to 'de-nazify' the Germans. Interestingly, and importantly, his wife

---

[119]   Herbert Marcuse Archive. https://www.marxists.org/reference/archive/marcuse/

161

worked for the Office of Naval Intelligence. Today that same
Green Party has been all but toppled in Germany as the party
supporting or at least dealing in paedophilia[120] but then, the FS
began with a man aggressively trying to sexualize kindergartners in
Hungary. A representative of the same, a man responsible for
driving a deeper wedge between students and their families and
culture than ever before, and who worked for the OSS (CIA)
during WWII, created the German Green Party when he was sent to
de-nazify Germany in 1950. In fact, Herbert Marcuse is the only
person who has ever held a US and German passport at the same
time. The same is happening today.

Marcuse co-founded the Frankfurt Institute for Social
Research with Theodore Adorno and Max Horkheimer. They
developed a model of Critical Theory, a type of Marxism
influenced by psychoanalysis and existentialism, and their theories
of capitalist culture. Marcuse became a US citizen in 1940. When
the War began, he joined the Office of War Information and the
Office of Secret Services as a specialist on German culture. Later,
he headed the State Department's Central European Bureau.

When he was sent by the US government to 'de-nazify'
Germany, Marcuse became an example of the poodle let loose in
the kennel created by Marxist insistence on removing traditional
and personal examples of authority figures from the lives of
individuals. The fascist moves right in. It was a janitor's job, in a
way, but with devastating later consequences for the German
people. It wasn't just a matter of taking the data and learning from
the takeover of the American psyche into Germany to try it out. It

---

[120] A Major Political Party Used to Support Pedophilia. The New Republic 2014
http://www.newrepublic.com/article/120379/german-green-party-pedophilia-scandal
Shadows from the Past:Pedophile Links Haunt Green Party
http://www.spiegel.de/international/germany/past-pedophile-links-haunt-german-green-party-a-899544.html Der Spiegel, 2014

was a matter of turning Germany into another social and behavioural laboratory. A laboratory it remains.

As a professor at the University of California in San Diego, Marcuse became important to the FS and Tavi-built generation of radicals coming of age. It was noted, for whatever reason, that enormous student uprisings in large cities around the world had one thing in common: the physical presence of Herbert Marcuse. Take that for what it may be worth.

Finally, Weaponized Political Correctness was a robust child of the FS in America – when one can gain some perspective and distance from this subject it sounds very much like something that would have come out of Lenin's Soviet Russia or Mao's China. A social straight-jacket, prescriptions from the top as to what can be said, what we are allowed to think, parented by the Frankfurt School and Franz Boas. "Thought Crimes." The bogeyman of the Cultural Revolution in China looms large here and my mind is my kingdom to do with as I will, thank you. Again, it should be clear by now that the separating of us into the smallest components of who we are and how we are part of a minority, while true, nonetheless, keeps us from embracing the very best thing we are: human beings. That would make us a dangerous majority.

It was in 1923 that the Frankfurt School began its work. Though it was not exclusively responsible, the cultural revolution which it inspired starting in the 1950s developed in the US and then Europe. About 20 years later, the cultural revolutions of 1968, under the influence of Marcuse, mark an important stage. About another 30 years after 1968 would be needed to see the triumph of the counter-culture which began 80 years earlier.

We are dealing with a long-term, brilliantly conceived,

deeply sinister operation. The men of thought and action who devised it had the foresight to understand what had to be done and to carry it out consistently by selecting priority sectors–universities, music, media broadcasting, psychological and educational action– to put at their service the networks which were offered to them. They succeeded beyond their wildest dreams.

To further the advance of their 'quiet' cultural revolution – but giving us no ideas about their plans for the future – the School quite literally recommended (among other things):

1. The creation of racism offences.
2. Continual change to create confusion
3. The teaching of sex to children
4. The undermining of schools' and teachers' authority (this happened in the 1960s and thereabouts. However, the school as *in loco parentis* is back in a big way.)
5. Huge immigration to destroy identity.
6. The promotion of excessive drinking
7. Emptying of churches
8. An unreliable legal system with bias against victims of crime
9. Dependency on the state or state benefits
10. Control and dumbing down of media
11. Encouraging the breakdown of the family

The prescriptions?

Undergo psychoanalysis as the secularized version of the confessional. (The Hawthorne Experiments and the Civil Religion of the School).

164

Eliminate all of the 'Christian' sexual prohibitions and there will be no stress in society.

Assimilate Psychoanalysis as a form of sexual liberation toward political control.

And so forth. It is a glorious form of insanity, like diamonds sparkling under the light of a supernova. Marxism is false in almost every area of life; that men and women are interchangeable (false); that the family is an enemy construction of man when it's the basis of human dignity in all groups. That economic activity between human beings is always a form of oppression when in actual fact almost everybody at one level or another gets something out of it otherwise it couldn't exist in the first place. (I did not say money. I mean the business of exchange and provision one human being to another). Human beings are kind and nasty. They're avaricious, but they have a capacity for self-sacrifice. They're endlessly cowardly and lying, but they also have a penchant for courage and glory. At least, we think these things apply to human beings. We have been so far severed from our true memories, our characterizations of the true nature of human beings is actually quite likely to be fundamentally flawed.

I came across a wonderful article on psychopathy, written by someone referring to themselves as 'Peace.' I want to share it here.

"It seems that everywhere you turn these days, there's some new study or book unveiling the wonderful qualities of dangerous personality disorders. Narcissists will simply tell you they are narcissists. Sociopaths can empathize, just like you and me.

Psychopaths are necessary for the progress & betterment of humanity.

These strange claims are on the rise as psychopathy awareness spreads. Some from self-proclaimed psychopaths, some from pop-scientists seeking a piece of the action, and some from perfectly well-intentioned people who are just hellbent on seeing the good in everyone. But regardless of the source, it's time to put an end to this misinformation.

Saying that a psychopath is "good" is like saying that someone with ADHD has great focus & attention skills. Or that someone with chronic depression is actually the happiest person in the world. And that's ignoring the fact that ADHD & depression are treatable, while psychopathy most certainly is not. The point is, you're literally describing the opposite of the disorder you're claiming to understand.

Let's review a few of the DSM criteria for diagnosing ASPD:

- **Deceitfulness**, as indicated by **repeated lying**, use of aliases, or **conning others for personal profit or pleasure**
- **Reckless disregard** for safety of self or others
- **Consistent irresponsibility**, as indicated by repeated failure to sustain consistent work behavior or honor financial obligations
- **Lack of remorse**, as indicated by being **indifferent to or rationalizing having hurt, mistreated, or stolen from another**

What about these qualities is Good? Wise? Empathetic?

Psychopaths aren't just regular human beings who are able to make tough decisions because of their low empathy. Nope. Read the diagnostic criteria again. Psychopaths are characterized by the *actual enjoyment of harming others*.

There's no way to twist that around into sometimes being good & virtuous. It does not matter whether they're a Wall Street CEO or a prison inmate. High-functioning or low-functioning. It makes no difference. They're still pathological liars who relieve their chronic boredom by hurting other people.

There are lots of disorders that have to do with low empathy, but this one specifically describes someone who actually gains pleasure from causing pain to others. If you take that element out of psychopathy, then you are no longer describing psychopathy.

The idea that psychopaths have empathy is a bunch of word salad garbage. Yes, psychopaths observe & mimic the behavior of others. They learn to understand human behavior because that makes it easier to manipulate it. But empathy isn't just about "understanding" feelings. It's about **feeling** those feelings. Sadness, because someone else is sad. Joy, because someone else is joyful. Find me a psychopath who has that ability, and I'll eat my hat.

Then there are the narcissists who will tell you they're narcissists, which seems like a bizarre thing to trust, considering that narcissists are liars. It's odd, because most of us found that when we confronted our abusers about their hurtful behavior, we were called "crazy" and "insane". Most psychopaths are narcissists, and questioning a psychopath's good nature is an effective way to make yourself enemy #1 and have your name smeared to everyone you know. A psychopath's greatest advantage is the illusion of normalcy. Do we really think an actual psychopath wouldn't notice which questions scream PSYCHOPATH on a self-assessment questionnaire?

Perhaps these studies are thinking more along the *Criminal Minds* type of narcissist—the blatantly arrogant womanizer who flaunts his money & flashy car for the world to see. But most of us met an entirely different monster. The person who started out exceptionally nice, as our mirror image. And that person would never admit their disorder. Certainly not in the middle of grooming a new victim.

What about "wisdom"? Maybe I'm a spiritual nutjob, but I thought wisdom was about turning dark experiences into light, and discovering what it is we can offer to this world. I thought it took adversity & compassion to develop wisdom. Call me crazy, but I didn't think wisdom was about working your way to the top because you didn't feel remorse for the people you steamrolled along the way.

And last but not least, there's this relentless suggestion that we're all "sometimes psychopaths", or that we have the ability to behave like psychopaths when the situation calls for it. What the actual hell? I assume these are the same sort of people who say "Omg I'm so OCD" because one day they decide to rearrange their shoe collection by size & color. Personality disorders are not jokes, and they don't just "sometimes" arise in healthy human beings. Yes, we're all capable of being angry or jealous or dishonest, but that's not born from an innate desire to harm other people. No normal human being sits there and *sometimes* thinks it'd be entertaining to watch an innocent person suffer.

These theories are normalizing psychopathy in society. There's no dancing around it. They're redefining good & evil to make room for people who are incapable of "good" as we know it. They're eroding our values and minimizing the damage caused by serious personality disorders. Are we really willing to sacrifice our integrity for people who have none? To change the rules so that psychopaths can get away with more than they already do?

Professionals will tell you that they feel like they're losing their mind when they interact with psychopaths, like their entire sense of self is falling apart with every moment spent in their presence. It's a lingering feeling that haunts you, long after the person is gone from your life. So if you really think these people are advantageous in politics, business, and relationships, then by all means, surround yourself with "psychopaths". But to those of us who have actually encountered psychopathic evil, we know that these predators have nothing to offer to this world except pain & devastation.

So please stop the bullshit. It's insulting to survivors of psychopathic abuse, and it's dangerous to the general public. One really begins to wonder what the motives are behind these "experts" (and the media outlets who promote them)." [121]

Thank you, Peace.

---

[121]

Recommended Reading

https://www.psychopathfree.com/showthread.php?19311-Article-Wise-Psychopaths-Honest-Narcissists-Empathetic-Sociopaths-amp-Other-Virtuous-Evil-People

Andrew Lobaczewski *Political Ponerology*: *A Science on the Nature of Evil Adjusted for Political Purposes*

Bolton, K. *Revolution from Above: Manufacturing Dissent in the New World Order*

The Schiller Institute *The Frankfurt School and Political Correctness* http://www.schillerinstitute.org/fid_91-96/921_frankfurt.html

Peace. *Wise Psychopaths, Honest Narcissists, Empathetic Sociopaths, & Other Virtuous Evil People* www.vortexcourage.me

Steinberg, Jeffrey. *From Cybernetics to Littleton: Techniques in Mind Control. 2000 The Schiller Institute.*

http://www.dailymail.co.uk/news/article-2315185/Five-year-olds-Germany-given-sex-education-book-achieve-orgasms-condom.html#ixzz3HHAWOOZn

Chapter Six

Homo Correctus Politicus: Redefining the Soul, Again

February, 2014. London. Producer, The People's Voice TV, to myself : "I think people who have a problem with political correctness are just looking for an excuse to be racist."

August 26, 2014. London. Asian gangs' 1,400 child sex victims in one town...social workers too scared of being branded racist to act. The victims were white, mostly girls. ***The social workers dared not report the crimes for fear of being labelled as 'racist.'*** The newspapers included the words politically correct in the headlines.[122]

July, 2014. A woman reads an article on my magazine site, at vortexcourage.me. It is an amazing article, written by an expert, on the feasibility of interstellar travel. The writer used the word, mankind, instead of humankind. The reader blasted the writer, took nothing else away from the article, and never came back again...over one word. The power of political correctness. It is a big, slamming door in the face of knowledge.[123]

What we see materially are expressions of thought. *Our* thought. The cultural environment is an expression of the Folk Soul, all the way down to colour, form and sound – vibration – which is something that can and should be taken up in the scientific discussion of the attack on/with frequency. Thus far, the

---

[122] http://www.amren.com/news/2014/08/how-fear-of-being-seen-as-racist-stopped-social-workers-saving-up-to-1400-children

[123] Vortex:Conscious and Courageous Magazine. Cara St.Louis, Ed. http://vortexcourage.me/

discussion has led us to understanding the school as both concentration camp and re-education camp; the overlay of industrial organization as intentionally fracturing, marginalizing and supremely dis-empowering; the examination of human nature such that an entire method of instilling fear and from that directing human beings in large groups one way or the other has been established and widely used; the fact of the establishment and power-mongering of social and cultural engineering organizations with global reach and two-pronged competing but complementary aims: war and how it serves the psychopathic oligarchs and the push for Freudo-Marxist conversion of the entire planet. In the end, we may feel like casualties in a war between the two. The question is whether we will actually be aware that is what's happening.

Whether the discussion centres on bloody combat or Marxist dialectic, both sides are enamoured of struggle and conflict as a way of life. That is an important thing to remember. This is not basic human nature. If it were, John Watson would not have had to teach a baby to fear. If it were, newspapers would not have had to be engaged in a mighty propaganda war to push the British and the Americans into World War I. No, this is not our nature. It is the nature of the psychopath, the Predator...who has rightly been referred to as an Infection. An infection insists on spreading. There are powers/factions who believe they can split up the world. There is a baseline strength and power, the one within us as human beings, that protects and resonates with the planet. The infection is topical but global. We have been trained to see the infection as life when it is just the infection.

We have not thought our way into this. No, indeed. Our thoughts have been blocked, shaped, mangled, fractured, assaulted and mostly distracted such that we have not been able to align the

cultures and in humane society. The rogue's gallery, the usual suspects, the Predator, are discussed above. We can, however, think our way out of it, and the Predator knows this. It may seem that the Noise Level is reaching unspeakable heights and intolerable levels. That is what is happening and this is why. They must keep us from thinking. They must keep us distracted. They must keep us confused. The Roman bread and circuses pales in comparison.

Sigmund Freud and his 'work' certainly constitute a redefining of the soul and in so doing, attempted to sever us and other cultural members from our Folk Soul, from their Folk Souls. That was important to the early Freudo-Marxists, as well, since the Bolshevik Revolution had not gone as planned on the heels of the First World War precisely because these people did not understand what the Russians were protecting. They were protecting the Russian Folk Soul, not the tsar, and not the proletariat. Hence, the Frankfurt School philosophers, in their quest to save Marxism (Bolshevism), adopted Freud's theories as a way to hopefully infiltrate that human capacity and disable it. It has worked fairly well and, of course, it was not the only target. It was also excruciatingly important to determine some way to prevent us from acting as a group, a majority, as the Predator is a slim bunch, to be sure. They are obscenely wealthy but throwing paper money at an advancing horde will not even slow them down much less stop them. So, the game plan has been to disable our Imagination (I Mage In, I Magician), and to alienate us from each other in ways that are so firmly rooted in our consciousness that we dare not transgress, even at the risk of our own lives. Welcome, weaponized political correctness.

A bit of history, first. We have discussed the hijacking of our childhoods via the schools and how that came about. Critics of the social climate of the 20th century have boiled political correctness down to a single thesis, which is not unwarranted. Over the last century, American education has been (additionally) subverted by ideas from three German sources – Nietzsche, Heidegger, and the Critical Theory of the so-called Frankfurt School, including Georg Lukacs, Herbert Marcuse, Walter Benjamin, and Theodor Adorno. In my estimation, this leaves out one of the major threads, from Plato through Fichte and Horace Mann, but that has been discussed in-depth in Chapter One of this book.

"Political Correctness" was a phrase originally used in the communist party intellectual circles in the 1930s and 1940s. It was revived around 1990 as an insulting characterization of the school of thought known as post-modernism. So what then is post-modernism?

The complete works of Frederich Nietzsche (15 October 1844 – 25 August 1900) had been edited, upon commission by his estate, around 1900 by the philosopher, Rudolf Steiner. In 1936, Nazi Culture Minister Josef Goebbels, formed a committee headed by the philosopher, Martin Heidegger, to 're-do' that. Immersed in Nietzsche's work, Heidegger declared that what he most shared with Nietzsche was the commitment to extinguish the last traces of what he called 'metaphysical humanism.' This goal was shared by The Frankfurt School.

'Metaphysics' is the study of that which generates the physical world or that which changes it. Many would call that God. (I suggest it is the **human imagination** in conjunction with a higher creator, and the planet Sophia). Nietzsche's statement 'God is Dead,' is the basis for all politically correct post-modernism. Nietzsche tried to prove that man's ideas of God, morality, of good and evil, are foolish and false – that there is no Universal Natural

174

Law, creator or no creator. He said the moral architecture we invented as a consolation to avoid the reality that our material world and physical bodies are all there is. Invented it may well be but not as a conolsation.

Nietzsche also proposed, very formally, the idea of moral relativity[124] – each individual will make his own concept of good and evil, based on 'physical' (?) and intellectual' strength. (Might makes right?) This is his man of the future, an 'artist of violence,' based on the Will to Power. A discussion of the different types of will is likely beyond the scope of this book. However, the Will to Power is extremely destructive and completely 'horizontal.' No 'As Above, So Below,' no indispensable spiritual respiration. It is the world view that has us trapped in material misery and distracted from the spiritual cosmos.[125]

Martin Heidegger (26 September 1889 – 26 May 1976) followed with this: if God is truly dead, then objects are all we have and therefore, the sole determiner of our will and ideas.[126] We, ourselves, would be the primary object then. So much contained in 20th century philosophies are both true and false at the same time, deliberately twisted or misunderstood, and most certainly not exclusive of a creator or natural law. The concept of 'both' or simultaneous never enters the conversation. This is, once again, the 'science' of a theory looking for substantiation rather than a set of phenomena looking for an umbrella theory. It is half of the whole, the ever-present fracture. Heidegger even said that life itself is inauthentic because we are mortal and there is no immortality. He completely invalidated our existence with that

---

[124] http://staffweb.hkbu.edu.hk/ppp/top/top19 from Hong Kong Baptist University

[125] Kaufmann, W. *Nietzsche: Philosopher, Psychologist, Antichrist.* Princeton: Princeton University Press, 1974.Nietzsche, *The Gay Science, Section 125,* tr.

[126] Heidegger, Martin. *Nietzsches Wort 'Gott ist tot* (1943) translated as "The Word of Nietzsche: 'God Is Dead,'" in *Holzwege,* edited and translated by Julian Young and Kenneth Haynes. Cambridge University Press, 2002.

statement. For the sake of argument, though, let us continue. The entire idea is to objectify ourselves within the material, or 3D world, which eliminates the mind and the soul.

The Frankfurt School – founded primarily by an Hungarian aristocrat called Georg Lukacs and funded by a wealthy German industrialist – is largely a Nietzsche-Heidegger program under a communist organization system.[127] After WWI, Lukacs veered toward Bolshevism and became Commissar of Culture in the doomed Hungarian Soviet in 1919. After 100 days, the attempt failed and he fled to Moscow. His obsession? Figure out why Bolshevism had succeeded in Russia but not in Hungary or the West, despite the presence of revolts all over Europe. To that end, in 1922 he gathered a band of Marxist intellectuals and philosophers together and formed the Institute for Social Research housed at Frankfurt University, aka The Frankfurt School. The *whole point* was to discover why Marxism had failed and what could be done about it.

"The (FS) determined that the answer was that Russia had been dominated historically by a peculiar gnostic form of Christianity that was ultimately pessimistic."[128] This sort of Christianity replaced the individual soul with the group or communal soul. They posited that the Bolsheviks had succeeded in Russia because their movement represented a 'secular messiah.' Hence, through this secular messiah, they could funnel resentment toward the aristocracy and the church. The FS asserted that despite the most pessimistic efforts of Nietzsche, the West was still

127
    The Political Philosophy of the Frankfurt School by George Friedman. *The Canadian Journal of Sociology / Cahiers canadiens de sociologie* Vol. 7, No. 3 (Summer, 1982), pp. 343-345

[128]   Minnicino, Michael. The Nazi-Communist Roots of Post-Modernism. p.45

dominated by a Judeo-Christian culture that elevated the unique, sacred soul. Pessimism at its most extreme was required to provoke world revolution.

From the standpoint of the FS, western culture maintained that the individual, through exercise of reason (as opposed to rationality, which is **not** the same thing), could directly discern the divine or universal will (as opposed to the Will to Power). This would mean that the individual had the power to change the physical universe. That is the very pinnacle of optimism. The certainty held by western populations that they had the power to solve the ills of society, no matter how large, meant the west simply could not give birth to a Bolshevik Revolution. In 1914, Lukacs issued his most famous query: who will save us from western civilization?[129] One must absorb the reality that the only goal was Bolshevism but this as a reason to bring down the west – too optimistic to allow communism in – was never going to be enough to kick that optimistic atom off the cell of the western physiology. So, what to do?

The FS' addition to post-modernism was to create a tool kit by which western culture could be engineered to self-destruct. Traditional cultural forms would be eliminated so that there would be nothing to support the population and new forms would be created; not to enlighten or uplift but to degrade, fracture, rationalize, divide, shatter. Weaponized Political Correctness was the outcome, the child of Bolshevik pessimism and post-modern bitterness. When the very bottom of the pit of pessimism and despair is reached in this way, they say, then a Bolshevik revolution is possible in the West. Lukacs regarded Nietzsche and Heidegger as amateur pessimists. What was needed was the abolition of culture to be replaced by a culture of pessimism. This

[129] Ibid.

is what is meant by optimistic pessimism; desiring the absolute soul poverty of a culture of pessimism but being absolutely optimistic that this could be created and put into place. Go team. Leave alone the absolute arrogance required to assume one has the right to do this to an entire planet, beginning with the west. For good measure, the paradigm was tweaked a bit for full potential effect and became Freudo-Marxism.

From 1922 until today, the (FS) spun out theory after theory (collectively known as Critical Theory),[130] designed to forcibly remove joy, for the divine spark, for our delight in art, literature and music...politically correct post-modernism...is the essential curriculum taught on today's campuses. It is the straight jacket that awaits us all. This is what explains encountering phenomena such as students at a northern California university chanting, 'hey, hey, ho, ho, western culture's got to go!' Western Civilization as a study offering is dubbed 'racist.' These are absolutely incoherent conclusions. Shall we eliminate Women's Studies as gender-biased? African Studies or Asian Cultures as racist? They are simply a slice of what it is to be human and, as such, must be honoured one as much as the other.

Here we must engage with the politically-driven contribution of the anthropologist, Franz Boas. It was his task to float every possible difference between us to the surface and make those the only things that counted. It was his protégée's task to present non-Judeo-Christian cultures of any kind as superior to the West despite the firm entreaty to be value-free. Hand-in-hand with the moral relativism of the Nietzsche and Heidegger as conscripted by the Bolsheviks, we have cultural relativism,[131] which is one of

---

[130]   *The Frankfurt School and Critical Theory.* http://www.iep.utm.edu/frankfur/
[131]   Rosaldo, R. *Of Headhunters and Soldiers, Separating Cultural and Ethical Relativism.* http://www.scu.edu/ethics/publications/iie/v1n1/relativism.html

those painful 20th century bastardizations of a truism. Cultural relativism, which is true, becomes toxic with the elimination of basic Universal Natural Law, the universal human being, that which joins us foundationally. Boas collected a young, willing, and *ambitious* cadre of acolytes to help the cause and spread the illness, including, as we have noted, Margaret Mead, who ended up an agent for both the Tavistock Institute and the Frankfurt School.[132]

Importantly, it must be stated again and again that politicizing the study of humanity in this way perverted a rich and beautiful course of investigation.

(Mead was trained by and opened a cell of the OSS. Her book has been debunked. Margaret Mead received then, after WWII, a $1 million dollar grant from the Office of Naval Research, which she used to assemble a team of 120 anthropologists. In addition, she maintained a personal relationship with MKSEARCH contractor Dr. James Hamilton. These numerous interconnections between Mead, Bateson, MKUltra and MKSEARCH, the OSS and the Navy illustrated how the mind control network involved in the field of anthropology as well as psychiatry and psychology.)

Cultural relativism is an opinion, just an opinion although an attractive one, that was established as axiomatic in anthropological research by Boas in the first few decades of the 20th century and later popularized by his students. Remember an axiom is, by definition, that highly unlikely and very improbable self-evident truth that requires no proof. These are always *tres* convenient.

Boas first articulated the idea in 1887, that civilization was not an absolute, that everything is relative, our civilization is

[132] Gregory Bateson and the OSS: World War II and Bateson's Assessment of Applied Anthropology. http://homepages.stmartin.edu/fac_staff/dprice/Price-Bateson-OSS-HO1998.pdf p.2

truly only our ideas and conceptions. A tangled web, that. Yes and no. There is such a thing as absolute. It is called Natural Law. Our civilizations are an overlay. This is obfuscation at its finest. However, Boas did not coin the term, cultural relativism. The first use of the term recorded in the *Dictionary* was by philosopher and social theorist Alain Locke in 1924 to describe Robert Lowie's "extreme cultural relativism", found in the latter's 1917 book *Culture and Ethnology*.[133]

The term became common among anthropologists after Boas' death in 1942, to express their synthesis of a number of ideas Boas had developed. Boas believed that the sweep of cultures to is so vast and pervasive that there cannot be a relationship between cultures and races on the one hand but insisted on the other that there are no differences between the races biologically. The greatest single equalizer then is that of our common biology; our fundamentally shared humanity. It is a modern stance that our cultures are so unlike one another that we have no real common ground and that we must invent categories of words and lists of acceptable speech balloons in order to communicate with each other. Indeed, it became a thought-crime and deep social transgression to stray outside these new 'norms.' It was a new penal code in a very real way

In a nutshell, here is the theory: there are no real differences between human beings based on biology. There are **nothing but differences** between human beings based on the culture in which each lives. (Way too black and white to be true, but...) We are unable to understand each other because of this, cultural relativism, and a prescription for both language and process must be devised by the anthropological and political elite

---

[133] Cultural Relativism.
http://www.princeton.edu/~achaney/tmve/wiki100k/docs/Cultural_relativism.html

as a tool so we can understand each other. This system will be set down and codified socially. Cultural relativity has been co-dependently merged with moral relativity, which theoretically ought to provide more individual freedom, whether it's a good idea or not. However, the social and linguistic straight jacket that is politically correct terminology and thought control served to nail us to our differences. It has become immoral, in a morally relative society, to be accused of being politically incorrect. To be accused is all that is necessary; to be afraid one will be accused is enough to silence most people. Has political correctness become a secular messiah, as well? Psychiatrists became the secular priests, schools became the secular churches and replacements for the Sacred Feminine, political correctness became the secular messiah, governments replaced the Sacred Masculine. And, all along, humanity was convinced that if it were not like this then we were being robbed. We were robbed, of that there is no doubt, but it is not of what they tell us it is.

The Predator has taken this system and uses it to hide behind deeply negative and damaging behaviour. Some even suggest and there is much evidence to the effect that the political arena has been manipulated so much that leadership is anchored in 'minority' and to criticize obvious and horrifying abuses, even for the sake of the rest of humanity, is to be accused of throwing racial and ethnic hand grenades. It is to commit thought crimes and worse, be politically incorrect. I cannot tell a minority politician, for example, to stop slaughtering human beings in my name without being shut up by accusations of racism. This is insanity. New priests, new churches, new definitions of the soul and natural law. What were once natural taboos are now engineered taboos, a la politically correct terminology. Generally speaking, these new social domains were meant to divide and separate, divide and conquer. Any given minority pitched against any perceived threat. The threat most often is that the minority won't be recognized as having the same 'rights' as everyone else. **Those rights are garnered by being a human being, one does not need to be a member of a minority.** We no longer know that because of cultural relativity.

In fact, it seems that the only time we are allowed to talk about a 'majority' of any kind is when we are referring to 'all' the Americans, 'all' the Germans, 'all' pick your nationality..and then let the disparaging begin. In these cases, we are really just doing the Predator's work for It. All Americans are a lost cause, all the Germans deserved what they got after the war, all this, all that and so on. Demoralize. Perhaps there is a 4th D. But, no, demoralizing people debilitates them, does it not? Remember our Heidegger: we are inauthentic because we are not immortal. De-moralize because it debilitates.

Political correctness serves this purpose. The thought police. If someone says or does something that causes the slightest emotional discomfort, they are charged with racism, ageism, sexism, or genderism to name a few "isms" on an ever-growing list of politically correct transgressions. Ironically, political correctness has evolved from a means to protect the emotionally weak to a powerful offensive weapon used by politically correct bullies to win losing arguments or suppress opposing ideas or ideology. Political correctness is now being marketed as automatic victory. If you are losing an argument or failing to bend others to your will, pull out a can of "automatic victory" – accuse them of racism, homophobia, anti-semitism or sexism. You win; they lose. *And society grows weaker with the suppression new ideas and opposing views.*

The new social sciences gather information, from the

seemingly banal to the deeply personal, as any gate-keeping body might do...or any security agency seeking to sway the masses by discovering just how the masses tick. They have taught us to call it science. It is the Science of Control, established in this guise by Lenin and the Bolsheviks, the conclusions or yields of which are Weaponized Political Correctness. In this case, language is fascism, and it certainly can be used that way. It is also Creation and Power when it is properly linked to our Imagination.

What can we do? Call a crime a crime, no matter who commits it. Insist on studying all of history and every culture in every context. Insist on value being placed on all the earth's creations. Renew the knowledge and understanding of Universal Natural Law. Redeem the sacred word: No.

Recommended Reading

Bloom, Allan. *The Closing of the American Mind*

d'Souza, Dinesh *An Illiberal Education*

Franz Boas 1963 [1911] *The Mind of Primitive Man* New York:
Collier Books.

Chapter 7

Cerebral Inhibition, Hypnosis and Programming...T.V.

Otherwise known as 'the media,' or the 'entertainment industry,' it's already got a big problem. It's an industry. From blood to dust, remember? Compartmentalize, fracture, rationalize, disempower, mind-numbing repetition, shatter the mirror into a thousand pieces...then elevate all of that within the context of a very low frequency, keep it hovering right there where the human subconscious can be played like a piano. Or, even better, move all of that onto a frequency that is slightly higher than normal for us, which is the frequency to which the earth itself resonates, and be like some distant fingernails on a chalkboard for us subconsciously as we listen and watch all of the 'programming' on frequencies that are abnormal for us.

The Critical Theory of The Frankfurt School has invented, driven and even named the Entertainment Industry.[134] Entertainment itself, as a word with meaning, isn't just about distraction. It also means to enter and train the mind.

One of the most important offshoots of the Frankfurt School's social engineering program was the takeover of the electronic media of radio and television into the powerful social controllers they are today. Two men were primarily responsible for that: Walter Benjamin and Theodor Adorno. One of Adorno's chief influences, in fact, was a Freudian extremist called Otto Gross,135

---

134   *Theodor Adorno.* http://www.iep.utm.edu/adorno/

185

a cocaine addict, who believed man's salvation lay in a return to the Cult of Astarte, which would sweep away monotheism and the 'bourgeouis family.' Adorno went on to become one of the biggest players in the media programming field. This man also became the chief manipulator and philosopher of the music industry in the United States.

We entertain thoughts and ideas, from outside in and, critically, from inside out. If we are kept buzzing at a strange frequency and our thoughts and ideas are nothing more than a barrage from the outside, it becomes difficult to entertain the thoughts coming the other direction.

The Tavistock Institute has provided the research on and implementation of propaganda to drive the masses one way or the other. This is the fatal embrace of the Predator. The FS, or Institute of Social Research, coined the term 'culture industry'[136] to indicate the process of the industrialization of *mass-produced culture* and commercial imperatives that drove the system. Adorno, who was to lead the way in this arena for the FS, "...was a philosopher who took mass entertainment seriously. He was among the first philosophers and intellectuals to recognize the potential social, political, and economic power of the entertainment industry. Adorno saw what he referred to as 'the culture industry' as constituting a principal source of domination within complex, capitalist societies."[137]

The FS created tools of social sampling (Fromm) to both determine how to drive the masses and how the mass entrainment was doing out in the population. Theorists scrutinized all mass-

---

[135] Otto Gross is an elusive but interesting figure, known to Freud and Adorno. http://english.umn.edu/contact/roth/freud.pdf
[136] Ibid.
[137] *Theodor Adorno.* http://www.iep.utm.edu/adorno/ part 5.

mediated results within the arena of industrial production...ie, sales figures, and applied these standards of success to all cultural products or substances as art and music and news and so on became commodities. At least the anaysis of such was conducted as if they were commodities. Edward Bernays concocted the recipe by which all things could be 'sold' to the masses, otherwise known as propaganda or, in modern terms, advertising and marketing.[138] One does not hear the term 'culture industry,' which has no meaning to the masses at all, one hears the term 'entertainment industry,' which has more meaning to the masses. In fact, it's a good bet these would be thought of as two separate things when they are not.

The culture industries had a specific function, however, of providing ideological permission and sanctioning of the planned society and of assimilating individuals into the same. The Tavistock Institute achieved this via its massive investigation of and experimentation with propaganda, hypnosis, subliminal suggestion, and subconscious prodding. The FS applied its critical theory to every aspect in an attempt to politicize these tools of unfathomable power.

The media itself, used in this way, was first unleashed upon the US by William Randolph Hearst during the Spanish-American War.[139] It was, as has so often been the case since, an effort to get the US into a war, this time with Spain over Cuba. It worked. "The Spanish-American War is often referred to as the first "media war." During the 1890s, journalism that sensationalized—and sometimes even manufactured—dramatic

---

[138] *Mind Control Theories and Techniques Used by Mass Media.* http://vigilantcitizen.com/vigilantreport/mind-control-theories-and-techniques-used-by-mass-media/

[139] *Yellow Journalism.* http://www.pbs.org/crucible/journalism.html

187

events was a powerful force that helped propel the United States into war with Spain. Led by newspaper owners William Randolph Hearst and Joseph Pulitzer, journalism of the 1890s used melodrama, romance, and hyperbole to sell millions of newspapers--a style that became known as yellow journalism."[140] It can be readily argued that it was a race between the British newspaper moguls toward the end of the 19th century and Hearst in the US as to who was the first to proagandize the desires of the elite and manifest war.

It is so different now and yet just the same. The newspapers were the only game in town then. The media now surrounds, envelops and saturates us in frequency, visual, auditory, and unconscious. It takes only a moment now to connect, to enter our mind (our brain really, which is different) and start to manipulate us. This has become the sole purpose of modern entertainment. It is an industry, indeed.

"...few could dispute Adorno's description of the mass entertainment industry. However, Adorno's specific notion of the 'culture industry' goes much further. Adorno argues that individuals' integration within the culture industry has the fundamental effect of restricting the development of a critical awareness of the social conditions that confront us all.[141] The culture industry promotes domination by subverting the psychological development of the mass of people in complex, capitalist societies."[142]

It is The Programming Industry. The programming industry sucks young talent in by dictating what constitutes 'good'

---

[140] ibid
[141] ibid
[142] ibid

188

film, writing, art, and music. Much of that, even subjects which seem controversial and topical, must stay within the bounds of what is considered to be politically correct or must support the cultural consumer agenda. The consumer angle is the easy angle: "David Held, a commentator on critical theory, describes the culture industry thus: "the culture industry produces for mass consumption and significantly contributes to the determination of that consumption. For people are now being treated as objects, machines, outside as well as inside the workshop. The consumer, as the producer, has no sovereignty. The culture industry, integrated into capitalism, in turn integrates consumers from above. Its goal is the production of goods that are profitable and consumable. It operates to ensure its own reproduction."[143]

Few can deny the accuracy of the description of the dominant sectors of cultural production as capitalist, commercial enterprises. The culture industry is a global, multibillion dollar enterprise, driven, primarily, by the pursuit of profit. What the culture industry produces is a means to the generation of profit, like any commercial enterprise. Every one of these portals of artistic expression is viciously guarded such that unwanted liberating or free-thinking expressions can be gagged, bound and buried in some cellar, never to see the light of day. I believe the Vatican Library is a spectacular example of this sort of prison. Every major publishing house plays a role in this, whether paper or online.

However, it is the behavioural programming that underlies the obvious and it is the most poisonous and insidious. When one entertains this notion in this sort of context, it becomes

---

[143] Held, D. *Introduction to Critical Theory: Horkheimer to Habermas.* Cambridge: Polity Press, 1980. (1981:91)

very easy to see a familial relationship to the Chinese Marxist Cultural Revolution, Bolshevism, Stalinism, Fascism, Catholicism and any other 20th century 'ism' in which thought police were employed. We can now truly mourn the 20th century as, in fact, The Stolen Century.

Prior to the first World War, Woodrow Wilson was instructed to and did use the fledgling media at hand to whip up support for the US to enter WWI. Woodrow Wilson acted always upon orders from the Tavistock Institute via his advisor Col. Edward House, who received his orders from Chatham House, London.[144] In this way and at this time the film industry as proaganda tool was born. Of course, we cannot forget the foundations of the Tavistock Institute and their war-mongering in England to the same end. Once the power of radio and then television was understood, even if merely on a frequency level and how that affects the human brain and neurological system, a great ring of power was forged and the quest to learn how to wield it in the plan to pervert humanity began.[145] This statement bears repeating:

"Since President Woodrow Wilson openly enlisted the cooperation of Hollywood film makers to create propaganda to stir war fever among Americans, Hollywood and US media have been intimately linked with shaping consensus for US national strategy. ...The US Pentagon and the military industrial complex, together with the elites at the New York Council on Foreign Relations and other select

---

[144] Coleman, Dr. John. Diplomacy by Deception.http://saxonmessenger.christogenea.org/book/export/html/643 p.1

[145]

http://www.medicalveritas.org/MedicalVeritas/Musical_Cult_Control.html

organizations of power brokers, developed a form of culture and media warfare..."146

Newspapers, books, the radio, films and eventually television and computer-driven forms of entertainment were the instruments of waging war on other nations. Now they are the instruments of waging war against the individual and his/her independent thought or choice within the idea of culture. Radio, film, television, the internet (which is also our best hope in many ways), and designed computer games are meant to enter our minds and affect us via the frequency match: theirs to ours. That's a little more like semi-conscious rape than Sunday morning reading over coffee and croissant.

It is now appropriate to discuss what was and what is. Thanks to the immoral and avaricious use of the media, the movement, which has already been discussed at length in this book, which could very aptly be called a counter-Renaissance, was born. The anti-light. One wonders what sort of soul, with what sort of agenda, would be interested in an antidote to the Renaissance and all it wove together, all the soaring accomplishments gained therein? What sort of soul would be interested in crushing optimism and joy and calling it a boon for humanity? Would a true soul even be involved? I don't think so.

The Renaissance of the 15th and 16th centuries was a spiritual and intellectual celebration of the human soul; a true climax of the heart, mind and soul in a preview of the ascension to come. It was a glorious image of humanity's potential for growth. Beauty in art, expressed as scientific principles, demonstrated by

---

146   Engdahl, FW, *Target China* p.153

the use and understanding of sacred geometry...these were the hallmarks of this period. Human beings truly began to express themelves as polymaths, what we would refer to as Renaissance Man. The boundaries were only the infinite Heavens, the dark and mighty Deep, the newly revealed Cosmos, and the undiscovered New World. About a century ago, it was as if a checklist had been drawn up, each accomplishment set to be reversed. The concept of the human soul was undermined by the most vociferously sclerotic intellectual-abstraction campaign in history. Some people call it mental masturbation. There is a level of intellectualizing and abstracting that borders on pornographic mental insanity.

The genesis of this vast mechanism of manipulation, after the newspapers, was The Radio Project (Little Annie). It was developed in 1937, not prior to the development of radio for the masses but rather in sync with its inception. This program was developed and funded by The Rockefeller Foundation to look into the effects of mass media on society. The Radio Project became part of the Psychology Department at Princeton University. At the same

time, an unholy alliance between the Rockefellers and Rothschilds was funding research into the military applications of sound (ie, music and so forth) upon populations. "Between World Wars I and II, accelerating during the 1930s, scientific studies in musical frequencies best suited for war-making were funded by the Rothschild-Rockefeller alliance, represented by the Rockefeller Foundation and U.S. Navy. A major objective of this war, and profitable population control, research was to determine the musical factors capable of producing psychopathology, emotional distress, and 'mass hysteria.'

Academically directed by grants provided by the Rockefeller Foundation, in concert with the US Navy and National Defense Research Council according to the foundation's archives, acoustic energy researchers, including Harold Burris-Meyer, an audio engineer and drama instructor at New Jersey's Stevens Institute of Technology, were commissioned. Burris-Meyer is best known for providing consulting services to the Muzak Corporation, 'which used his expertise to optimize sound installations in factories so that emotional motivation of workers achieved through music would not be adversely effected by factory noise . . ,' wrote James Tobias, a Professor of English at the Univ. of California.

Tobias reviewed Rockefeller Foundation (RF) archives, and documented investigations leading to psychological warfare applications of acoustic vibrations, ultimately advanced militarily and commercially.

Burris-Meyer, according to Tobias, contributed to the Department of Defense during World War II, "including building speaker arrays deployed on warplanes such that enemy combatants could be addressed from the air" to produce psycho-emotional

193

affects leading to "mass hysteria." Additionally, the Princeton Radio Project played a role in this research. This occurred precisely at the time the atomic bomb Manhattan Project was beginning at Princeton involving Albert Einstein at the Institute for Advanced Study.[147]

At the same time, the BBC was testing Tavistock techniques on the British general population to see if their behaviour could be altered. In fact, the devlopment os such things as serials (series) and cliff-hangers came about simply to see if, as B.F. Skinner later described, humans beings could be programmed en masse to be in a certain spot doing a certain thing on command. Skinner also postulated that some 'thing' could be inserted into people's physical environment that would convince them to change their behaviour.

The analysis and harnassing of radio came first followed by television. One of the data collection projects – dubbed 'Little Annie' – was created to analyze mass listening habits. There is only one real reason to care and that is if one wants to program the masses.

Because the germinal group behind these efforts fancied themselves philosophers first and foremost, they exercised intellectual conceits which would go far toward translating to a cultural destruction tool. Walter Benjamin dwelt on Art and Artistic Creativity. Theodor Adorno took on Music. Essentially, these were just deeper studies of what creates a culture, makes it strong, and how to destroy it. The fact that cultures remain at their

[147] Tobias J. *Composing for the Media: Hanns Eisler and Rockefeller Foundation Projects in Film Music, Radio Listening, and Theatrical Sound Design.* Rockefeller Archive Center Research Reports Online, 2009. http://www.medicalveritas.org/MedicalVeritas/Musical_Cult_Control.html

194

bases...have a look at the crumbling European Union for a brilliant example of the strength of the individual folk soul. Both said they were determined to settle the question proposed by Georg Lukacs: how to give aesthetics a firmly materialistic basis.

Unfortunately much of the foundational philosophy these two brought to a discussion about aesthetics or arts, assuming those are the same thing which, in my opinion, they may not be, has to do with the profound pessimism of the Mraxist movement coupled with the unkillable Freudian tenet of pansexualism. Hedonism and despair, this is a lethal cocktail. (Not surprisingly, Walter Benjamin went on to commit suicide.) Adorno worked with Bertrand Russell to decorate the 1950s and 1960s culturally via the new electronic media toward the pruposes of cultural revolution via social engineering. The senior man on-hand for the Tavistock Institute within the Radio Project was Gordon Allport as well as Frank Stanton, the future head of CBS in America.

The Frankfurt School, in their effort to snuff out the divine spark within, was patient and found its own means of conveying material 'art,' until what was once considered to be base and ugly was common popular fare. The goal was to strip away the belief that art comes from a divine or cosmic source, to release the idea of the good old days and build everything from the 'bad new days.' They felt this would, in the end, force man into political revolt as there was no divine reason for anything. The mangling of art and literature and music was meant to develop into a sphere reserved one hundred percent for images that could be used and channeled into political action.

The neutralization, in whatever way possible, of the content in images and the transmission of that content (its

original potent content with which we as human beings resonate naturally and correctly, on a deeply spiritual level), was a critical mission of the FS, particularly via the routes of art and music. In terms of theatre, Bertold Brecht worked closely with Benjamin and intended his audiences to leave his plays demoralized and angry. Benjamin worked with Brecht on films, created radio plays, and attempted to use the media as an organ of social change. One is reminded of a battery, a source of energy to be tapped into and consumed. No matter what, mass media and entertainment in the present day creates the profoundly passive, deprived well and truly of independent energy.

Importantly, we must know that **Rockefeller destroyed music to make it military based.148** Prior to the standardization on 440 Hz, many countries and organizations followed the Austrian government's 1885 recommendation of 432 Hz. The American music industry reached an informal standard of 440 Hz in 1926, and some began using it in instrument manufacturing. In 1936 the American Standards Association recommended that the A above middle C be tuned to 440 Hz. This standard was taken up by the International Organization for Standardization in 1955 (reaffirmed by them in 1975) as ISO 16. Although not universally accepted, since then it has served as the audio frequency reference for the calibration of acoustic equipment and the tuning of pianos, violins, and other musical instruments.149 432 is divisible by 12, coming to 36. 440 is a decimal, but when one divides it by 12, one sees 36.6666666666666 etc. This frequency has been proved to agitate human beings inwardly. Tesla said it, Einstein agreed, frequency is

148 Musical Cult Control: The Rockefeller Foundation's War on Consciousness through the Imposition of A=440hz Standard Tuning. Volume 7, No. 2 Jan. 2011 http://www.medicalveritas.org/MedicalVeritas/Musical_Cult_Control.html
149 A440 http://en.wikipedia.org/wiki/A440_%28pitch_standard%29

the secret to energy and matter generation.**150** Changes to our frequency is everything. This is the fundamental purpose of the GWEN towers dotting the countryside. These are the results of a decades-long discipline called 'acoustic war studies.' "Analyzing the antecedents of current geopolitics and economics, this dirty fact of musical history may be foundational to the status-quo, and instrumental to contemporary sociocultural crises, including modern pandemic psychopathology."**151**

We will have delved deeply into this dialectical potential and the actuality of the takeover by the Programmers by the end. However, it is here we will pause for a moment and touch base with the original question from the introduction yet again. How did we become people, human beings, who could and are allowing all of this to happen to ourselves and, importantly, at times actively and happily participating in the physical demise of our brothers and sisters?

My research into this phenomenon began with the death of my mother, who had worked as an editor for Operation Paperclip scientists at the Office of Naval Research in London. There is a mountain of circumstantial evidence that points to her having been eliminated. What follows is an exerpt from an article I wrote in October, 2013, in which I examined some of her life as an example that might help answer that question**152**:

I am certain the woman would be glad to volunteer as

---

[150] Ibid

[151] Musical Cult Control: The Rockefeller' Foundations War on Consciousness Through the Imposition of A=440hz Standard Tuning. Rockefellerhttp://www.medicalveritas.org/MedicalVeritas/Musical_Cult_Control.html

[152] St.Louis, C. Flyboys in Hell. Originally pulished in Veteran's Today. http://vortexcourage.me/2014/08/08/flyboys-in-hell/

the artist's model, the subject in an examination and rendering of how we were fractured in the 20th century such that we could and would be clay, placid and moldable. The contemplation of a life lived with the fractures and a terrible death has made her story fundamentally one of redemption. It doesn't get any better than that in my estimation.

The frightening first fact may be that hers was/is not an unusual story. In fact, it is common. As we turn the pages of the second half of the 20th century, it is the back story and while the back story for what came then was written, arguably, centuries prior, the basic framework looks like this: World War II and the war of propaganda launched against all of us everywhere so that our understanding of events were what those few driving the conflicts wanted them to be.

Ponder a nine-year-old girl in this case, sitting in a dim movie theater in a little town in the west on a Saturday afternoon, completely surrounded, enveloped by the images running before her. Dazzled, heart swelling with pride, as the stories of unfathomably courageous men and women stood between her and the end of the world.

Here's where it gets a bit sticky, manuevering through this image. In order to understand the effects on a wartime population, one risks deeply insulting the same men and women who did step up when they truly believed the US military was all that stood between a nine-year-old girl and the end of the world. Acknowledged. Respected.

Nonetheless, this very successful boondoggle, almost unbearably tragic, has to be brought out, lifted up and added to the mix that, in the end, has made people who will fly airplanes willingly drop poisons on their friends, their family, their children.

So there it is, with my deepest sympathy/empathy for every one of us who has been duped and all of our children who continue to dissolve before our eyes. That's the first bit of the puzzle.

The second bit: this was a nine-year-old girl with no father. The parents had split up, the father ran off and joined the army no less, the mother worked miles and miles away where there was actually some work to be had. So many longed-for authority figures. In loco parentis, indeed, and the military/government were happy to comply, trained to comply, this impulse having been prepared and planned. Deeply prepared to do so, in fact.

Add more to the mix, because it had to be so: poverty. Poverty as befitted a rural, post-Depression community juxtaposed once again to the 'moving' images of wealth, glamour, bravery, Big Business smoking an expensive cigar. Most of us reading this know this drill. Moving Images, indeed. In loco parentis plus images that 'move' equals a nine-year-old girl – let's just call her America – in desperate need of parents, authority figures and security, both emotional and material. Safety and clear parameters of behavior...what's inside the rules, what's outside the rules.

The latch-key kid called America who just wants to locate someone in authority who seems to know what they're doing. How easy to present an image of authority; yes, this is how to view the world, even if as a grown adult with a moral, ethical or intelligent compass, we would find the parameters repugnant. Horrific. Nightmarish. And, with some perspective accompanied by different 'moving' images, the move might just be away. Far away.

The other location of much-needed authority and feedback for the child, America? The school. And don't they know it? A continuation of behavior modification and brain-washing tinkered with and honed over decades. Add things they want us to rely on, subtract things that encourage independent thought. Year after year. Drip. Drip. Drip. Citizen. Want to save your children? Get the government corporatocracy out of their education.

So, this little girl we've nicknamed America, born in 1936, becomes an adult, vulnerable in all the right ways, longing for all the right missing parts, dazzled by all the right narrative. The Narrative we have all been immersed in for so very long. A Made Creature ripe for the picking. Add immigration, marginalization over decades, ever-increasing and pressurized 'moving' images, the wedge driven into families brutally and relentlessly as funds dry up and every able body goes out to work. Drip...drip...drip. In loco parentis.

Back now, gratefully and with deep love, to the woman; the one who gave her life and her permission to use her as a lens through which to see clearly what has happened. Grateful, she was, as a single mother, to have a government job. Security, health care, retirement benefits.

It was a completely known quantity. Boring but next to impossible to screw up. The rules? Clear. The parameters? Set in stone. The price? Way too high. But, of course, this is what we never know until it's too late. We could know, especially today, if we would unplug, step out of our automaton role. (Hence, the oncoming wave of drones? Yes, but other things, as well, far more scary).

So, yes, back to the little girl. Add the dazzle of the US military and many dreams are realized; implanted dreams but again, we won't realize that until it's much too late. What makes the story much more shiny is that she is adept and intelligent and ambitious and so gains ever-higher security clearances and...the cage door swings shut. Exciting and glamorous according to her very well-groomed ideas of excitement and glamour – remember those newsreels of 1945 – and service to her country. The Greatest Nation in the World. In loco parentis. Citizen. Drip...drip...drip."

This story pulls several of our threads together. Creat a vacuum everywhere it is possible in which to create a vaccuum in a person, preferably a young child. Then fill it with whatever one wants to fill it with. In the case of the post-Depression mid-20th century child it was the newspapers, radio and films.

The human being is a creature of habit on many functioning levels. Some call our array of habits the Morphic Field, which we will discuss in the next chapter. It could be looked at that way. The behaviourists identified and set loose the demons of classical and operant conditioning and the Predator uses that on the world via the media. This changes what we define as normal, all the time. Normal is constantly being tweaked, changed and re-pitched not for our benefit but to produce a herd that will move in a desired direction and generally a herd that is agitated at a desired level to produce a desired reaction or put to sleep in order to be suggested subliminally. Normal becomes constant war. Normal becomes living with shortage and scarcity. Normal becomes ill health from cradle to grave. Scientists call this the Normalcy Bias.[153] **As well, the public has been trained to ignore critical thinking since the assassination of President Kennedy, the time at which the CIA coined the phrase 'conspiracy theory.' What would have caused a national uprising beofre TGV now goes right over our heads.** The Normalcy Bias condition is well known to psychologists and sociologists. It refers to a mental state of denial in which individuals enter into when facing a disaster or impending

[153] Ingles-Arkwell, E. The Frozen Calm of Normalcy Bias. http://io9.com/the-frozen-calm-of-normalcy-bias-486764924

danger. Hence, like an infant with a security blanket we cling to our habitual, repetitive, and normal way of life, despite overwhelming proof.

Even when the evidence of a conspiracy is massive, we have been awash in the conditioning of debility, dependency and dread for so long that we watch, passively, convinced we have no power to change anything. Many times, that idea never even crosses our minds.

Debility, Dependency, Dread.

This is how present day America has been conditioned to not act in the fact of absolute criminal behaviour coming from the government, for example. Today, we lay down in the face of the abject criminality of our government. We accept GMO's, chemtrails, CPS sponsored child sex trafficking, the theft of our mortgages, the murder of dissidents, constant surveillance, unsafe medicines and foods, and the privatization of our most vital resources which are being priced out of our reach (e.g. water). We simply give up as a country in trying to change things because the system has been so unresponsive to the demands of the public, we have become conditioned to believe that our actions will not make any difference. We have the ability to fight back. We have done it before (e.g. Revolutionary War, Civil War). However, this was before the laboratory conditioning of the main stream media came onto the scene. Importantly, though, we in the United States and elsewhere suffer from a very strong underlying malaise, a self-disgust, if you will, because the one thing we cannot be disconnected from is The Folk Soul, which is part of the Morphic Field, and so we do indeed know who we are and what we can do.

It is a bit like sleep paralysis.

There is little to say at this point other than turn off your television. Now. Turn off your radio and watch films, if you must, with a truly educated eye. You may find yourself horrified, shocked and disgusted but, as all mammals teach their young what constitutes a predator and how to avoid it, this is just what human kind needs to see.

Chapter 8

The Folk Souls and the Morphic Fields

Time and a again, a question has arisen for me, as I have acquiesced to the inevitability of this journey and allowed myself to be thrown into the deep water of this quest for simple answers. There are names and places that are inextricably woven through this path of the 20th century social engineering and the Adversaries would have us believe that this is so largely due to the nature of the people or the nations involved. Indeed, that is something we can trace and prove about individuals, one way or the other. It is easy but rather incorrect to apply the same methods and conclusions to the nations. It isn't even correct, when looking for the source of embattlement, to say 'nation,' for nation is the artificial construct, an economic entity.

When one really wants to discuss and understand how a People is acted upon, one has to open up the chest and get to the real beating heart of such: the Folk Soul. Then when the Folk Soul is identified, one must be given the facts of the relationship between the Folk Soul and the Morphic Field. In doing that, it is necessary to understand the field in simple terms and what an individual and nation are independently. Aside from my own personal experience of such, for the purposes of discussion herein, my research resources are Rupert Sheldrake, John Lamb Lash, and Rudolf Steiner, a man who understood the reality of the folk soul very deeply and who lived and wrote about the realities of the pre and post World War I Germany.

There are three situations which deserve to be looked at here because of both the puzzles and answers demonstrated: first, why didn't World War I cause an immediate and successful communist revolution? Second, why is it always Germany used as the club with which to beat the rest of the world into a fearful uproar? Third, why is it absolutely imperative to subdue the United States and make this citizenry blindly obey? All of these questions, the 20th century history of each of these nations, goes directly back to dashed hopes of a group of Freudo-Marxists, directed by the insatiable greed of the Predator, as I have discussed here. However, the layer beneath that has to do with absolute control of the planet, Sophia, and her caretakers and children, humanity. That requires an understanding of the theory of how this reality is created and from whence it is created. In the end, what I hope it really causes is a remembrance of who we really are. An amnesia has been placed upon us from which we must awaken.

The idea for our Predator has been to move entire peoples. To a much larger and more frightening extent that has been possible. The 'hows' we have already covered in previous chapters. However, remember that at the beginning of the 20th century, and as one of the desperately desired outcomes of World War I, the Marxists and the Bankers were sure that, as a result of Communist propaganda, the Russian population would not fight for their country, would not turn and repel the invader but would rather turn all its mighty energy toward enacting a new communist for of government. That did not happen. The question in this case, is why? My answer was and remains that the Russians reacted as they did to the German invaders not out of loyalty to their nation and not our of loyalty to their Tsar. They reacted as a unit from the fabric of the Russian Folk Soul. Every Folk Soul has a mission and every dweller within that folk soul is there to be part of something greater than themselves. When that is the case, the organizing authority, if you will, is the morphic field. Once again, the deeper levels have to do with light and darkness, with spirit and anti-spirit, and with taking over control of creation by entities who have no capacity to create, only mimic. The true way to break Humanity is to infiltrate and gain control of the field. This is not truly possible although untold misery has been caused in the attempt.

Just as the morphic field is the etheric or pattern of the adult tree to an acorn, the morphogenetic field may be the prototype for the Folk Soul. The fields are not 'made' from anything. In fact, according to Dr. Rupert Sheldrake, matter is generated from the field. How? I suspect that this is where the human being enters. Humans are both filters and conduits. It is a great spiritual tenet that we are co-creators in the universe. Our thoughts are spirit and what we think we manifest. Many great teachers and philosophers state this. In the beginning was the Word, after all. In Form Ation. In Forma? This is the sister idea to I Mage In, Imagination. The entire life cycle of the human being begins with the child as a purely imaginative creature and the adult who is able to manifest what is imagined into the material, In Form. Information. I believe as do many others, that we act as the bridge between the morphic field and the material plane. This is how the material is formed, from the field, via our imagination then words and actions. Therein lies our power of creation. This is why we are referred to as co-creators. This is a power that the Predator has not got but this is an ability that the Predator wants, for many reasons. In the absence of the ability to become that co-creator, then subjugating humanity and using us to manipulate the field would be one of the paramount goals. We have seen that discovering how most powerfully to move entire populations is one of the prime goals of the social engineers. There are many ways to do this and nationalism itself can be stoked to the point of madness.

It would have been quite the task to understand why this is easily accomplished in some ways and ultimately we remain uncapturable in others. This has to do with the Folk Soul. Sheldrake discussed the idea of the phantom limb and also of actual material regeneration of physicality due to the affects of the field, which holds an etheric template always for us. Cut a worm in half...one has two whole worms, not a top half of a worm plus a separate bottom half a worm. Break a magnet...each piece becomes a whole magnet, not a half of a magnet and a half of a magnet, a north pole and a south pole. Try to break or shatter a folk soul. It cannot be accomplished. One does not fracture a Folk Soul, as the dismal experiment with the European Union has demonstrated so ably. The Folk Soul and the Nation are not the same thing. One also does not take Folk Souls and jam them together to make a bigger sandwich, so to speak, as in the ideas of Pan-America and the Pan-Slav goal. These have not been accomplised even after a hundred years or more of planning and trying. Break down the borders of the nations; this does not erase the container edges of a Folk Soul.

The Folk Soul is...the template, the prototype and, more importantly than anything else the karmic mission. Since the morphic field organizes anything that is more than the sum of its parts, the Folk Soul is certainly that, and resides in the field. Each folk soul is a collection of missions, tasks, strengths and weaknesses. These are set us just so that each of us gets and gives what is needed because of the folk soul we have chosen for that particular incarnation. There is a school of thought that we are now prisoners of reincarnation. The jury is still out on that one. The most suspicious part of that debate is that the very idea of reincarnation has been removed from our waking consciousness for so long by the Catholic Church that it must be something empowering, something to be kept from us by the controlling forces. Now that its existence has burst forth into consciousness again, there is a new spin on the phenomenon. There is this idea that it is part of our emprisonment. However, this is not the subject of our tale and will be left for now.

My personal experience is that there is, in fact, an underlying cultural backbone and it is known as The Folk Soul. It has nothing to do with nationalism. According to the philosopher and mystic, Rudolf Steiner, nationalism is nothing other than a consequence of the lack of ideas, not just of spiritual ideas but of the imprisonment of the imagination. It is simply to be completely grounded in the material; in lateral thinking. Nationalism is a game of borders and territories and economics...a distraction. The only legitimate use for nationalism, in my view, is to be the loose identifier of the primary location of a Folk Soul. Since the Folk Soul is absolutely more than the sum of its parts, however, one will find the strength of this carried with the individual and group as migration occurs from outside a national territory. The Folk Soul is much more, much stronger, than a nation of country. The Ukraine in 2013 is a modern example of such as it cries out for and to its Russian Folk Soul in the midst of the carnage being heaped upon it by demonic greed and those who would destroy, not just ancient seats of wisdom, but for the pure demonic pleasure of destruction.

And, as we have shown, it was this potential for enslavement through nationalism that was played upon by the Predator just prior to the turn of the 20th century and certainly in the years leading up to the first World War. It Russia, the experiment was to try to replace the Nation with the abstract notion Proletariat. That failed dismally. Abstract notions are not ideas either. Nationalism appeared to be working and so was used beyond reason until it became its pathology in many places during World War II: fascism. The United States is an example of nationalism headed toward, if not firmly ensconced in the lap of fascism now. These are the nationalistic and material principles, writ way, way too large. These are the material support of economics, industry and material sciences.

If the morphic field holds the prototype for that which is bigger than the sum of its parts, then this is where we can locate the Folk Souls. It is theorized that the prototype, for example, of a tree or a human or anything else that is actually living is already in existence. Steiner referred to this as the 'etheric.' Some might locate it in counter-space...the thing we see as emptiness around anything material, such as the inner concavity of a bowl which is actually anything but empty...it is filled with counter-space, with the etheric, with the field....

Britain goes to war with Germany while Russia twists itself into a socialist knot, breaking its own bones in the process. Then the United States became the next great seat for social experimentation. In his series of lectures, *The Karma of Untruthfulness*, delivered in 1916, Dr. Rudolf Steiner puts together a compelling and well-researched case for the destruction of modern Europe, planned well in advance and then fomented by a now-rabid press.

"If the British Empire wants to draw its colonies closer together, if it wants to generate impulses there which lead towards going along with the motherland, then it needs a war...and whenever such thoughts are thought, the end justifies the means." (Steiner, TkofU, 1916) and...

"British Empire by placing before their souls and the souls of their pupils maps which showed what still had to come about if the British Empire was to beam its forces over the whole world." (Vol.2)

(by means of maps): Arthur Polzer-Hoditz says in his book, *Kaiser Karl*, Zurich-Leipzig-Vienna 1928, p.19: I conclude that the breaking up of the Hapsburg monarchy had been a foregone conclusion among the politicians who – by the way – after the collapse of the Central Powers intended to share among themselves the chief roles in world politics. I refer in particular to a map showing the divisions of Europe, which was published by an Englishman Labouchere in his satirical weekly journal, *Truth*, in 1890 (The Christmas Number dated December 25, 1890, not the regular number for that week which is also dated December 25) that is 24 years before the outbreak of the World War. This map is virtually identical with that of present-day Europe (1916): Austria as a monarchy has disappeared and way for a republican member of the League of Nations. Bohemia is an independent state in the incidental shape of Czechoslovakia. Germany is squeezed into her present confines and split into small republics. Where Russia would be is written 'Russian Desert,' Countries for Social Experiments." (KofT, Vol 1, Lecture 1 Note 5)

See also – C.G. Harrison, *The Transcendental Universe. Six Lectures on Occult Science, Theosophy and the Catholic Faith.* London. 1894. 'A powerful empire which unites under a despotic government a number of local communes – Russia. The remains of a kingdom – Poland, whose only cohesive force is its religion, and which will be ultimately reabsorbed in the Russian Empire in spite of it. A number of tribes who, oppressed by the alien Turk, have thrown off the yolk and have artificially consolidated into little states, whose independence will last as long as, and no longer than, the next great European war. The Russian Empire must die that the Russian people may live, and the realization of the dreams of the Pan-Slavists will indicate that the sixth Aryan sub-race has begun to live its own intellectual life, and is no longer in its period of infancy.' (KofT, Vol. 1 Lecture One, Note 5)

Nations are economic entities which purportedly act on behalf of the individual. However, this is never the case. Nations are the tools of economic powers and sovereign heads-of-state and that is all. Nations exist to both serve despotism and form a citizenry that complies with the will of the strongest power behind the nation-state, whatever or whoever that happens to be. It is imperative then that the manipulating powers understand how to implement control over an entire population. Nationalism and the jingoism that goes with it, very much like religious sloganism, affects the blood. The Folk Soul, on the other hand, affects an individual. It is the difference really between ceremonial magic (i.e., the church or the state) and true spiritual magic, the vertical connection between, for purposes of this discussion, the Morphic Field and the materialized human on this plane, the body, soul and mind operating here on the behalf of the morphic field with Sophia, the cosmic spirit that is this Earth. This is not a new age speech...far from it! There are terrible things in play here on the material plane and we must summon our ability to use our anger and say No. Nothing New Age about that. We must discern again, see through the horrible hologram surrounding us, admit that we are being poisoned, eliminated and say no to it.

How does the Individual then fit into the Folk Soul on this side? The Individual resonates with the particular frequency of a given folk soul and does so no matter where they are or when. The so-called melting pots end up being a symphony then of folk soul gestures and movements into the general population and toward each other and the planet. However, I believe that just one of the many things that the artificial electro-magnetic frequencies we are drowning in is supposed to do is thwart the resonances of the folk souls. The electro-magnetic swamp we exist in is there simply to change frequency. Alter the good and add the bad. So simple.

Germany Fact from just prior to WWI...(RS)...

"Germany's exports started to catch up with the British, not many years ago (*this was written in 1916*) a comparison showed that Germany's export figures were very low and Britain's were very high.(Sir Roger Casement, *Ireland, Germany and the Freedom of the Seas* Munich 1916)...the figures for January through June, 1914. For this period Germany's export figure was 1,045,000,000 British pounds and that of Britain was 1,075,000,000 Brisith pounds. If another year had passed without the coming of the World War, it is possible that the German export figure might have been larger than the British. This was not to be

212

allowed to happen!'"

There is ample evidence that the events of the beginning of the 20th century, emanating from Britain, were well-planned and had to do with re-carving the map of Europe. Germany itself, land of a solid will and the great philosophers must have been subjugated and harnassed to the imperial will. That would only happen if, as in the case oif the United States, the German spirit was broken. That was done in true sociopathic style. Many events were presented to a people...a gaslighting, if you will...and the German people were taught not just to question what they had lived through or seen with their own eyes but to subsequently hate themselves.

The Russians simply could not be convinced to turn on themselves and so the Freudo-Marxists moved on to Germany and from there to the United States. What lies within the Folk Soul of the US? The sovereign individual. That must be broken and then used and, as such, we have become the military arm of the new Rome, like it or not. The Folk Souls, however, cannot be broken, no matter how much or how poisonous the attack on our morphic field. This is where the tidfe will turn.

As John Lash suggests however, there must be an awakening of the Sorcerer. This is the direct line from Imagination to Manifestation. Information into the morphic field is a cleansing, a protection and an awakening. Yes. The manifestation of the disabling and neutralization of the Predatory impulses on the material plane is the No. And we must have balance at all costs. Hence the information in which has been polluting, or trying to pollute, the morphogenic field must be countered with true information. This is a situation in which it takes only a little to affect the great whole. Then then manifestation of change can and will occur because the Sorcerer has awakened. We are those forces. And we will have the strength of Sophia with us.

Recommended Reading

Steiner, Rudolf. *The Karma of Untruthfulness*, Vols. 1 and 2 1916

Lash, John Lamb. *Not In His Image: Gnostic Vision, Sacred Ecology, and the Furutre of Belief* 2006

Sheldrake, Rupert. *Morphic Resonance: The Nature of Causative Formation.* 2009

Chapter 9

Sacred Space, Sacred Imagination

(Babylon is Falling)

I said at the very beginning of this piece I would not talk about money. I didn't. Forget money. It is both the Grand Illusion perpetuating a black art and a gaming addiction at the artifical intelligence level.

The other thing I won't talk about is the debate over CO2, greenhouse gases, and global warming. This is a meme, a mental hamster wheel on which they have purposefully placed us so that we cannot think of anything else and certainly cannot think of either the whole or any context. This is the meme that convinces human pilots to spray their fellow humans with poisons from the sky. The goal is to shake it all off, reclaim intellecual clarity, yes, and operate especially with our heart-mind. It is time to understand and digest the fact that we think with the heart mind and be grateful because this is a frequency the Predator cannot locate. It is truly safe and private, closed to the National Security Agency, a fact which makes the demons gnash their teeth!

What I will come back to is Humanity as Creator and the Imagination to Manifestation process the Predator wants to eliminate in us and usurp for itself. Barring that, the idea is to harnass the morphic field through us by controlling information in and out. We project reality via our physical eyes based on what we've tapped into in the morphic field. It makes sense that a power play would be made by a non-human entity to wield this magic wand. The entire process can be seen in microcosm in the imaginative play of a child and traced through the manifestation of our vision and thought and wonderings in the physical world, the material. So many indicators point to the vulnerability and targeting of our youngest children. This is where the imagination is most free, innocent and beautiful. Nailing the youngest children to the three lowest chakras, a crucification of the purest and most innocent imagination, via early exposure to sexually explicit material in any form and through sexual assault, as well, is one way the Predator seeks to destroy us. Remember this is a technique brought by every social engineering group in the 20th century from Georg Lucasz in Hungary in 1919 and forward. We see it now in the USA, in England and in Germany, just to name a few. These countries are experiencing horrifying, catastrophic changes in the protective status of the youngest children. So wake up and protect the children and do it now.

The enemy strategy is clear. Isolate children from their parents as early and completely as possible. Teach them fear as early and completely as possible. Wire them into a computer as early as possible to by-pass the neurological development they would ordinarily experience left to their own developmental calendar in accessing our profound capacities. The capacities would have become realities and these connections atrophy in the face of the dim substitute of the computer, which is only a tool, a mere shadow of a glorious human being. Expose them to sex education (or worse) and nail them to the lower chakras hoping that higher consciousness is either delayed or thwarted entirely.

Teach them, then, that we have no commonalities among the cultures but only our differences and that there is a law of communication, called political correctness, which will stop us early and often from questioning the obvious. Remove art and music and oral learning – everything that helps keep the brain hemispheres working together, as is natural, such that the Imagination, our seat of power, becomes profoundly hamstrung. Teach by rote, remove play and times of rest and recreation and joy. This adds an element of mind control technique in weariness and overload. All inhale and no exhale. Convince the children and the adults they become that they are mere machines, organic machines of bone and blood, meant for assembly line production, moving bits of paper around in a never-ending circle, divorced completely from process and context and wholeness. Compartmentalize all that they are and all in which they live such that they are fractured, made of rations...pieces...that do not communicate with each other – a mirror shattered into a thousand pieces. Attack their neurology via injections and poisonous gases, food that contains within it the very mechanism of physical destruction, numb their minds with flouride and tranquilizers and anti-depressants (which include a large portion of flouride). Put a musical, tinkly, colorful box in front of them to capture their attention and 'program' their actions, emotions, needs and wants. Learn to tune it and all music to a frequency that causes them to fall into a semi-hypnotic state, very tractable and suggestible. Dot the landscape with electro-magnetic pulse machines, emitting frequencies at demonic proportions which cause the saline in their very cells to vibrate and scream out in agitation....create illnesses which require drugs, customers until they finally give up and succumb in abject exhaustion like worn rugs who used to be human beings. Relentlessly remove natural healing substances and marginalize complementary medical schools until they have to cross national borders for safety lest jail be their lot. Create war after war after war, demand blood sacrifices and energy sacrifices to feed the insatiably vampiric nature of the Predator. Trauma and fear. Dependence, debility and dread. Yes, this is the plan dialed up to super-demonic levels in the 20th century, a final gambit for victory and total control.

Thanks to the 'journalists,' the battle is being made to seem fierce, fiery, hopeless and panicked at the moment. However, something appears to be going awry. False flag operations, while they are ongoing and relentless and everywhere, appear either to be found out almost immediately or die in mid-flight. Whatever all the variables may be to explain this, I propose that the most formidable foe is now the Collective Unconscious. The Morphic Field. It can only get stronger and, since the control of information appears to be absolutely paramount as a goal of the opposition, I also propose that there is no real way to destroy it. The opposition can only try to keep people ignorant of its existence and of our role as partners of the morphic field.

Babylon, the state of being within which there is no understanding between people, artificially created as such, highlighted at the beginning of the 20th century, alas, by the budding field of anthropology. Definition: any society or group in a society considered as corrupt or as a place of exile by another society or group. I believe the reality for us now is both: the state of illusion created by those of Babylon, convincing us we have no common understanding or common being as well as the predator group which will fall, due to the divine nature of humanity and its relationship to the morphic field which cannot be captured, not really, and certainly not eliminated. The same phenomenon that allowed us to be put to sleep can be used to wake us up. People already think they know the truth but they do not on a conscious, material level. In the morphic field, of course, they remember. Dis-member in the material, re-member in the morphic field. The question is: where is memory located? The predator assumes it is in the head, in the body, mechanistic and computer-like and material. This is an erroneous assumption and will be the downfall of the predator. Babylon will be forgotten because it cannot locate or destroy the source of the memory.

The secret is in the act of creation. Those who have erected the 3D world, the trauma-saturated holograph in which they have trapped us, have no souls and thus cannot create. In fact, it is in the search for the soul and some way to harness or subdue the human soul, that the Predator gives itself away. What is every phase of the jagged edge of 20th century social engineering if not the redefinition of the soul? Every social engineering cannon has been aimed at this. They cannot find it. They cannot identify it much less take it because it resonates at a frequency to which they are blind. They can only attack and degrade and shred the periphery, the fruits of the human soul labour, for by its fruits shall ye know it.

They can conjure up something they believe is 'like' the soul but it is not. It's all a guess. None of their 'creations' have life for they cannot bestow life, they cannot create as a human creates. The only real issue is that they would rather kill us off than give up. We have strength and wisdom, ancient wisdom, available to us in the morphic field as we have not had for a very, very long time.

Collective unconscious, collective memory, morphic resonance or field...these are the dwelling places of humanity. This is why information is the battle arena. There is a certain percentage of the morphic field that has to house information for it to then spread like wildfire. I believe this is mostly for the good as I believe there are protections against evil or black information to some extent. This is why there are so many artifial constructs (TV, movies and so forth) developed to deliver information to large collections of people. The Predator hopes the artificial constructs invade the morphic field, as well. Our consent is necessary to work their will, engineered or seduced or programmed or forced. So, turn off your television as it is the major engineering tool for consent of the masses. Now.

The strength of the true collective unconscious is that it requires no such contrivances. We are life with consciousness whereas these entities are consciousness without life, soul or spirit. It is in the forgetting, the trance, the hypnosis, the coma...we have been made to forget who we are and how truly powerful. We have, above all else, been made to forget the sacred word: No. Short, sweet and powerful. Use it. It belongs to you.

The signs of desperation and destruction are all around us, some of it is ours, most of it is theirs. It is because of the strength of the collective unconscious and the morphic field. Some refer to it as the 100th Monkey Phenomenon – one hundred monkeys who understand something means all the monkeys in the rest of the world learn it and, many times, spontaneously. This is proved science.

On a material level, the Predator has rewritten our history and our past, placed the lies in books and force-fed it to us from childhood. Literacy is truly important to those who would control us through the written word, is it not? The ancient truths were corrupted, buried or changed. Wars are fought in the Middle East especially to destroy antiquities, symbols powerful to our collective unconscious, keys to turn the locks in the doors of our awakening. It would be paramount for everyone to have a computer, for every child to have a laptop, if the point was to control us through what we see on these. It would be important, not to hear live music or see live theater as was the absolute way of life for humanity, but to see what is canned and controllable. In fact, it would be paramount to make that available, cheap and cast a very, very broad net of thought direction and manipulation. It would be impoirtant to take live music, what there is of it, and make it jar our resonance fields, disrupt us at a cellular level, rip what remains of our social fabric to shreds.

Fortunately, the idea of a mass lie has a reverse and that is the mass truth in the morphic field. Just enough of us have to place it there and we all have it. It works in reverse of the mass media manipulation. This is what is happening. This is what is meant when we talk about raising the consciousness. Maybe it would be better to say, wake the sleeping consciousness. We have this metaphor in Sleeping Beauty and in many, many archetypal tales kept and handed down, despite being bastardized by Hollywood and Walt Disney. These co-opted fairy tales were attacked and leached by putting them on the big screen, not preserved and propogated. Stop watching them. Start reading these, the original versions...right out loud...to your children. They are meant to awaken in us what needs to awaken.

And remember the Water. Water is the holder of memory for Sophia (Gaia). Water memory. Water Being, an intermediary, at a frequency between solid earth and ephemeral air and light. Fracking and such is the attempt to damage the deeper memory of the earth and us. Underwater nuclear testing, deep water drilling and all its subsequent 'accidents,' are all an attack on the water itself and, of course, the creatures who inhabit it. So we must turn our attention to protecting the water and to understanding what it really is, all the kinds of water. Most human beings have lost conscious sight of the fact that there are different types of water. That which the earth generates and regenerates as the living being she is have been hidden from us (such as this thing which was renamed petroleum at the beginning of the 20th century, the black liquid the earth regenerates in plenty). Interestingly, one of the best ways to protect water is to not force it through a right angle, as there are no right angles in nature and this does much to kill the water, which can be revived via the process of vortexing. Dowsers also clean water, they don't just find water...the masters dowsers restore water. Our cities and houses are networked with water systems built to kill the living water that heals and nurtures us. Luckily, it responds to us, to humanity, when we seek to enliven it again. We must turn our attention, as well, to understanding that thought is fequency according to many scientific minds now and that frequency causes water to vibrate. Hence, how much of water could be classified as thought?

It is best if we have direct access to the Soul of the Sun, from which we draw so much of our strength but, in the end, it is the Qi (the chi) that is our spiritual water and that is always accessible. Since it is always accessible, the only recourse for the predator is to disrupt our receptors. Hence they attack our body, our bodies' frequency receptors, the organs, the neurology, everything about us in the physical in an attempt to sever us from that which they cannot destroy.

Rupert Sheldrake has done much work on the idea of the morphic field and suggest the idea of non-local fields, meaning that a family of sentient beings would remain in a collective field even at a distance. I wonder how the destruction of the physical nuclear family perpetrated so successfully by the Frankfurt School, and the New Age idea that blood does not make family, may have affected this morphic field phenomenon. My guess is not at all. Sorry, opposition.

Morphogenic Fields as a counter to Industrialization and Man as Machine: What are Morphic Fields? I suggest studying the works of Goethe on *Urpflanzen*. An alternative to the mechanist/reductionist approach, which has been around since the 1920s, is the idea of morphogenetic (form-shaping) fields. In this model, growing organisms are shaped by fields which are both within and around them, fields which contain, as it were, the mold of the organism. This is Platonic, this idea that fields evolve and the forms from them evolve but only mechanistic, mathematical constructs. Goethean science stated that there is an Ur form of everything, an archetype. I do believe Jung followed up on that with his notions of the collective unconscious and archetypes. So some theorists take almost a Darwinian mechanistic view of the field and some take an archetypal view. I certainly fall into the latter category as I think it is still part of the Great Lie to attach any of this to a mechanistic process. This is where I and the Great Sheldrake part company. As a tree develops, the seed is connected to the tree field, whatever species, like some sort of mold. There are forms of restorative medicine in which a holographic model of the affected organ, albeit a healthy and whole model, is created. If the soul is willing, then the organ or system can and will restore itself.

Additionally, plants and some forms of life (worms of some kinds, for example), will become several of the same thing if broken into many pieces. This is something a machine simply cannot do. This is the wholistic property of the morphic field, which could be another nail in the coffin of the Predator. No matter how fragmented we become, we are still part of the whole and can be made whole again. In fact, we *are* whole in the field.

There has been such a push to control or destroy natural frequencies in every way. Music and the frequencies from the earth being interfered with through man-made electro-magnetic frequencies, the largest we know of at this point being HAARP. Why? The earth's resonance has been tuning upwards, rising to a higher frequency, for awhile. Vibrations increase. Why? And why try to stop the evolution?

Some of the questions can wait. The thing is to stop the

madness now. We are whole in the morphic field. We can communicate with that. We can use our own sacred word...you know, that word which has all but been bred out of our vocabulary? No. I have tried to present solutions at the end of each chapter to the conundrums traced within. Therefore, no solutions will be presented here just the reacquaintance with our own creative, raw material; where it is located and how we use it.

So, here we are. Why cannot we get past asking the question: What's the difference between a contrail and a chemtrail? And, too many people would have to know about it. It couldn't possibly be happening. How is it we became people who could stay on this merry-go-ground, who could breathe deep the aerosols, who could blithely saturate our fellows and stew our beloved Sophia in the same? It is my belief that I have just answered these questions. As my friend and co-author says, this is a no-excuses book. Namaste.

224

Further Reading

Rupert Sheldrake Resonance Field Studies via
http://www.sheldrake.org/

Oslo, Berlin, Reykjavik, November 19th 2014:

The Chemistry in Contrails

Assessing the Impact of Aerosols
from Jet Fuel Impurities, Additives and Classified
Military Operations on Nature

by

Harald Kautz-Vella

I would like to thank all the people who have
contributed to this study by gathering detailed information
about the single aspects of this big jigsaw puzzle.
Without their dedicated work this paper would not have been possible.

Special thanks to:

- Kristin Hauksdottir, who carried my soul through the first half of
  this research, made it grow with endless remarks and questions;
  and contributed chapters and knowledge where my own skills
  failed to deliver.
- to Cara St. Louis that revealed the transhumanistic background of
  the chemtrail-agenda and handed me over a beautiful book to
  translate.
- Manuela Binieck, who has solved the mystery of the Morgellons
  disease with her photographic skills.
- to my partner, my family & friends who lived with the burden of

all the negative things I attracted during the time I researched to the topic Black Goo.

Abstract

The starting point of this study was to research damage occurring on crops in Norway in the year 2012. Chemical analysis of the crops as well as associated soil and rain samples showed relative high values in barium and strontium. Together with aluminum and titanium this is known to be the chemical fingerprint found when analyzing dying crops and trees in areas with frequently occurring persistent contrails. Thus this damage is often associated with aerosol spraying i.e. geo-engineering as a possible source for the damage observed. However the total amounts of heavy metals measured in the samples were too low to explain the damage as the impact of intoxication by bio-available metals i.e. metals in solution.

From the historic development of geo-engineering techniques as well as from technologies utilized within the military domain the mixture of both amorphous and mono-crystalline Al_2O_3 and mono-crystalline $(Ba, Sr_x) TiO_3$ can be derived as the two most common compounds that should be in use. But these crystalline particles do not show up in standard chemical analysis, unless one uses hydro-fluorine acid, which is hardly ever the case. Regarding the fact that these crystals can be manufactured on-board in spray-pyrolysis within the jet engines, the widely measured fingerprint could be understood as the rejects of the Al_2O_3 production as well as the of the $(Ba, Sr_x) TiO_3$ nano-particle production, or as deriving from additional chemicals that could not be identified yet.

The nano-particles themselves may stay up in the atmosphere up to 18 months, but will eventually come down with rain. Due to their tiny size they can cross cell membranes of leafs and roots and enter the plant tissue. Beyond the known mechanisms of intoxication by bio-available elements as observed and researched in the context of acid rain, this opens up a second set of mechanisms possibly leading to plant damage.

(Ba, Sr_x) TiO_3 nano-crystals are non-soluble and would thus accumulate both over the time and in the food chains. (Ba, Sr_x) TiO_3 has piezoelectric properties, the highest optical refractivity of all minerals known and cancels out UV-light, which leads to outstanding effects within non-linear optical systems. When embedded in the plant tissue they very likely would affect plant growth by actively canceling out exactly the frequency of ultra weak biophotons exchanged between the DNAs, which is responsible for the regulation of cell division. Additionally, these piezo-electric nano-crystals ionize when hit by terrestrial electromagnetic radiation. This should heavily interfere with the electric cell potential, making the plant vulnerable to the attacks of fungi. When found as mono-crystalline nano-particles, also Al_2O_3 has some outstanding optical qualities, as well as an "informational" impact on biological systems. Thus both (Ba, Sr_x) TiO_3 and Al_2O_3 are reducing the ability of nature to self-organize. These three theoretical derived mechanisms would exactly mirror the effects observed with plants: retarded plant growth, "burned" dots on the surface, death by fungus infections. Additionally, (Ba, Sr_x) TiO_3 and Al_2O_3 nano-particles bio-accumulate in the food chain and show up in mammals and humans. Research has been found where they are suspected to play a key role in diseases related to the nervous system.

Climate change and the urgency to lower the earths temperature has been used officially as a reason to look seriously into the topic of geo-engineering. Actual execution of the program is denied. Behind this public discussion there is a broad spectrum of military applications already utilizing a piezoelectric particulate plasma, as well as applications connected to the intelligence community, utilizing the same plasma background to track and influence single individuals and possibly apply methods of collective mind-control. These technologies used by the intelligence community involve synthetic biology as a part of self-assembling nano-machines that are able to form a technological interface to the human DNA light communication. The entire concept is referred to as smart dust. These technologies are widely marketed in the framework of "integrated geospatial intelligence solutions".

Since there are so many indications that these military and intelligence programs are up and running without democratic influence, information about classified operations and organizations will be presented and discussed.

Detailed Summary

During the last few years there have been many reports from concerned citizens about a new type of damage occurring to plants that is different from the damage known from acid rain: Grass simply stops growing; trees drop their bark and die. It has been speculated that these damages could be caused by high values of aluminum, barium, strontium or titanium found in the chemical analysis of affected plant tissue, rainwater and soil-samples. There has been an increasing suspicion and worry among people, of a possible link between these high metal findings and the increasingly frequent occurrence of persistent contrails.

In order to discuss the chemistry in contrails and its impact on nature one needs to distinguish between

-   the impact of lead, sulfur and halogens from fuel impurities or additives in civil and military jet propellants,
-   single, bio-available ions to artificially create cloud formations as well as reflective particles released by intended geo-engineering programs designed to combat climate change
-   and the spraying of high-tech aerosols for military and intelligence purposes.

In order to explore a possible link between one or more of these sources to retarded plant growth we decided to perform a chemical analysis on damaged grass *(phleum pretense)* and associated soil samples from the Oslo area. The results from this chemical analysis showed slightly elevated levels of barium and strontium in the grass, and an surplus of barium in soil exposed to rain in comparison to soil not exposed to rain, which makes it likely that the barium found in the ground partly comes from aerosols.

On one hand the link of retarded plant growth and elevated values of barium and strontium as reported by other environmental groups in connection with aerosol-spraying could be confirmed. Regarding the mechanism of bio-accumulation the content of heavy metals was in a range to be considered as being dangerous to mammals and humans. Still, compared to countrywide values and experience with heavy metal pollution from the early times of industrialization as well as the acid-rain area in the 70s, the total values of aluminum, barium, strontium and titanium were in a range that had to be considered as not toxic enough as bio-available elements to explain the damage observed at the plants themselves. Under the premises that there is a connection between the values in heavy metals found and the affection of plant growth the only solution was to look for non-soluble particles containing aluminum, barium, strontium and/or titanium that were affecting plant growth not due to their chemical, but due to their mechanical, electromagnetic or optical properties.

The method of chemical lab-analysis we used did not reveal in which form the metals found were present, but there is a number of indications that make it very likely that a part of them might be brought in as aluminum oxide (Al_2O_3) and barium-strontium-titanate $(Ba, Sr_x) TiO_3$.

- Al_2O_3 is mentioned as a reflective particle in the Welsbach patent as the main compound in climate engineering by aerosol spraying.
- US military sources mention besides Al_2O_3 also $(Ba, Sr_x) TiO_3$ piezo-electric crystals to be in use as an aerosol for military purposes. This nano-crystal could very likely be formed during

the combustion process when various barium, strontium and titanium salts are added. At least one can state that the synthesis of (Ba, Sr_x) TiO_3 in spray pyrolysis at 750 deg. C, declining to 600 deg. C, like given in a jet engine, would highly resemble one established industrial production method of these nano-particles.

(Ba, Sr_x) TiO_3 has a melting point of 2000 deg C and is not soluble in water, thus it would not appear very soon as barium, strontium and titanium in bio-available form, but does have electro-physical properties that theoretically could lead to plant damage.

Once we were thinking about the topic of solubility, the question arose, whether these non-soluble particles would show up in chemical analysis at all. Barium-titanate is soluble in sulfuric acid, strontium titanate only in hydro-fluorine acid. Interviews with a number of institutes conducting heavy metal monitoring for state authorities revealed, that they all use nitric acid in their testing method, which would neither reveal barium-titanate, nor strontium-titanate, nor mono-crystalline aluminum oxide. Amorphous Al_2O_3 would show up to a certain percentage only. This means that from the state side there is no reliable monitoring of these nano-particles happening at all. Privately gathered values need to be co-checked on the measurement-method. Only analysis' with hydro-fluorine acid delivers valid results.

These nano-crystals would be taken up by plants as a whole and would remain unaltered, and thus also would have the potential to bio-accumulate. Embedded within the plant tissue these crystals will keep their intrinsic and electromagnetic properties. As an unintended side effect, this nano-crystal is likely to cause retardation of plant growth when absorbed by plants following three possible different mechanisms:

- Plant growth may be inhibited due to interruption in cell communication. When hit, the $(Ba, Sr_x) TiO_3$ nano-particles absorb 90% of the weak inter-cellular UV signals, also known as biophotons, exactly on the wavelength responsible for cell division.

- The electromagnetic cell potential in plants may be disturbed and set out of balance when $(Ba, Sr_x) TiO_3$ nano-crystals within the plant tissue are hit by terrestrial EMF, microwave or radar-radiation. Due to the piezoelectric properties of $(Ba, Sr_x) TiO_3$ such radiation induces a change in the crystal-geometry that releases free electrons. This would dis-balance the cell potential. A balanced cell potential is fundamental for plant health and growth.

In addition to these possible damages done to plants single publications have been found that report on negative effects of aerosols like (Ba, Sr_x) TiO_3 on mammals and humans. Two studies discuss the bio-accumulation of these nano-crystals in mammals and humans that leads to a damage of the nervous system. The crystals attach to the sensory receptors and trigger them by releasing electrons and/or photons due to an external acoustic or electromagnetic impulse. A third report anecdotally showed how the presence of something that was detected as containing barium on the surface of snow was associated to weakened biophoton activity of humans, accompanied with symptoms of non-treatable headache.

Taking this as a working-hypotheses, the next step was to find out how much of these piezoelectric particles might be deposited to see if the total amount could be in a range of being of any danger to plants. Of cause, a direct measurement is not possible, however it is possible to monitor heavy metal-depositions. Assuming that the titanate-synthesis in jet engines will be as accurate as in industrial processes and that there should be some excess metal that will be measurable in nature, it made sense to monitor the official data. From the metals contained in barium-strontium-titanate only barium has been sufficiently monitored by state authorities. The data from Germany covering the last 15 years show that the values of airborne barium referred to as dry deposition went down by 95%. This is accredited to improved industrial standards and reduced industrial exhaust. There is also a significant reduction seen in other heavy metals. Pollution deposited with rain is measured through the absorption of the pollutants in grass and referred to as wet deposition. This is a bit misleading because actually it covers both wet and dry deposition. During the same period, values for this composite wet and dry deposition of barium have been almost doubled. For the year 2012 the data gathered from private rain samples directly reveal an average of 0.003 mg barium per liter from which one can calculate a wet deposition of 865 t of Barium on the German territory per year – this value is supported by the data of the state authorities for wet deposition, last published for the years 2009-2011. Being specifically bound to rain, the detected barium must be considered as originating from aerosols of unknown origin, since industry and mining can be canceled out as sources.

As mentioned, this is barium showing up on testing methods involving nitric acid. The amounts of nano-particles deposited can only be estimated based on these measurements. Estimating an affectivity of 85% for the nano-particle synthesis this would hint to a total of 4901 tons barium, or 14.873 t of $(Ba_{0.5}, Sr_{0.5}) TiO_3$ that are deposited but not detected by the state run heavy metal monitoring. Besides $(Ba_{0.5}, Sr_{0.5}) TiO_3$ also $(Ba_{0.25}, Sr_{0.75})TiO_3$ is a widely used formula. In this case the total values estimated would need to be doubled.

Official values from Germany as an industrialized country in the middle of the continent were compared to values collected by the State Veterinary Institute in the less populated Norway. Total values in Norway were in average about 4 times higher than the ones measured in the German grass samples, but it turned out that in Norway a big part of these metals are from natural sources. High values of barium found in Norway are mainly associated to the uptake of dust from barium-rich soils; strontium is associated to the uptake from salts from the Atlantic. The chemical analysis of moss done to gather the values does not distinguish between natural barium compounds and artificial barium compounds. Again, barium-strontium-titanate nano-crystals would not show up at all. These results hint again to non-toxic levels of barium compounds as bio-available metals, however the data were of no value to detect the total amounts of nano-crystals deposited in Norway.

Concerning the impact of these nano-crystals on mammals and humans we reviewed a few papers and scientific lectures published to this topic.

Once dealing with aerosols sprayed for military purposes we felt the need to look into a second topic, referred to as the Morgellons disease. It turned out that the same nano-particulate plasma utilized by the military community, that leads to the negative effects on plant growth, is also part of a program run by the intelligence community involving synthetic biology and self assembling nano-machines as part of a system to track and influence civilians. The entities involved can be found when one looks for the term "Integrated Geospatial Intelligence Solutions". Due to the existence of the Morgellons disease, which is nothing else than the explosive spreading of this synthetic biology within single individuals, who's immune system is unable to handle the growth, the documentation and the proof of the existence of this program seems much easier than the proof of the particulate plasma. The components of this artificial biology could be described from air samples, from the lesions of Morgellon victims as well as from the scientific papers of the official transhumanistic research, that precisely describes how the system works. Observation of components of this transhumanistic technology showed that the controlling signals are transmitted, i.e. that this system that is designed to influence the DNA-light communication – thus controlling all aspects of human life – is in action.

Due to the fact that there is a partly irrational discussion going on around the term "chemtrails", we felt the need to add a chapter about the political aspects of geo-engineering. This chapter both tells a brief history of geo-engineering and analyzes the layers of belief systems the entire topic is surrounded by in the public reception. The crossing lines of these two ways of approaching the topic of geo-engineering hopefully will help to free the numbers in the scientific part of this study from belief systems like stating that "there is no geo-engineering done at all" or "just on an small experimental scale".

Besides the officially announced state-run programs heading into the direction of geo-engineering, we monitor a number of companies who are involved in the network conducting the recent activities discussed in this paper: apart from the driving forces CIA and US-Navy intelligence with no information available to the public, we monitored the private company Raytheon being responsible for HAARP Alaska, the production of radar, microwave and ELF transmitters as well as for laser weapon systems and satellite based aerosol monitoring as part of the star wars program. In the civil domain the company is into flight control and weather forecast. Also, Raytheon was for a few years into aircraft manufacturing of airplanes specialized on aerosol spraying. Smoking gun evidence recorded via satellite lead to the Marion Island Meteorological station, that turned out to be involved in privately funded, South Africa-state-run scalar wave applications very likely used to ionizes the local aerosol layers, to turn them into a controllable plasma.

We have found no published peer-reviewed research on the effect of (Ba,

Sr_x) TiO_3 and of mono-crystalline Al_2O_3 on plants, mammals and humans. Equipment and infrastructure to implement these technologies even on large(r) scale is already in place.

As to the Morgellons disease, despite – according to different sources – up to 300.000 registered victims, this disease is officially declared to be "delusional parasitizes". This statement is a slap in the face of the people who suffer, who dye of a disease that can be shown and verified under any simple microscope, and this clearly proofs the involvement and guilt of state authorities, that obviously went far beyond any democratic control.

We urge for proper research on the impact of aerosols on plant growth, microorganisms, plankton, insects, and animals under controlled lab conditions. Aerosols need to be found safe for every aspect of our biosphere before they are released into nature.

We urge for proper research of damage done by transhumanistic technologies that have been released onto mankind without knowledge and agreement of the victims, and call for investigations regarding the violation of the Nueremberg Treaty, of not into bio-terrorism.

CONTENT

1.   Introduction

- to the term geo-engineering

The topic of geo-engineering has three aspects that need to be first differentiated before we can look at how they are historically interwoven:

1.   There has been an ongoing development of jet propellants and their additives by the US-air force and the NATO. The chemistry of the additives currently in use is classified information – some of the additives have been identified by civil-right-initiatives and private researchers as 1,2-dibrom ethan (EDB), perfluoroctane sulfon acid (PFOS), perfluor octane acid (PFOA) and lead tetraethyl. These additives contain fluorine, sulfur and brome and must be regarded as an important source of the aerosols H_2SO_4, HF, $HBrO_3$, which lead to persistent contrails[154]. These additives

---

154

240

are highly toxic contact poisons and are suspected to be responsible for multiple-chemical-sensitivity (MCS) and the gulf-war-syndrome (GWS).

2. There is an official line of research that mainly evaluates options of climate engineering to combat global warming. This research processes huge amounts of money but officially projects all "practical applications" into the future. It claims to conduct "small experimental programs" only. It mainly propagates sulfur oxide and reflective particles like Al_2O_3 flitters as possible aerosols.

3. There is a strong involvement of the US military in the development of both geo-engineering in the classical meaning and advanced military applications involving piezoelectric nano-particles $((Ba, Sr_x) TiO_3)$ and mono-crystalline aluminum-oxide varieties for 3D battlefield monitoring, radar-range-enhancement and advanced defense and weapon systems, including the star wars program. There are similar programs run by the intelligence community.

In the jet fuel development the main aim is to adopt the jet fuel to the low temperatures at high altitudes, to adjust the point of ignition to the engine technology and to lower the consumption as much as possible.

The geo-engineering idea roots back to WWII with German scientists which after the end of the war were taken over by US military to do

PATRICK MINNIS, J. KIRK AYERS, RABINDRA PALIKONDA, AND DUNG PHAN: Contrails, Cirrus Trends, and Climate. Atmospheric Sciences, NASA Langley Research Center, Hampton, Virginia.

research mainly in the framework of the *Project 'Paperclip'* that transferred about 10.000 German top scientists to the US intelligence community.

The official aim of geo-engineering is weather manipulation to protect the agriculture and civil society, although on scientific level from the very beginning ideas like melting the poles to get access to natural resources played a major role[155].

The main military applications today seem to depend on nano-size piezo-crystals creating a controllable plasma background for 3D radar monitoring as well as a plasma layer for advanced applications like weather manipulation, earth quake weapons and, when combined with satellite based laser technology, the star wars program. The idea to create an artificial plasma layer very likely popped up after successful research on weather manipulation by the HAARP device in Alaska and other HAARP-like transmitters, utilizing the natural ionosphere as a controllable plasma layer. From this point the idea to create a artificial plasma layer at lower altitudes than the ionosphere was not very far out.

In the US the borders between governmental research, military research and applications, the activities of the intelligence community and university- and company based research and applications are difficult to define. In this financially interwoven network a growing number of whistle blowers are drawing attention to a classified project "Cloverleaf". It is supposed to serve military-, agency- and governmental and privately-owned-company-aims by spraying large amounts of aluminum and titanium based aerosols using the infrastructure of the CIA, NASA and the

---

155

Derived from private discussions with people who had family members involved in these research programs.

US-Navy as well as civil airplanes altered for additional spraying.

However approaching the topic from this angle at this point of this paper would lead to discussions involving belief systems. This will be discussed in greater detail in the last chapter, for now we just want to mention one of these whistle blowers, the person who is known as the inventor of the titanium-based aerosol system. Since the 1980s Jim Phelps from the Oak Ridge laboratories in the USA had researched the impact of aerosols from airplanes on nature and climate and had found out that jet-fuel-impurities and additives were responsible for the following:

1. the loss of ozone at the poles due to fluorine-compounds
2. global dimming due to persistent contrails and enhanced formation of cirrus-clouds
3. global warming, because these cirrus-clouds hold back infrared radiation from the ground and
4. growing problems with toxic flour-aluminum compounds forming in the soils.

In 1996 Phelps suggested solving 3 of these problems by adding titanium oxide, which forms less toxic compounds than aluminum, to the jet fuel. This concept was meant to prevent the ozone loss and the forming of toxic flour-aluminum compounds by binding the fluorine to titanium-oxide already in the sky, and additionally reduce global warming by seeding reflective particles, that would block even more sunlight and let through infrared from the ground. Additionally, when combined with Barium and Strontium, these piezzo-crystals photo-ionize, thus they block sunlight during daytime and let through infrared during the night. Jim Phelps today openly accuses the US military as well as the intelligence community to abuse his invention, which was meant to solve jet fuel related environmental problems.

- to the damage on plants

There have been many reports from concerned citizens about a new type of damage occurring with plants. It is different from the known damage by acid rain in the 1970s, where large areas of spruce forests died in Germany. The symptoms observed back then were first the dying of the tiny roots of the trees after suffering from heavy metal poisoning, followed by a loss of the needles and the death of the tree. Now grass is reported to simply stop growing, trees to drop their bark and die. It has been speculated that these damages could be associated with the increasing occurrence of persistent contrails on one hand, and presumably linked to the high values of aluminum, barium, strontium and titanium found in chemical analysis of plants tissue, rainwater and soil-samples on the other hand.

During the year 2012 we were confronted with the problems of a number of Norwegian farmers who lost parts of the second harvest of hay. Additionally, the increased appearance of striped clouds was a cause for unease. These clouds appeared in the morning and eventually in the afternoon covered the normally blue summer sky with a milky haze at a high altitude. One of the farmers associated the drizzle falling later on such days to damage done to tomato-plants and lettuce. The farmers, who had taken chemical analysis of rain samples and the grass retarded in growth, asked for help interpreting their lab results.

- to our scientific approach

Our starting point was the worry that aerosols could disturb plant growth to an extent where it affects the harvests and thus the livelihood of mankind. At the same time, we were aware that the topic of geo-engineering, also referred to as chemtrails, was controversial and caused heated discussions. From the information available in public, it was hard to get a picture of what was actually happening. In this context we felt the need to search for consistent information, and to check the theories against scientific data. This meant in detail: to find out if high atmospheric spraying is already taking place, if yes which aerosols are in use and how big the amounts actually sprayed might be. The second task would be to find out in what way these aerosols might affect plant growth to explain the damage observed.

The only anomalies showing in the results near Oslo concerned high aluminum in rainwater samples, increased barium in soil exposed to rain. Strontium and titanium were present within the countrywide average. These are elements discussed as parts of aerosols used for military purposes. The measured amounts of the elements themselves had to be regarded as chemically non-toxic to plants. We therefor took a closer look into the patents and papers involving these methods to see if there could be some overseen mechanisms affecting plant growth. It became clear that the optical and electro-physical properties of these nano-crystals could be essential in understanding how plant growth can be severely affected by these aerosols.

A six-fold line of research has been undertaken to examine the possibility of a relationship between slowed plant growth and deposition of aerosols released by airplanes for military purposes and eventually for purposes of geo-engineering

1   Going through the patents and papers about aerosols for geo-engineering, the patents of aerosols for military purposes and the normal jet-fuel and jet-fuel additive-chemistry in order to see what substances to look for, and look for research proving their safety.
2   Review research on plant communication and growth.

3   Discussing the physical properties of aerosols regarding possible mechanisms that could damage plants.

4   Analyzing samples of grass with reduced growth and of the earth underneath to define what part of the findings could have an aerial source.

5   Reviewing official data of wet and dry deposition of heavy metals.

6   Look at the operational and political aspects of aerosol-spraying.

In the following chapters we will first summarize some scientific background knowledge about toxicology in general and discuss the additives used in Jet Propellant 8, the Jet fuel used by US army and NATO forces. Additionally we used the only available original paper on "chemtrails", to understand the basic mechanisms of this technology and name some of the compounds that might be involved today. This paper is the course material for a course in chemtrail-chemistry at the US Air Force Academy dating back to the year 1990.

As a second topic we will summarize some background information about biophoton-research and the non-linear optical properties of $(Ba, Sr_x) TiO_3$ nano-crystals. Against this background we will discuss possible mechanisms of damage that $(Ba, Sr_x) TiO_3$ nano-crystals cause to nature. These effects will be discussed regarding plant growth, marine life and possible effects on mammals and humans. Following this theoretical part we will review the data available of barium, strontium, and titanium depositions in Germany and Norway over the period of the last 15 years and try to distinguish between industrial pollution, natural deposits and other aerosol deposits. To backup the scientific finding we will then again look at historical and political aspects to evaluate the probability of our data.

2. Direct toxicity, synergistic effects of toxic elements, subsequent damage in the ground

The entire topic of toxicity is rather complex. We start by taking a look at some basic principles:

- ### The level defining toxicity

Plants and all living beings need most metals in minute amounts to be healthy. In a way, nature on the continents is still addicted to the statistic distribution of rare metals as found in sea water, where we all came from, and is trying to stabilize this statistical pattern in the chemistry of the cell water. The metals we need, can be absorbed in so called bio-available form, in solution as cations, or from organic decay products as organic complexes. Up to certain levels higher amounts of metals will be tolerated by the plant or living being without any harm done. Above these levels the metals will cause damage and function as a toxin.

- ### Lead and Mercury

To this rule there are two exceptions: lead and mercury. Neither lead nor mercury is good for any living being. They are toxic already in the minutest level, cause serious damage with higher levels and are eventually lethal. The tolerance for lead varies between plants and mammals. Plants tolerate more than mammals.

- ### The compound defining toxicity

Metals can be present in nature in many forms. Due to their structure and reactivity they can react with other elements and form many different compounds. The same metal can be toxic in one compound and neutral in another compound. For example the uptake of aluminum can happen in form of 200 different known compounds, from which especially the fluorine-compounds are known to be highly toxic, while both fluorine and aluminum can appear in compounds that are less toxic than the direct combination of both.

- **Synergy of metals can manifold the toxic and lethal effect**

Toxicity does not always add up the way one would expect. Sometimes the combination of two toxins multiplies in an extraordinary way. The following experiment shows this synergistic effect clearly: 1/20 of a lethal dose of lead (Pb^{2+}) that kills 1 of 100 mice, was combined with 1/20 of the lethal dose of mercury (Hg^{2+}) that also kills 1 of 100 mice. The combination did not kill 2 mice, but all 100 of 100 mice.[156]

- **Complex synergies caused by lack of other essential minerals**

A second type of synergistic effect occurs when there is a lack of an essential element with similar atomic structure. Strontium, which is regarded as non-toxic[157] to humans, is even given as a medicine to strengthen bones. However if the body suffers from a lack of calcium[158],

---

156

Boyd E. Haley: "Mercury toxicity: Genetic susceptibility and synergistic effects", p. 537

157

First draft Peter Watts; Paul Howe: England. Concise International Chemical Assessment Document 77: STRONTIUM AND STRONTIUM COMPOUNDS. WHO publication

158

Lara Pizzorno: The Truth about Strontium Supplements, Side Effects, DEXA Results, Efficancy and More. Online at: http://www.algaecal.com/Blog/the-truth-about-strontium-supplements-side-effects-dexa-results-efficacy-and-more/11333 on Jan. 3rd 2013.

the uptake of strontium can lead to bone deformation.

- **Magnitudes of released toxins – nature vs. man made**

To get a feeling for what is normal in nature and what is man made we will look at general amounts of pollution, with the example lead. There is a natural worldwide pollution by volcanoes and bush & forest fires that amounts to 19.000 tons lead per year set free into the atmosphere. The amount of lead released by the burning of coal and fuel in the early industrial period exceeded this natural amount by more than 100 fold. Up to the 1960s these amounts were mostly blown into the atmosphere via high chimneys, without filtering units. Since then at least in the US and Europe filtering technologies have been introduced that reduce the output – comparing the early 80s to today – by an average of 95%.

- **Direct metal pollution vs. secondary release of metals via acid rain**

If one compares the content of heavy metals against the content of sulfur and halogens in coal and oil derivatives, one finds that sulfur and halogen concentrations are far higher than concentrations of metals. Coal of bad quality can contain up to 3% sulfur, while the heavy metal content might be in the range of a few mg/kg. 1 mg/kg equals 0,0001%.

The sulfur and the halogen compounds released by burning will connect with water droplets and result in acid rain. Following the forest decline in Germany in the 1970s the mechanisms of damage by acid rain have been thoroughly studied. The main consequence is that the acidity brings SiO_2 in the soil into solution, and thus releases metals into bio-available forms that used to be bound to the SiO_2. This can affect soils as well as rivers. In soils this leads to a dying of the tiny roots of trees. In rivers these released metals, mainly aluminum, caused death of fish.

Looking at total values, this means that when sulfur and halogens are turning into acid rain they can release about their molar equivalent of metals once getting into the ground. Thus the amount of metals released by acids can by magnitudes higher than the amount of metals directly released by the same amount of fuel. Thus the first thing to have a look at when talking about heavy metal intoxication with bio-available metals is the quality of the jet fuel itself regarding sulfur and halogens. Among the different known fuel types especially one draws attention: Jet Propellant 8. It is the fuel used by the US air force and the NATO and is also about to enter the market for civil air traffic.

2.1. Back-engineering JP-8

The aim of the US military was to have one fuel for all purposes: to fuel the kitchen stove to cook a meal in the army camp, to run the jeep, the tank, helicopters and airplanes. It should be possible to use the same fuel no matter if the action was happening in the arctic, the desert or at altitudes of 40 000 feet. A second aim was to have a fuel that in the situation of combat would not ignite so easily when one was attacked. A third aim was to have this fuel available commercially – which reduces the internal logistics. This resulted in what is called Jet Propellant 8. The so-called JP-8 is identical with normal Jet-Fuel Jet-A1, except of 0,02% additives.

The chemical formulas of the additives used in JP-8 are classified.

However, it is possible to deduct some of its content from the information available.[159] The military turbo prop transporters run their engines on a compression of 25 bar. This demands fuel with lead tetra ethyl, as unleaded fuel would already explode at a compression of 20 bar. As a second additive leaded fuel needs dibrom or dichlor ethan[160]. Up to the early 80s lead and halogens were used in car fuel in much lower concentrations. The exhaust from cars in this period resulted in levels of lead in the air causing widespread health damages. Due to the high toxicity of lead it became forbidden to use it as an additive to fuel.

Due to this toxicity the military developed a system where higher amounts of these poisonous additives would be added in situations of high risk only: whether it was when refilling airplanes in the air or being in combat, in certain situations the fuel needed to be less explosive[161].

It is known that during the first Iraq war the US airplanes added 25 liters of halogen based additives to the fuel at each tank filling in order to lower the flame point. Depending on the size of the plane this equaled 2-5% of the total fuel consumption. It is not known how often nor under what conditions these extra-additives are used during times of peace.

159

       Marion Hahn: Umweltkrank durch NATO-Treibstoff? Neues zu einer umstrittenen Theorie. umwelt·medizin·gesellschaft | 16 | 4/2003

160

       Marion Hahn: Umweltkrank durch NATO-Treibstoff? Neues zu einer umstrittenen Theorie. umwelt·medizin·gesellschaft | 16 | 4/2003

161

       Air Force Times 18.1.1999

To have these additives fast and equally distributed when injected it needs a tenside that is already contained in every regular tank filling: perfluoroctane sulfonacid (PFOS) and/or perfluoroctane acid (PFOA) would be solutions to this task. PFOS and PFOA are among the most toxic chemicals known.

Both PFOS and PFOA nowadays happen to appear in nature and in the blood of humans. To convey a sense of the size of the problem we refer to the study "Survey of PFOS, PFOA and other perfluoroalkyl and polyfluoroalkyl substances" by Carsten Lassen, et al[162]. The paper is Part of the LOUS-review from November 27th 2012. There is a *Version for Public Consultation* available. Values of lead were measured in the soil near to US-military airports and reached up to 1.767 mg/kg. 30-40 mg/kg was the average countrywide pollution at the time of measurement.[163] Thus this back-engineering of JP-8 seems to make sense.

World production of JP-8 was back in the year 2000 already at 4.5 billion gallons (17 billion liters) per annum. Assuming these additives were used in high dilution (0,02%), the amount burned together with JP-8 back in 2000 amounted to 3.4 million liters concentrated poisonous liquids. The measured pollution at the ground might come from burning residues as well as from the release of un-burned fuel when taking up fuel in the air, where the last pipe filling is lost after disconnecting, or when intentionally releasing fuel from the tanks for security reasons before landing.

162

      Carsten Lassen, Allan Astrup Jensen, Alexander Potrykus, Frans Christensen, Jesper Kjølholt, Christian Nyander Jeppesen: "Survey of PFOS, PFOA and other perfluoroalkyl and polyfluoroalkyl substances". Danish Ministry of the Environment. Environmental Protection Agency.

163

      Marion Hahn: Umweltkrank durch NATO-Treibstoff? Neues zu einer umstrittenen Theorie. umwelt·medizin·gesellschaft | 16 | 4/2003

In addition lead and halogens are added (2-5%) in combat, eventually combat simulations or maneuvers like refilling during the flight[164]. The total amount is unknown, however this technique is increasing the output by the factor 100 to 250 when applied, depending on plane size.

The cocktail of EDB, PFOS, PFOA and lead tetra ethyl is known to have synergistic poisonous effects on mammals and humans, probably leading to the gulf war syndrome (GWS) and multiple chemical sensitivity (MCS). These additives are also associated to the depletion of the immune system and reduced fertility.

Following this "back-engineering of JP-8, there are a number of compounds released into nature by exhaust from airplanes:

1. From the burning of the fuel itself (CO_2 and NO_x forming H_2CO_3, H_3NO_4),
2. the burning of fuel impurities (mainly SO_2 forming H_2SO_4)
3. and the burning of fuel additives (forming H_2SO_4, HF, $HBrO_3$, PbO).
4. If the burning process is not fully happening we eventually will have to look at additive residues (dibrom ethan (EDB), perfluoroctane sulfonacid (PFOS), perfluoroctane acid (PFOA)).
5. The acids, H_2CO_3, H_3NO_4, H_2SO_4 and HF are of great concern as they set free secondary toxic compounds when they are absorbed in the ground, following the mechanisms referred to as acid rain.

All sulfur and halogen compounds burned with the jet fuel act as aerosols

164

Marion Hahn: Umweltkrank durch NATO-Treibstoff? Neues zu einer umstrittenen Theorie umwelt·medizin·gesellschaft | 16 | 4/2003

253

leading to persistent contrails and increasing the appearance of cirrus clouds. Due to the fact that this phenomenology is regarded as contrails in the public discussion it becomes obvious that the distribution of nano-particles for geo-engineering and/or for military purposes might be hiding within these sulfur- and halogen induced haze.

According to an longer interview with an employee of the German military the entire organization of the jet fuel supply within the NATO forces is aimed to serve the key role of JP-8, i.e. the three different JP-8-classes with their classified components. Everything is organized in a way that JP-8 is used without having people asking questions about the ingredients. Apparently the chemistry of JP-8 does not seem to be what it is claimed to be: dirty diesel of low quality. According to the former employee of the German Air Force we interviewed, JP-8 is burning much faster then both kerosene or diesel fuel, smells different and extracts the oil from the skin when being in direct contact, leaving the skin completely white. Additionally it causes heavy headaches when breathed in.

During the Gulf war JP-8 has been used to hide the US troops following the first row of tanks in clouds of smoke by evaporating the fuel on the hot exhaust pipes of the tanks. This has been suspected to be the most important cause of the so-called gulf war syndrome when it comes to US soldiers.

254

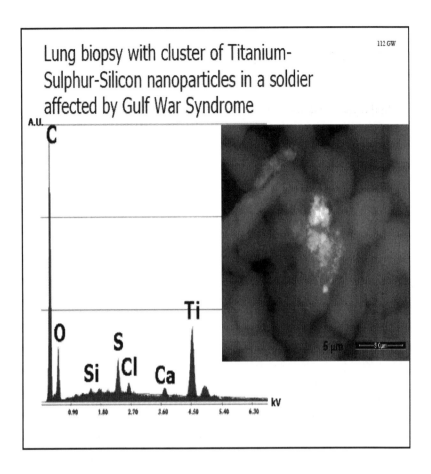

Picture and analysis taken from the lung biopsy of a gulf war veteran.

Besides the carbon-black from the smoke Analysis of the particles in the lung tissue of a soldier effected by the gulf war syndrome shows sulfur, titanium and oxygen. Like the interview with the German military employee this hints to the possibility that the metal salts for the nano-particle production within jet engines that is going to be discussed in the next chapter are part of the JP-8 additives.

2.2. Nano-particles from special military applications

In the year 1990 the U.S. Air Force Academy, Department of Chemistry, created a script for the chemtrail class, including the examination-forms. This script is available to the general public on microfiche. Of cause this script does not provide the precise formulas used in chemtrailing, but the combination of basic knowledge, the chemical reactions taught and repeated and asked for in the exams, give a rather clear picture of the chemical processes the students are trained to get creative on.

The script names HCl, NH_4OH, and NaOH, $KMnO_4$, $Al(NO_3)_2$, $Ba(NO_3)_2$, $Cu(NO_3)_2$, $Fe(NO_3)_3$, $FeSO_4$, $Pb(NO_3)_2$, $Mn(NO_3)_2$, $AgNO_3$, Na_2CO_3, NaCl, NaI & $NaNO_3$[165] as metal salts to be added to the combustion process. The script discusses the oxidation and reduction in the burning process and the examination forms ask for the possible interaction of these metal salts, when following the rules of chemistry during the combustion process. This is what in civil industry is called spray pyrolysis. Further it separately discusses the possible reaction with halogen acids, especially HBr, apparently being an outcome of the combustion of JP-8. The goal of spray pyrolysis is to create defined nano-particles. The injection of the compounds mentioned in the manuscript into jet engines will lead to the

---

165

Chemtrails. Chemistry 131 Manual Fall 1990, Department of Chemistry, U.S. Air Force Academy. See also: Kammler, Hendrik K.; Mädler, Lutz; Pratsinis, Sotiris E.: Flame Pyrolysis of Nanoparticles. WILEY-VCH. Chem. Eng. Technol. 24 (2001) 6. See also: M. Enhessari, A. Parviz1K. Ozaee, H. Habibi Abyaneh: Synthesis and characterization of barium strontium titanate (BST) micro/nanostructures prepared by improved methods. Int.J.Nano Dim.2(2): 85-103, Autumn 2011

256

production of nano-particles with an unknown range of properties formed as a result of the pyrolysis of the metals and metal oxides during the combustion process.

Another topic that is part of the chemtrail-script is the polymerization of nylon and electrolytic coating of surfaces with thin metal layers. This corresponds with findings of aluminum coated nano-nylon fibers in rain samples that have been reported by many concerned citizens taking and analyzing rain samples. In the military language these fibers are referred to as spoofer sprays.

Including nylon based fibers into the overall concept shows that already back then two different distribution systems must have been established, pyrolysis in the jet engines and spraying through extra nozzles, because substances like nylon cannot stand temperatures higher than 250 deg. C.

It needs to be stated at this point, that the script is from 1990 and it is not possible to say precisely in what way the technology has been further developed, and from this script only it is also not possible to say to what extend the technologies described have been applied. The titanium-based method to bind fluoride introduced by Phelbs six years later, in 1996, obviously is not yet part of that script, just like the development of titanium based nano-crystals formed during the pyrolysis as intelligent ionizable particles that can be controlled by radio-transmitters.

To get an idea of the state of the art we assume that according to the method introduced by Phelbs Titanium is added to the set of chemicals in use, and that the pyrolysis must meet the conditions within a normal jet engine.

Spray pyrolysis is a promising technique for producing various materials in a wide range of composition, size and morphology. Powders and films can be successfully prepared. The powders characterization confirms that powders are composed of spherical submicronic particles with internal nano-crystalline structure.Spray pyrolysis involves passing an aerosol of a precursor solution through a graded temperature reactor, in which the individual droplets are thermally decomposed to form the oxide particles. In this work, the precursor solution for BST ($Ba_{0.8}Sr_{0.2}TiO_3$) was prepared starting from titanium citrate, barium acetate and strontium acetate. Stoichiometric amount of strontium and barium acetate were dissolved in water and two solutions were mixed together. (…) To obtain dense particles, without carbonate, it was necessary to optimize temperature and heating rate of thermal treatment (temperature at the first chamber of the furnace, 750 °C; temperature at the second chamber of the furnace, 600 °C). The powder mixture was prepared from 47.95 wt.% of BST and 52.05 wt.% of SiO_2. Results of X-ray diffraction analysis showed that almost single phase BST powder, with traces of (…) was obtained under the optimal processing conditions.

The script from 1990 only mentions NO_3 as an anion associated to the metal input. Recent sources report that methane is used to introduce the metal salts into the combustion process. Regarding this, one might assume that the formula recently used is based on titanium-citrate, barium-acetate ($C_4H_6BaO_4$) or strontium-acetate ($C_4H_6SrO_4$). If this is not connected to the medium used for the dispersion it could as well be barium nitrate ($Ba(NO_3)_2$) and strontium nitrate ($Sr(NO_3)_2$) instead, as it has been in 1990. Of cause, other metals like iron or lead can be in use to dote the resulting crystals for special applications.

As it looks like there are two different methods of spray pyrolysis: Infrasound dispersion of water-soluted salts and the use of methane based additives that are mixed with the jet fuel before use. Maybe the NO_3^- system relates to the water based pyrolysis and the methane-based system to the additive-system used in military context.

Besides (Ba, Sr_x) TiO_3 also Al_2O_3 can be created in spray pyrolysis. However within the temperature range of a jet engine in normal flight the nano-particles should come out in an amorphous structure. To achieve a mono-crystalline quality it needs temperatures in the range of 1700 deg. C, that are present in normal jet engines only in the starting phase. In military applications the temperatures needed to melt and recrystallize aluminum-oxide should be achieved in rocket and afterburner technologies. This technology seems to be standardized: Afterburner and rocket-propulsion requires so-called Aluminum-fuels. Additionally aluminum oxide crystals can be doted with other metals during the process of creation to achieve defined qualities. Dotation with for example chrome would create ruby nano-crystals, dotation with iron and titanium would lead to the creation of sapphires. Sapphires for example are known to be non-soluble in all acids, which could be a desired attribute for particles that are meant to be stable in nature for a long time.

2.3. Understanding particle sizes

The understanding of what is possible especially with nano-crystals has not yet reached the general public.

To convey a sense of what actually is possible we calculated the values for the aerosol barium-strontium-titanate with a particle size of 10nm. This aerosol is already in military use but also is in discussion for civil geo-engineering to combat climate change as a separating agent to prevent aluminum-oxide-flitters to agglutinate. 1 gram of these $(Ba, Sr_x) TiO_3$ nano-crystals has the amazingly large surface of 2500 square meters. It is possible to spread these nano-crystals so unbelievable thin that 1gram can totally seal 685 square meters. 300 tons would be enough to cover a country of the size of Germany with a optically sealed one particle thick layer.

When it comes to the measurement of particles and the metals they contain after being released to nature one faces a few difficulties: The measurements refer to the basic elements detected in chemical analysis, not to different compounds. Additionally one has to choose whether to have only bio-available metals measured, which is metal elements in watery solution, or if one wants to detect all metal present. The latter analysis does not show if the compounds the metal comes from is already in solution, is soluble but still solid, or if a detected metal is part of a non-soluble nano-crystal or particle. The result from a lab analysis therefore delivers a limited knowledge of the chemical toxicity the plant, soil, microorganisms and other living beings are exposed to. Additionally the values given can lack precision. If the matter analyzed contained crystals not soluble in nitric acid or fluorine acid, depending on the analytical method used, the content of these crystals will not show in the values delivered by the labs.

Such an analysis will to a certain degree indicate the degree of pollution, especially when comparisons are made between exposures of different places or over a long time-span. One cannot read possible toxic synergies directly from this type of data nor can the mechanical and optical qualities of crystals be detected.

2.4. Chemical vs. elector-physical effects of barium-strontium-titanate

When it comes to heavy metals connected to geo-engineering, especially barium, strontium and titanium, the first logical reaction would be to say that even if considerable amounts would be sprayed today, it would still be minute compared to levels of industrial pollution in the late 1960s, early 70s, when filtering technologies were not applied in coal and oil power plants, and that it would be minute to the levels of heavy metals released in the ground by acid rain.

This might be the case as on the German territory about 100 tons of Barium are deposited per year coming from natural sources, i.e. resulting from volcanism, uptake of minerals from the ground, the ocean as well as from bush and forest fires, and 100 times more, about 10.000 tons of barium was the estimated deposit from industrial sources in the 1960s and 70s. And another two zeros could be added to the numbers when one calculates the heavy metals (incl. Al) released in the ground as the molar equivalent of the sulfur and the halon causing the acid rain[166]. These are higher amounts than what one can imagine to be sprayed into the upper atmosphere.

166
    For detailed explanation see Chapter 4.2.

We can't know in advance the threshold of nature's ability to adapt to known toxic or other compounds. From the data available it does not look like there is a direct damage done to plants by barium, strontium and titanium as bio-available elements in the present magnitudes.

If we would assume that the high levels of Barium are coming from military applications, it is difficult to say how much of it is raining down in a bio-available form as metal salts, and how much of it is coming from insoluble nano-crystals. Barium-strontium-titanate nano-crystals are not soluble and would not be expected to become part of the bio available chemistry.

What one should expect is bio-accumulation of the non-soluble crystals in the food chain, with possible mechanical, optical or electrochemical effects.

In chapter 3 and 4 we will have to go to physics to understand the process.

3. Scientific background to electro-optical effects

3.1. Non-linear optics

Light is scientifically defined as being both a transversal electromagnetic wave and a number of particles, photons, traveling together, carrying a defined amount of energy each. Actually the photon, the particle aspect, becomes relevant for abstract calculations and for the case the light stops traveling, is caught, absorbed, then the entire energy of the wave that had been scattered in space is manifesting at one defined spot, is transferred into heat or electric potential when exciting an electron, or further up in complexity into chemical bound energy like in photosynthesis. The wave aspect of light is very useful and precise when observing continuous transmission of large amounts of photons from one random/chaotic source of light. For this type of light, science knows the possibility of polarization. Light is polarized when the direction of a transversal wave structure is reduced onto one optical plane. Polarization occurs due to reflection or is produced by special filters consisting of a grid of parallel lines with a distance smaller than one wavelength, so that waves that are not parallel to the grid cannot pass through. Another, separate phenomenon is coherence. It occurs when the wave pattern of all photons involved are in phase. The light quality created by laser technologies is coherent.

Polarization is order in space. Coherence is order in time.

Going back to the origins of electrodynamics, one finds that the definition of light not always was limited to include transversal[167] electromagnetic waves only. Maxwell, the father of modern electrodynamics, tried to describe the transmission of light from the very basic mathematical principals known to be valid for any wave-transmitting medium. He observed waves in water, both acoustic under water (longitudinal := parallel to the direction of propagation) and surface waves (transversal := perpendicular to the direction of propagation), acoustic waves in air (longitudinal), waves in solids like seismic waves (both longitudinal and transversal), observed continuous, harmonic waves following the sinus-form, standing waves being the result of two transversal waves traveling in

---

167

     In transversal waves the motion of the particles is 90 degrees to the direction of propagation. A typical example would be waves on the surface of the ocean. In longitudinal waves the particles move in the direction of propagation. A typical example would be sound. Some media can carry both wave types. The distance of the core of an earthquake is analyzed by the time difference between the arrival of the longitudinal (quick) and the transversal (slow) wave.

opposite direction, wave fronts, shock waves, and hovered all this onto an abstract mathematical level. From there he stepped back and assumed that the same mathematics should apply on the transmission of electro-magnetic waves traveling in some kind of transmitting ether. Thus he described electromagnetic waves with all three, theoretically given possible solutions to the general wave equation he had developed from watching plain nature, naming transversal, longitudinal and scalar wave functions. For the calculation of this complex system he used quaternions[168].

So light is understood as an electromagnetic wave consisting of a number of units with defined energy content, called photons. "Single photons", understood as particles, of cause always add to each other in a way, as one would expect from "particles" to do so,

but their ability to interact with matter, their visibility in our reality, adds to each other or deletes each other according to their field effect. The interference of large amounts of photons from a chaotic source results in transversal waves. The other two solutions to the general wave equation that occur only at wave fronts and by interference of different wave fronts, were dropped by mainstream science. Only a few researchers like E. T. Whittaker[169, 170] followed up the full notation. Later this side-path became

---

168

A Treatise on Electricity and Magnetism, in 2 Volumes, Oxford 1873, 2. Auflage 1881 (Hrsg. W. D. Niven, noch mit Maxwells Änderungen in den ersten acht Kapiteln), 3. Auflage 1891 (Hrsg. J. J. Thomson).

169

E. T. Whittaker, "On the partial differential equations of mathematical physics," Mathematische Annalen, Vol. 57, 1903, p. 333-355. 11 V.K. Ignatovich, "The remarkable capabilities of recursive relations," American Journal of Physics, 57(10), Oct. 1989, p. 873-878.

170

E. T. Whittaker, "On an expression of the electromagnetic field due to electrons by means of two scalar potential functions," Proceedings of the London Mathematical Society, Series 2, Vol. 1, 1904, p. 367-372.

264

a specialized field within non-linear optics[171].

With the introduction of pulsed laser technologies in the early 1990s, the
first experimental set-ups and applications were developed utilizing
properties of longitudinal electromagnetic fields[172, 173], appearing at the
wave fronts of the laser-pulses, as well as scalar waves in the interference
of two different pulsed laser sources. The shorter and sharper the pulses,
the higher the relative amount of longitudinal and scalar field-structure
becomes.

Pulsed lasers were utilized mainly for cutting materials with less heating
up of their surface. They are state of the art by now. Due to the bio-
relevance of scalar fields further advanced research was mainly kept in the
military domain, and was not allowed in civil research and application.
The only exception to this rule, as mentioned, is some research in non-
linear optics done in the civil university domain, as well as medical
research, where scientist try to influence biological processes with ultra
weak pulsed laser signals.

Scalar waves can been produced by wave coupling[174] of two longitudinal

---

171

Amnon Yariv, Optical Electronics, 3rd edn., Holt, Rinehart and
Winston, New York, 1985. Chapter 16: "Phase Conjugate Optics -- Theory and
Applications."

172

David M. Pepper, "Nonlinear optical phase conjugation," Optical
Engineering, 21(2), March/April 1982, p. 156-183. On p. 156

173

See also David M. Pepper, "Applications of optical phase
conjugation," Scientific American, 254(1), Jan. 1986, p. 74-83. See particularly
the striking photographic demonstration of time reversal of disorder on p. 75.

174

Wave coupling is a special effect in optics. Normally longitudinal em-

265

waves, generated by two pulsed laser beams. It was possible to observe a fusion of the two beams resulting in a partly optical annihilation of those beams, a process in which one wave behaves like a "master wave", the other one as a "slave". Annihilation does not mean the waves completely cease to exist, but they transfer a part of their energy content into a state that is not measurable, they are mathematically spoken pushing the energy content into another dimension, into scalar potential. Scientifically one would say that during such a fusion of two longitudinal waves a "pump wave" controls a "time reversed replica wave", which means it makes this replica wave act as if it is flowing backwards in time[175].

The experiments in non-linear optics back in the 1990s were a very exciting moment for science because it was the first controlled process that involved effects of virtual time reversal[176, 177] in electromagnetics and

waves are adding to each other, are overlaying without influencing each other. If they get to similar to each other in frequency and direction of propagation this can change. Suddenly they relate to each other, merge into one wave-set whose components are not able to propagate independent from each other. This is called coupling. Wave coupling happens mostly at 0 and 180 degree, some more complex coupling phenomena also occur at 30, 60 and 90 degree. One beautiful example for wave coupling comes from acoustics. Acoustic waves are longitudinal and thus able to couple.

175

An example to understand the special properties of longitudinal waves: When a sound studio is set up normally the size and form of the room generates some resonant frequencies that are comparably to loud when things are recorded. To lower the intensity of these resonant frequencies a little absorber-box is build that has exactly the same frequency defined by its internal geometry as the unwanted frequencies in the room. The box has a hole and is stuffed with rock wool. Now this box that is normally hung up in one of the corners starts to resonate, sends out a signal to the room, and this signal turns into a pump wave, forcing the unwanted frequencies into the state of time reversed replica waves that then directly flow into the little hole in the box and are there being absorbed by the rock-wool. Hard to understand – but reliable in practice. And it is obvious that all this sound can not disappear in this little hole by chance quick enough to kill the slightest echo.

176

Robert G. Sachs, The Physics of Time Reversal, University of Chicago Press, Chicago, Illinois, 1987.

thus made it possible to utilize this negentropical process. Negentropy is the opposite of entropy. Entropy is the tendency in nature that things loose order; that heat equally distributes, that everything tends to the lowest possible level of energy in equilibrium to the surrounding. Negentropy is the ability to spontaneously build up order and concentrate energy. Negentropy is naturally occurring in biology and in fluid dynamics – generally spoken in non-linear systems, that show some kind of self-reference and thus are able self-organize and to build up fractal order.

These experiments are important because they give the scientific base, understanding and proof that touches many other fields of research, opening science up to a broader, holistic understanding of nature.

- It gives a basic understanding of mental processes like telepathy and the so-called synchronicities in life.
- This understanding can also lead to a completely new generation of energy technologies[178, 179].
- Scalar waves – created by a set of two coupled longitudinal waves optically annihilate each other – are the key to

---

177

     Carl Barus, "A curious inversion in the wave mechanism of the electromagnetic theory of light," American Journal of Science, Vol. 5, Fourth Series, May 1898, p. 343-348.

178

     T. E. Bearden and Walter Rosenthal, "On a testable unification of electromagnetics, general relativity, and quantum mechanics, Proceedings of the 26th Intersociety Energy Conversion Engineering Conference (IECEC '91), Aug. 4-9, 1991, Boston, Massachusetts, p. 487-492.

179

     Floyd Sweet and T. E. Bearden, "Utilizing scalar electromagnetics to tap vacuum energy," Proceedings of the 26th Intersociety Energy Conversion Engineering Conference (IECEC '91), Aug. 4-9, 1991, Boston, Massachusetts, p. 370-375.

understanding the non-local interaction observed in quantum physics, referred to as quantum entanglement. The most outstanding property of scalar waves i.e. quantum entanglement is that they don't transfer energy, but instantly transfer information. The word "instantly" here means not only far beyond the speed of light, but of information being here and there "at the same time".

- So negentropy is the physical process that is the basis for the ability of self-organization, especially of organisms, and thus gives understanding of the basic principles of life. Especially the term scalar potential is of big importance. Scalar potential is what also is called "life force", a measure for vitality of nature, for its ability to self-organize. Shape in nature, beauty that is connected somehow to the rules of the golden ratio, is the tendency of this life force to manifest in what science would call "scalar potential eddies", vortices, that develop a fractal order and display the rules of the golden ratio as part of the self-organization of their fractal order.

In this context single photon emissions – like observed with biophotons we are going to discuss in the next chapter – can be regarded as the most "pure" longitudinal waveform consisting of one longitudinal wave front only, with a very high potential to get involved into scalar interaction. This is not simply light. This is light looking for possibilities to fuse, merge, build up order.

And when it comes to the discussion of piezoelectric nano-crystals, we should remember that one type of optical applications utilizing these physics is referred to as self-pumped phase conjugation (SPPC) applications.

268

3.2. Biophotons

The concept of biophotons dates back to the work of Alexander Gavrilovich Gurwitsch. The Russian biologist observed root-growth of neighboring onion-roots and found out that some kind of emission deriving from the tip of one root strengthened the root-growth of the neighboring root. To find out more about the quality of this emission he separated the two roots with glass of different optical properties and found out that there must be a signal in the range of 260 nm[180] (UV) emitted from the tip of one root that is triggering cell division in the other root.

For a number of years this research has been widely ignored. Later on, measurement devices for ultra week and single photon emissions were developed. The most important researcher who re-introduced the topic into science was Fritz-Albert Popp, a late German scientist and professor with a PH.D. in Theoretical Physics. He is the founder of the International Institute of Biophysics in Neuss (1996), Germany. Popp established biophoton measurements as an indicator for the health and age of living organisms. As an example, in Germany biophoton-measurement is today used by the health-authorities as the only possible way to detect the real age of chicken eggs. According to the measurements carried out by Popp the entire range of biophoton-activity happens within the band of 200-800 nm[181].

180

Nissen, Ted M.A. M.T.: Ultra-weak Photon (Biophoton) Emissions (UPE)-Background Introduction, Copyright © September 2006 Ted Nissen, online October 23rd 20012 at http://www.anatomyfacts.com/research/photonc.htm

181

Nissen, Ted M.A. M.T.: Ultra-weak Photon (Biophoton) Emissions (UPE)-Background Introduction, Copyright © September 2006 Ted Nissen, online October 23rd 20012 at http://www.anatomyfacts.com/research/photonc.htm

269

During the 1990s in the western scientific community biophotons have
been discussed mainly as a result of oxidative processes in cell-tissue, and
biophoton emission was for a long time assumed to be random with no
functional importance in biology. But during the last decade the complex
function of biophotons have been explored with advanced measuring
equipment and statistical methods of evaluation. The findings showed in
addition to the random photon emissions from chemical processes that
biophoton-emissions – light signals – contain information of value to
biological systems.

The breakthrough was achieved by the Indian researcher Ram P. Bajpal
from the Institute of Self-Organizing Systems and Biophysics, North-
Eastern Hill University, Shillong, India. Conducting experiments with
germinating seeds, he clearly could link biophoton activity to biological
order[182].

Bajpal also linked this biophoton-activity to non-linear optics and
quantum physics. Citing the abstract of one of his latest publications:

> Coherence is a property of the description of the system in the
> classical framework in which the subunits of a system act in a
> cooperative manner. Coherence becomes classical if the agent
> causing cooperation is discernible otherwise it is quantum
> coherence. Both stimulated and spontaneous biophoton signals
> show properties that can be attributed to the cooperative actions
> of many photon-emitting units. But the agents responsible for the

---

182

Bajpai Ram P., Bajpai PK, Roy D.: Ultraweak photon emission in
germinating seeds: a signal of biological order. J Biolumin Chemilumin.1991 Oct-
Dec;6(4):227-30.

cooperative actions of units have not been discovered so far. The stimulated signal decays with non-exponential character. It is system and situation specific and sensitive to many physiological and environmental factors. Its measurable holistic parameters are strength, shape, relative strengths of spectral components, and excitation curve. The spontaneous signal is non-decaying with the probabilities of detecting various number of photons to be neither normal nor Poisson[183]. The detected probabilities in a signal of Parmelia tinctorum[184] match with probabilities expected in a squeezed state of photons. It is speculated that an in vivo nucleic acid molecule is an assembly of intermittent quantum patches that emit biophoton in quantum transitions. The distributions of quantum patches and their lifetimes determine the holistic features of biophoton signals, so that the coherence of biophotons is merely a manifestation of the coherence of living systems.[185]

Major progress in the measurement of the visible part of biophoton-activity was achieved by the Russian researcher Dr. Konstantin G. Korotkov [186, 187, 188, 189], with the development of the Gas Discharge

---

183

Both Normal and Poison Distribution are typical results from the measurement and statistic evaluation of random values concentrated around one central mean value.

184

Type of lichen used for the experiment

185

Bajpai Ram P.: Quantum coherence of biophotons and living systems. Indian J Exp Biol. 2003 May;41(5):514-27.

186

Korotkov K. Measuring Energy Fields. Proceedings of the International Conference "Vastu Panorama", Indoor, India, 2008.

187

271

Visualization Electro Photonic Capture Camera, that can capture images of corona discharge i.e. gas excited when hit by electrons leaving the plant or the human body along with its biophoton activity. The tradition of research Korotkov based his studies on first caught wide attention with the Kirlian photography in the late 60s.

This research started with the visualization of the visible part of biophoton activity. If one looks at the entire concept of biophotons of cause this is only a fraction of what is happening, especially if one includes the annihilated part of biophotons that would optically not show up. It is exciting how science slowly discovers the important role of this invisible part, the high amount of bi-directional, annihilated biophoton pairs that via quantum entanglement interconnect biological systems also on long distances.

Like one would expect from quantum entanglement or in other words scalar waves, the information carried by such a wave is transmitted instantly, and is not limited by the speed of light. This effect has been proven concerning communication within biological systems – like with

Korotkov K. General principles of electrophotonic analysis. Proceedings of the International Scientific Conference "MEASURING ENERGY FIELDS", Kamnik, Tunjice, 2007, pp. 87-92.

188

Korotkov K., Williams B., Wisneski L. Biophysical Energy Transfer Mechanisms in Living Systems: The Basis of Life Processes. J of Alternative and Complementary Medicine, 2004, 10, 1, 49-57.

189

Bascom R, Buyantseva L, Zhegmin Q, Dolina M, Korotkov K: Gas discharge visualization (GDV)-bioelectrography. Description of GDV performance under workshop conditions and principles for consideration of GDV as a possible health status measure; in Francomano CA, Jonas WB, Chez RA (eds): Proceedings: Measuring the Human Energy Field. State of the Science. Corona del Mar, CA, Samueli Institute, 2002, pp. 55-66. 2003

blood taken out and deposited thousands of kilometers away from the former owner. Still this blood instantly reacted on emotional stress of the body it belonged to – showing a transmission of information far beyond the speed of light.

The latest findings where delivered by Konstantin Meyl. Together with medical researchers in Spain he successfully treated terminal cancer by introducing modulated scalar waves into the body of the patient, which carried the information of killed cancer cells. According to Meyl the biophoton-exchange within the visible spectrum is the highest order of a number of frequencies modulated on top of each other, starting of with the low frequent brain waves on one end, being crowned by the biophoton exchange within the visible spectrum on the other.

To give a more precise picture: When technology utilizes waves of different frequencies to transport information a low-frequency-signal is modulated on top of a high-frequent signal. According to Meyl, in biology this is the other way round. In biology, wavelength's that stand to each other in a relation defined by the factor 3 are modulated onto each other in a way, that the higher-frequent signal is overlaying the lower frequent signal. This exactly is the mathematical formula to create sharp, rectangular and thus longitudinal signals: by adding sine waves of 3, 9, 27 fold frequency. These sharp, i.e. longitudinal signals, have the ability to couple to scalar waves of an intensity that goes beyond the annihilated single photon emissions.

Scalar waves are not visible and can't be shielded – which means that everything appears transparent for these waves. This might be the main reason why science was blind to the major role of optics in biological self-organization.

Another fact illustrating the major role of the annihilated part of biophoton activity is that when a being dies, in the moment of death there is a burst of biophotons leaving the body – originating from the biophoton activity dis-tangled at that very special moment – when cell communication is loosing its coherence.

3.3. Optical properties of nano-crystals

In the discussion about geo-engineering, $(Ba, Sr_x) TiO_3$ nano-crystals are mentioned as one possible compound of the aerosol mixture.

Barium-strontium-titanate is an advanced nano-crystal. To get an idea of this crystallographic family we might look at barium-titanate that is described in Wikipedia as followed:

> Barium-titanate is a dielectric ceramic used for capacitors. It is a piezoelectric material for microphones and other transducers. The spontaneous polarization of barium-titanate is about 0.15 C/m^2 at room temperature and its Curie point is 120 °C. As a piezoelectric material, it was largely replaced by lead-zirconate-titanate, also known as PZT. Polycrystalline barium-titanate displays positive temperature coefficient, making it a useful material for thermistors and self-regulating electric heating systems.

> Barium-titanate-crystals find use in nonlinear optics. The material has high beam-coupling gain, and can be operated at visible and near-infrared wavelengths. It has the highest reflectivity of the materials used for self-pumped phase conjugation (SPPC) applications. It can be used for continuous-wave four-wave mixing with milliwatt-range optical power. For photo refractive applications, barium-titanate can be doped by various other

elements, e.g. iron.

Thin films of barium-titanate display electro-optic modulation to frequencies over 40 GHz.

The pyro-electric and ferroelectric properties of barium-titanate are used in some types of uncooled sensors for thermal cameras.

High purity barium-titanate-powder is reported to be a key component of new barium-titanate capacitor energy storage systems for use in electric vehicles.[190]

Regarding the non-linear optical properties of these crystals, there are a number of interesting qualities and applications. They can "up-convert" photons, transforming input of a number of photons of a lower frequency into output of one photon of a higher frequency[191]. They can also alter the spin of photons[192].

Being distributed in a cluster of relative large distances between nano-crystals, like in aerosols or as an equally distributed pollutant in cell tissue, they can show optical qualities of second and third order[193], a quality that

190

 Wikipedia, online at http://en.wikipedia.org/wiki/Barium_titanate on Nov. 22nd 2012.
191

 G. Chen, T. Ohulchanskyy, A. Kachynski, H. Ågren and P.N. Prasad: Intense Visible and Near-Infrared Upconversion Photoluminescence in Colloidal LiYF(4):Er(3+) Nanocrystals under Excitation at 1490 nm. ACS NANO 5, 4981, 2011.C. Yuan, G. Chen, P.N. Prasad, T.Y. Ohulchansky, Z. Ning, H. Tian, L. Sun and H. Ågren: Use of colloidal upconversion nanocrystals to energy relay solar cell light harvesting in the near infrared region. J. Mat.Chem. 22, 16709, 2012.
192

 Jha, P. C., Rinkevicius, Z. and Ågren, H.: Spin multiplicity dependence of nonlinear optical properties. ChemPhysChem. 10, 817, 2009.
193

is connected to the ability to create holographic pictures.[194] These properties are utilized for holographic screening technologies utilizing 4 lasers turning a cloud of $(Ba, Sr_x) TiO_3$ nano-crystals into a holographic screen[195].

4. Nano toxicology

Nano toxicity, Nano pathology, Ecotoxicology are emerging fields researching the possible negative effect of nano-particles on plants, microorganisms and all living beings including humans[196]. Natural

---

Second and third order as a phenomena can easiest be explained with some pieces of modern art. Everyone has seen these pictures where every "pixel" is formed by a picture that has the everage color and brightness of the pixel it represents The content of these little pictures would be the first order, the picture they create as a cluster of pictures would represent the second order. And so on. The term is thus associated to "information".
194

Y. Fu, S. Hellström and H. Ågren: Nonlinear Optical Properties of Quantum Dots - Excitons in Nanostructures. J Nonlinear Optical Physics & Materials, vol.18, p.195-226, 2009. Z. Rinkevicius, J. Autschbach, A. Baev, M. Swihart, H. Ågren and P.N. Prasad: Novel Pathways for Enhancing Nonlinearity of Organics Utilizing Metal Clusters. J. Phys. Chem. A, vol. 114, pp. 7590-7594, 2010.
195

Heid, Christy A.; Ketchel, Brian P.; Wood, Gary L. (Sensors and Electron Devices Directorate, ARL)
    Anderson, Richard J. (National Science Foundation); Salamo, Gregory J. (University of Arkansas):3-D Holographic Display Using Strontium Barium Niobate. Army Research Laboratory, Adelphi, MD 20783-1197, ARL-TR-1520. February 1998.
196

Mytych Jennifer, Wnuk Maciej: Nanoparticle Technology as a Double-Edged Sword: Cytotoxic, Genotoxic and Epigenetic Effects on Living Cells. *Journal of Biomaterials and Nanobiotechnology*, 2013, 4, 53-63 53 doi:10.4236/jbnb.2013.41008 Published Online January 2013 (http://www.scirp.org/journal/jbnb)

occurring nanoparticles are found in volcanic ash, ocean spray and forest-fire smoke, nanoparticles exist also as a by-product from diesel emissions and depleted uranium weapons.

Research and production of engineered nano-particles and nano-fibers started in the late 1990ies. There is now an enormous push towards engineered nano-particles. Nano technologies can be used in fields like pharmacy, mobile phones, computers, industrial coatings, chips, sensors, cosmetics, clothes, solar cells, agriculture, seeds, pesticides, packaging, bioremediation, aerosols and new fields like re-engineering by building bio-inorganic complexes for crops, animals and other living beings, an advanced form of GMO.[197]

Information around the opportunities within the nano-technologies were collected and discussed by Gyorgy Scrinis, RMIT University, and Kristen Lyons, from the Griffith University:

> Nanotechnology is attracting large-scale investment from global food corporations, is backed by academic science, and has captured financial and ideological support from many governments around the world.

> In terms of economic relations, nanotechnology provides new opportunities for the extension and further integration of corporate ownership and control within and between sectors of the agri-food system.[198]

197

C. Remédios, F. Rosário, and V. Bastos: Environmental Nanoparticles Interactions with Plants: Morphological, Physiological, and Genotoxic Aspects University of Aveiro, Portugal (2012),
198

Nano technology opens a new field of biotechnology, which is the technology of merging of biology and technology creating synthetic life forms, which can self-multiply and regenerate.

'This enhanced capacity to reconstitute nature at the nano-scale also introduces novel kinds of hazards and new orders of risk. There may be an inherent unpredictability and unmanageability associated with atomic and molecular level manipulations of nature. '

Dupuy and Grinbaum, (2006)

'Studies so far have focused on how we can use engineered nano-materials in the environment for remediation of toxic chemicals. No one has yet looked at the possible consequences of these nanomaterials on organisms. We're leaping before we're looking.'

Dr. Eve Oberdorster, biologist, Southern Methodist University, Texas

'We must be careful about injecting loose nanoparticles into the human body and the environment. Exposure to large numbers of these particles could be harmful.'

Anthony Seaton, professor, Aberdeen University

'Science is not done in a vacuum; it is not done in isolation. I would say it is a social function. Although scientists like to think that they are independent and doing their own thing, science does have wider consequences.'

Gyorgy Scrinis: The Emerging nano-corporate paradigm: nanotechnology and the transformation of nature, food and agri-food systems. RMIT University, Kristen Lyons, Griffith University (2007).

278

Andrew D. Maynard. Ph.D. Chair of the Environmental Health Sciences Department, director the UM Risk Science Center. University of Michigan

Much of the research done shows adverse impact on plants and other living organisms. Other studies show a neutral or a positive impact on germination, root length and biomass on the plants tested. Nanoparticles are researched on for enhancing harvest, it is pursued with great force, and many patents are filed. Still the broader environmental consequences are not being researched sufficiently. How will natural life forms react? It is worth to notice that again and again the scientists in their abstracts urgently call for caution. What nanoparticles do to nature may be irreversible.

At nano scales, the basic rules of chemistry and physics are not applicable.[199]

The width of the human hair is 80,000 nm, so nano-particles with a diameter of just a few nm can pass cell membranes, enter and interfere in ways previously unknown.

> 'A key concern regarding human exposure to nano-scale particles is that they have many pathways for entering the body, such as through inhalation, digestion and through the skin. From there they may be able to pass into the bloodstream, penetrate cells, by-pass immune responses, lodge in the lungs, and cross the blood-brain barrier.' [200]

199

In the ancient Greece the philosophers distinguished between form-forces and matter-forces. Nowadays the form forces are rediscovered under the term Meta-Materials. In nano-materials these form-forces dominate the physics.
200

In a presentation at OECD, University of Modena, Italy showed photos of nanoparticles that have entered and are present in different organ tissues severely compromised by illness.

It is important to keep in mind that what might be positive in the first phase of plant growth, may have adverse effect when reviewing the total impact of that nano-particle on the full plant life cycle. As described in the following paper from University of Texas at El Paso, USA: Interaction of nano-particles with edible plants and their possible implications in the food chain. (2011):

> The uptake, bioaccumulation, biotransformation, and risks of nanomaterials (NMs) for food crops are still not well understood. Very few NMs and plant species have been studied, mainly at the very early growth stages of the plants. Most of the studies, except one with multiwalled carbon nanotubes performed on the model plant *Arabidopsis thaliana* and another with ZnO nanoparticles (NPs) on ryegrass, reported the effect of NMs on seed germination or 15-day-old seedlings. Very few references describe the biotransformation of NMs in food crops, and the possible transmission of the NMs to the next generation of plants exposed to NMs is unknown. The possible biomagnification of NPs in the food chain is also unknown.

Most of the excising research on nanotechnology relating to the environment, plants and humans were assessed in a study made at the University of Aveiro, Portugal. The authors felt the need to communicate

---

Friends of the Earth, 2006; Royal Society and Royal Academy of Engineering, 2004; Scrinis 2006b

the following:

> It is urgent not only to further elucidate the effects of NPs in plants
> in order to characterize the uptake, phytotoxicity, and accumulation
> of NPs, but also to understand how nanoscale materials can affect
> food chains and, ultimately, to human health risk assessment.[201]

Though, the toxic impact of nanoparticles is so far to be related to their
large surface, and also the fact that nano-particles can pass through the cell
membranes in organisms. Nano fibers like carbon fibers or silver fibers, is
shown to have comparable detrimental effect on health as asbestos,
working in a similar way, the length of the fiber being important.[202]

A question with large implications can be asked: Is it really so that normal
cell defense mechanisms cannot protect against nanoparticles and nano-
fibers? Scientific testing shows that nano particle can damage cell
membranes; nano-particles enter also through the blood brain barrier that
should protect the brain, nano-particles are shown to pass through the
placenta that should protect the unborn baby from unwanted interference.
It is shown that nano-particles and fibers can cause ROS and oxidative
stress, which is the beginning stage of many illnesses.

In this paper we will mainly look at the possible mechanisms of damage to
plants by aerosols associated to geo-engineering. Large scale dumping of

201

Environmental Nanoparticles Interactions with Plants: Morphological,
Physiological, and Genotoxic Aspects. University of Aveiro, Portugal (2012)
202

The threshold length for fiber-induced acute pleural inflammation: shedding
light on the early events in asbestos-induced mesothelioma. *University of
Edinburgh, Centre for Inflammation Research, United Kingdom, 2012.*

nano-particles on our biosphere is a risky endeavor. We will analyze the possible impact of nanoparticles from a theoretical viewpoint, looking at the interaction between the physical structures of nano-particles and biological communication within plants. We will move into the realm of quantum physics, biophotons, the special effects of clusters and global scaling.

4.1. Damage related to barium-strontium-titanate

In this chapter we will try to apply the knowledge about non-linear optics, biophotons and the optical properties of the $(Ba, Sr_x) TiO_3$ nano-crystals to theoretically derive possible effects on nature. This will cover effects on plants, plankton, mammals and humans.

4.1.1. Effects on plants

Plants take up nano-crystals as a whole. This may happen via the roots as well as via the leaf surface. The effect is utilized for example in leaf-fertilizers like Megagreen®. There are variations depending on the plant size, but particles smaller than approx. 100nm-particles can pass through most of the membranes.

On one side we have the concept of biophotons as a second grade non-linear-optical system, a field-structure of invisible light, one could call it energetic body, a surplus of visible light emitted by the DNA cluster, building up a real body of organic matter as a fractal projection of the order stored as information in the DNA. As a result of a holographic projection of the DNA clusters this system creates the blueprint for plants, animals and humans. The non-visible part of light signaling (photo emission) within the plant has stored the order, mainly by just being there,

282

hidden in the background. The visible biophotons are triggering cell division in a way that the plants repair missing cells and grow at defined areas – thus showing the main characteristics of self-organization.

Up to here this is biology as it is supposed to be. Now we introduce piezo-electric nano-particles to the system, scattered in space as the DNA is. We know that a cluster like this would be capable of non-linear holographic projection with $(Ba, Sr_x) TiO_3$ nano-crystal-clusters using coherent pulsed laser light.

Both systems, plant DNA and piezo-crystal-cluster, work with coherent light. Both systems work with longitudinal wave-forms (pulsed laser light and single photon emissions). Both systems work at the same range of frequencies. Both project holographic blueprints of higher order via clusters.

Thus it becomes obvious that one should expect some interference when both DNA- and nano-crystal-clusters are positioned in the same place.

The properties of the nano-crystals could result in the following effects when absorbed in plants:

- Barium-strontium-titanate nano-crystals absorb UV light with wavelength shorter than approx. 250 nm, taking away 90% of the light passing the crystal[203, 204]. The absorption of signals shorter

203

VIJAYALAKSHMI, R.; RAJENDRAN, V. *(Department of Physics, Presidency College, Chennai, TamilNadu, India)*: SYNTHESIS AND CHARACTERIZATION OF CUBIC BaTiO3 NANORODS VIA FACILE HYDROTHERMAL METHOD AND THEIR OPTICAL PROPERTIES. Digest Journal of Nanomaterials and Biostructures. Vol. 5, No 2, May 2010, p. 511 – 517.
204

Compare to entire concept - Sarney, Wendy L.; Oliver, Kimberley A.; Little, John W. (Sensors and Electron Devices Directorate, ARL); Livingston, Frank E. (The

283

than 260 nm is likely to eliminate the mono-directional signals responsible for cell division.

- The up-conversion of absorbed photons would take two or three photons of a defined frequency and convert it to one of a higher frequency, resulting in disruption of cell communication and maybe cause cell damage due to the higher energy of the single resulting photon.

- The refraction would geometrically disorder bidirectional biophoton-waves before being established.

- The disorder induced regarding the non-linear qualities of second and third order could possibly alter the entire blueprint of nature causing pseudo-genetic deformations.

To understand the quantitative relationship between this special type of opacity the nano-crystals creates and the harm done to the plants, it is useful to have a look at the optical density the particles may create in the plant. 1 kg dried organic matter equals a volume of about 3 l = 0,003 m^3 living organic matter. The average distance of plant DNA resp. cell diameter is about 0,75 mm. This means that in a plant containing 70 mg (Ba, Sr$_x$) TiO$_3$ per kg dried organic matter the optical density of the nano-particles would be high enough to even interrupt the communication between neighboring cells. 35 mg would disrupt at a distance of 0,125 mm.

Aerospace Corporation), Niesz, Kriszian; Morse, Daniel E. (Institute for Collaborative Biotechnologies, University of California, Santa Barbara): Progress in Materials Synthesis and Processing of Barium Titanium Oxide (BaTiO$_3$) and Barium Strontium Titanium Oxide (Ba, Sr$_x$) TiO$_3$ Films for Uncooled Infrared (IR) Detector Applications. Army Research Laboratory, December 2011. P. 9.

4.1.2. Effects on plankton

Phytoplankton builds up a very highly organized biotope that mainly covers the upper layer of the oceans. Phytoplankton is the basis for all life in the oceans.

Rain containing nano-crystals falling into the ocean would be distributed within the storm wave horizon. This layer of the ocean-surface is practically identical with the layer that is reached by sunlight.

It is known that nano-crystals due to their miniature size can stay up to 18 months in the atmosphere after being released. A similar mechanism would take place close to the ocean-surface.

Due to their size the particles would hardly sink further down, unless absorbed by dying bio-forms. Due to the comparable long distanced between single cells phyto-plankton-organisms this could very quickly lead to a concentration of nano-crystals that would be high enough to interrupt parts of the cell communication between single phytoplankton cells.

If in means of biophotons the phytoplankton is reacting as one biological unit deriving the impulse for cell division from the biophoton exchange within the biotope, the discussed nano-crystals could eventually reduce or disturb the production of biomass in the oceans and thereby affect the marine food resources.

4.1.3. Setting the electromagnetic cell potential of plants out of balance

The immune system of all cells is determined by a highly defined curve of electromagnetic cell potential. Plant cells have defined potential differences between the core and the inner membrane surface as well as between the inner and outer cell membrane surface. Any alteration of these cell potentials weakens the "immune system" by disturbing the equilibrium of oxidant and antioxidant processes.

Barium-strontium-titanate, as a piezoelectric substance, changes its crystal geometry when exposed to external electromagnetic fields[205]. Any change in crystallographic structure is accompanied by a release/absorption of electrons.

With regards to barium-strontium-titanate used as aerosols in the atmosphere, this effect could be used to "switch" clouds "on and off" by applying electromagnetic fields as used by HAARP and ICECAT devices or other radar or microwave-radiating antenna systems. These research- and military installations have equipment with sufficient strength to alter the crystal geometry of the barium-strontium-titanate while in the atmosphere, which in turn leads to free current that would charge the aerosol particle and create an ion. An ion will attract vapor and instantly lead to the forming of a droplet in the then forming cloud.

The nano-crystals remain unchanged when absorbed by plants. One would therefore expect the same effect to happen when a plant is hit by low and high frequency radiation.

In other words terrestrial mobile, WIFI, microwave or radar transmission as well as the EMF-pollution by power lines and transformer stations would be expected to cause a spontaneous release of free electrons, which would alter the cell potential and thus weaken the immune-system of the plant.

205

Wada, S.; Tsurumi, T.: Enhanced piezoelectricity of barium titanate single crystals with engineered domain configuration. British Ceramic Transactions, 2004, Vol. 103, No. 2.

286

4.1.4. Effects on mammals and humans

A study in North America has examined the impact on mammals caused by the presence and exposure to three elements:

1. naturally occurring barium,
2. barium pollution originating from drilling in barium-rich mud by the oil/gas industry and
3. downfall of piezoelectric nano-crystals. In these regions of North America aerosol spraying is conducted to enhance/refract radar signals for military purposes.

The study showed a connection between exposure to a combination of these and neuronal diseases like the chronic waste disease (CWD) and other transmissible spongiform encephalopathies (TSEs).

The study examined the chemical toxicity of silver, barium and strontium, which bio-concentrate in the food chain. It also studied the more complex mechanisms connected to nano-crystals used in aerosol spraying. In the examined cases the piezoelectric properties were believed to be triggered by acoustic pressure energy from incoming low frequency shock bursts from low flying jets, explosions, earthquakes, etc., additionally to high frequent electromagnetic fields. The magnetic fields on the surface of the crystal surface were also discussed.

The mechanism of damage caused by excited piezoelectric crystals should be the same for plants as for mammals.

Because of the precisely described biochemical processes we here render the full abstract:

High levels of Silver (Ag), Barium (Ba) and Strontium (Sr) and low levels of copper (Cu) have been measured in the antlers, soils and pastures of the deer that are thriving in the chronic wasting disease (CWD) cluster zones in North America in relation to the areas where CWD and other transmissible spongiform encephalopathies (TSEs) have not been reported. The elevations of Ag, Ba and Sr were thought to originate from both natural geochemical and artificial pollutant sources--stemming from the common practice of aerial spraying with 'cloud seeding' Ag or Ba crystal nuclei for rain making in these drought prone areas of North America, the atmospheric spraying with Ba based aerosols for enhancing/refracting radar and radio signal communications as well as the spreading of waste Ba drilling mud from the local oil/gas well industry across pastureland. These metals have subsequently bioconcentrated up the foodchain and into the mammals who are dependent upon the local Cu deficient ecosystems. A dual eco-prerequisite theory is proposed on the aetiology of TSEs which is based upon an Ag, Ba, Sr or Mn replacement binding at the vacant Cu/Zn domains on the cellular prion protein (PrP)/sulphated proteoglycan molecules which impairs the capacities of the brain to protect itself against incoming shockbursts of sound and light energy. Ag/Ba/Sr chelation of free sulphur within the bio system inhibits the viable synthesis of the sulphur dependent proteoglycans, which results in the overall collapse of the Cu mediated conduction of electric signals along the PrP-proteoglycan signalling pathways; ultimately disrupting GABA type inhibitory currents at the synapses/end plates of the auditory/circadian regulated circuitry, as well as disrupting proteoglycan co-regulation of the growth factor signalling systems which maintain the structural integrity of the nervous system. The resulting Ag, Ba, Sr or Mn based compounds seed piezoelectric crystals, which incorporate PrP and ferritin into their structure. These ferrimagnetically ordered crystals multireplicate and choke up the PrP-proteoglycan conduits of electrical conduction throughout the CNS. The second stage of pathogenesis comes into play when the pressure energy from incoming shock bursts of low frequency acoustic waves from low fly jets, explosions, earthquakes, etc. (a key eco-characteristic of TSE cluster environments) are absorbed by the rogue 'piezoelectric' crystals, which duly convert the mechanical pressure energy into an electrical energy which accumulates in the crystal-PrP-ferritin aggregates (the fibrils) until a point of 'saturation polarization' is reached. Magnetic fields are generated on the crystal surface, which initiate chain reactions of deleterious free radical mediated spongiform neurodegeneration in surrounding tissues. Since Ag, Ba, Sr or Mn based piezoelectric crystals are heat resistant and carry a magnetic field inducing pathogenic capacity, it is proposed that these ferroelectric crystal pollutants represent the transmissible, pathogenic agents that initiate TSE.[206]

Later Purdey associated the same biological effect of piezoelectric nano-crystal also to human diseases:

This paper exposes the flaws in the conventional consensus on the origins of transmissible spongiform encephalopathies (TSEs) which decrees that the protein-only misfolded 'prion' represents

206

M. Purdey: Elevated silver, barium and strontium in antlers, vegetation and soils sourced from CWD cluster areas: do Ag/Ba/Sr piezoelectric crystals represent the transmissible pathogenic agent in TSEs? US PubMed, US National Library of Medicine National Institutes of Health Online at: http://www.ncbi.nlm.nih.gov/pubmed/15236778?ordinalpos=1&itool=Entre zSystem2.PEntrez.Pubmed.Pubmed_ResultsPanel.Pubmed_DiscoveryPanel.Pu bmed_Discovery_RA&linkpos=1&log$=relatedarticles&logdbfrom=pubmed on Dec. 16th 2012.

the primary aetiological transmissible agent, and then reviews/presents the emerging data which indicates that environmental exposure to metal microcrystal pollutants (sourced from munitions, etc.) represents the heat resistant, transmissible nucleating agents which seed the metal-prion protein (PrP)-ferritin fibril crystals that cause TSE. Fresh analytical data is presented on the levels of metals in ecosystems which support populations affected by clusters of variant Creutzfeldt-Jacob disease (vCJD), sporadic/familial CJD, and the scrapie types of TSE that have emerged in the UK, Sicily, Sardinia, Calabria and Japan. This data further substantiates the abnormal geochemical template (e.g., elevated strontium (Sr), barium (Ba) and silver (Ag)) which was observed as a common hallmark of the TSE cluster ecosystems across North America, thereby supporting the hypothesis that these microcrystals serve as the piezoelectrion nucleators which seed the growth/multireplication of the aberrant metal-PrP-ferritin fibril features which characterise the neuropathology of the TSE diseased brain. A secondary pathogenic mechanism entails the inactivation of the sulphated proteoglycans which normally regulate the mineralisation process. This can be induced by a rogue metal mediated chelation of free sulphur, or by contamination with organo-sulphur pollutants that substitute at natural sulphur bonds, or via a mutation to the S-proteoglycan cell line; thereby enabling the aberrant overgrowth of rogue fibril crystal formations that possess a piezoelectric capacity which compromises the ability of the contaminated individual to process incoming acoustic/tactile pressure waves in the normal way. The crystals transduce incoming sonic energy into electrical energy, which, in turn, generates magnetic fields on the crystal surfaces that initiate chain reactions of free radical mediated spongiform neurodegeneration. Metal microcrystal nucleating agents provide a group of plausible aetiological candidates that explain the unique properties of the TSE causal agent - such as heat resistance, transmissibility, etc. - which the protein-only prion model fails to fulfill. This paper also discusses the possible nutritional measures that could best be adopted by populations living in high risk TSE ecosystems; as a means of preventing the successful implantation of these rogue microcrystals and their consequent hypermineralisation of the soft tissues within the CNS.[207]

In 2006 Purdeys hypotheses was substantiated at Auburn University.[208]

Like with plants, also in Mammals we look at an interference of clusters of natural and of artificial electro-optically active crystals. With plants we have seen that nano-crystal clusters can produce signals that may interfere with the plants DNA.

In mammals and likely in humans artificial crystals can take the place of natural ferro apatite crystals in the body. These natural ferro apatite crystals are also piezoelectric crystals and play a major role in the transmission of signals in the central nervous system.

If the natural ferro apatite crystal is displaced by artificially made piezo-

---

207

 M. Purdey: Metal microcrystal pollutants: the heat resistant, transmissible nucleating agents that initiate the pathogenesis of TSEs? US PubMed, US National Library of Medicine National Institutes of Health Online at: http://www.ncbi.nlm.nih.gov/pubmed/15908137 on Dec. 16th 2012.
208

 M. Purdey: Auburn university research substantiates the hypothesis that metal microcrystal nucleators initiate the pathogenesis of TSEs. PMID 16226390 [PubMed - indexed for MEDLINE]

electrical crystals, it appears to open the biological system to respond to a greater extent to artificial electromagnetic signals, both low and high frequency.

Wireless technology that uses high frequency radiation randomly causes high frequencies of different strength in our surroundings, which penetrates plants and living beings. Examples on such devises are; mobile phones, mobile towers and Wi-Fi technology, wireless routers, bluetooth technology, cordless phones, smart meters, tetra system, radars and digital terrestrial broadcast systems.

However, radio-signals also could be intentionally generated by transmission stations under the control of the intelligence community and weapon manufacturers who offer security solutions to governments. As to this theoretical possibility to apply mind control with piezo-crystals, we should consider the fact that there are technical facilities to apply microwave fields on every populated area of this world, and that this technical equipment is in the hand of people who are very much into the philosophy of control.

Following another article describing effects on humans, the bio-concentration in the food chain does not even need to reach dangerous concentrations, because the agent already does harm even if it is not located inside the body. In November 2010 after a snowy day in Aachen, a town in North-West-Germany, the healing practitioner Wolfgang Creyaufmüller[209] registered a widespread appearance of headaches among his patients. They could not be successfully treated with recipe-free painkillers like ASS, Paracetamol or Ibuprofen.

209

Wolfgang Creyaufmüller: Wie kommt Barium ins Regenwasser? Aachen. Online at http://www.sauberer-himmel.de November the 17th 2012.

As a healing practitioner he was using bio-field-measurement with the nosode FSME as part of his diagnostics. The device is measuring biophoton activity of the human body. All patients with the abnormal headaches showed significantly weakened biophoton fields.

Creyaufmüller knew that normally snow has a positive effect on biophoton activity of humans – supporting the levels of humans and being at +8 on the scale itself. So he went out measuring the snow and found a biophoton activity of -8 on the snow surface. As an anti-nuclear power activist he has been following up the contamination deriving from the Chernobyl accident for years. He expected some radioactive fallout, thus he decided to have chemical analysis conducted of the snow. However, the snow instead showed high levels of barium isotopes instead which could not be related to any known nuclear accident.

The source of the effect could have been barium-strontium-titanate, since these nano-crystals absorb biophotons. It is an indication that also humans might be affected by the interruption of biophoton activity, and that humans might feed their biophoton field with refracted (polarized) sunlight.

Additionally, it could hint to the ability of nano-crystals to affect life on the continents in a way similar to the effects suspected for plankton. This could regard all biotopes, when being optically open and interconnected systems.

In general, a weakened biophoton activity results in weakened ability of self-organization in the biological system. This touches all degenerative diseases as well as the subjective well-being.

In this context a very likely possibility of a synergistic toxicity could be given with mercury. It has been reported that the swine flue vaccination campaign in Scandinavia lead to a high number of cases of narcolepsy with children. Vaccines are often preserved with organic mercury compounds, and if they are not, sources from the industry report that still during production process the needles delivered with the vaccines are disinfected and preserved with mercury compounds. This mercury has been suspected to have caused the many cases of Narcolepsy in Scandinavia.

The main cause of mercury intoxication is the damage done to the tubulin of the nerves. The tubulin is the skin that separates the nerve as well as the sensitive receptor cell from the surrounding tissue.

Mercury degenerates the tubulin leading to diseases like autism and ADHS, literally driving the souls out of the body with the background-pain released by the permanently triggered receptor cells.

If there is any correlation between tubulin degeneration and the likelihood of the integration of an artificial piezo-crystal into the receptor cell like described by M. Purdey, we would indeed have a second case of synergistic toxicity.

The mercury prepares the ground, the "piezo" seeds are laid into the field and the HAARP, radar and ELF transmission could infiltrate the internal communication of the human body causing electrosensitivity.

Another possible impact of barium-strontium-titanate concerns signal enhancement. This is a term derived from information-medicine.

Dietrich Klinghardt, who has been voted to the Physician of the Year back in 2011, developed a special system for autonomic response testing (ART), where he uses laser light and refracting Plexiglas cubes as signal enhancers. The Plexiglas is meant to have optical qualities that are similar to those of barium-strontium-titanate nano-crystals, just on the macroscopic scale. By positioning a poison or a remedy on these Plexiglas cubes close to the patients head, Klinghardt tests if substances are setting

294

the body into a state of stress, or lead to relaxation – something that is possible to test via ART, where the tension of arm muscles is mechanically detected. The idea is that the coherent, polarized light created by laser and cube can carry both the information of the poison and of a possible remedy into the patients cell communication, triggering the same reaction that the real chemical would trigger once it is in the body.

Against this background the possibility that barium-strontium-titanate nano-crystals could act as signal enhancers is striking. They would enhance any kind of biological information above their absorption lines, i.e. above UV, just like Klinghardts Plexiglas cubes, but being millions of them.

This would be a classical case of synergistic toxicity, enhancing the information field of various toxins within the body. This could be one explanation of Multiple Chemical Sensitivity (MCS).

4.2. Damage related to Aluminum Oxide

The last time Europe experienced large scale consequences from airborne pollution was in the 1970s and 80s. The fume from burning of fossil fuel by large industries was permitted to go unfiltered into the atmosphere, causing acid rain. In the late 1970 large forest areas in Germany, Poland and Czech Republic started dying, and mass death of fish was reported from rivers in Norway and Sweden.

Burning fossil fuels releases SO_2 and NO_2 into the air, when it connects with the humidity in the air H_2SO_4 and H_2NO_3 is formed. In addition burning carbon creates extra CO_2, which forms extra H_2CO_3. All these are acid agents, which turn the humidity in the air acid. This acid can damage plants directly via fog or indirectly via the rain entering the ground and releasing heavy metals from the soil, among them aluminum oxide which can harm plants and other organisms.

Al_2O_3 as well as other heavy metal compounds occur as a mineralogical unit with the SiO_2 in clays and many other minerals. In this form it is harmless. The acid rain has the capacity to dissolve SiO_2 and thus release Al_2O_3 and other heavy metal compounds into a bioavailable form. In addition the Al_3^+ can form toxic compounds with for example fluorine.

The sulfur-content of coal can be up to 3%, where as heavy metals content amounts to only 0,003%, so the amounts of aluminum brought up into the atmosphere by burning fuel used to be of minor importance compared to the amounts of aluminum released in the soil as a result of acid rain.

Aluminum-oxide was found to attach to the membranes of the tiny roots of the trees, blocking the uptake of nutrition and causing the roots to die off. Aluminum ions were identified to attach to the gills of fish and disturbing the uptake of oxygen.

The vague scientific memory of the acid rain problem causes a number of misunderstandings. Sometimes in discussions it is said that aluminum turns the rain acid. This is not correct. Large presence of Al_2O_3 in the rain would bring the rain further into the alkaline state. When rain comes down acid it is an indication of fuel impurities or additives containing sulfur and halogens. Rainwater has a natural acidity at 5,5 when it is in equilibrium with the natural CO_2 content of the air. Acid rain is rainwater with acidity below 5.5.

Interestingly this release of Al_2O_3 in the soil is part of the self-regulation mechanism that protects the soils itself from getting too acidic by acid rain. In this way it can protect the microorganisms in the soil itself.

The problem today is that it is not known how much of the aluminum deposited is deposited as amorphous flitters in micron-size, amorphous nano-particles or mono-crystalline nano-particles.

Al_2O_3 as mentioned in geo-engineering-patents, would form thin flitters in the range of 10-100 micron. However, even the micron size flitters when being thin enough might brake down and produce nano-size particles. But anyway it seems to be more likely that the particles observed come from military application and are produced by spray pyrolysis within the jet engines[210]. When run through normal jet engines during normal flight-condition at stable altitude the temperatures in the engine should create amorphous spherical aluminum-oxide nano-particles. With military planes we see the possibility to utilize afterburner technology, with very similar conditions to rocket propulsion, that reaches higher temperatures and would be able to melt and re-crystallize amorphous aluminum oxide nano-particles to mono-crystalline corundum nano-crystals in the second chamber, with the varieties ruby as a result if doted with chrome, and sapphire if doted with iron and titanium.

Conditions like found in afterburners could eventually create a particles-form called "whisker". Back in the 80s engineers tried to create ultra-light concrete with nano-particles created in spray pyrolysis at high temperatures. The crystalline particles formed shapes with hundreds of sharp radial orientated mono-crystalline needles. The concept was meant to achieve low weight when bound in concrete. The technology was abandoned because these particles turned out to cause cancer.

~~Aluminum oxide is not only mentio~~ned as reflective particles but also is

210

A.I.Y. Tok, F.Y.C. Boey, X.L. Zhao: Novel synthesis of Al2O3 nano particles by flame spray pyrolysis. Journal of Materials Processing Technology 178 (2006) 270-273. M.I. Martín, L.S. Gómez, O. Milosevic, M.E. Rabanal: Nanostructured alumina particles synthesized by the Spray. Pyrolysis method: microstructural and morphological analysis. *University Carlos III de Madrid, Avda. de la Universidad, 30, 28911 Leganés, Madrid, Spain. Institute of Technical Sciences of Serbian Academy of Sciences and Arts, K. Mihailova 35/IV, 11000 Belgrade, Serbia.*

known to improve the efficiency of the combustion process by up to 40%
as a combustion accelerator. This technology is especially utilized for
fuels used in afterburners. It also relates to the experience with JP-8
reported to burn easier and faster then kerosene or diesel fuel. Especially
the rocket- and afterburner fuels can contain up to 40% aluminum.
American environmental activists suspect the same properties of the
material to enhance the violence of bush- and forest-fires once these
particles are accumulated within the plants and in the ground, and
especially lead to very aggressive fires, especially in the root area of the
trees, a phenomenon that has not been observed before.

However, the only thing possible at this moment is to theoretically
evaluate what type of particle would have what effect when entering plant
life and mammals.

Below are examples of studies involving nano-aluminum-oxide, like the
one proposed for geo-engineering.

A peer reviewed research paper from the department of biology at the
University of East Carolina, USA, researched the effects of aluminum-
oxide nano-particles on the growth, development, and microRNA
expression of tobacco (*Nicotiana tabacum*), demonstrating negative effect
of Al_2O_3 nanoparticles on plants:

> In this study, we exposed tobacco (*Nicotiana tabacum*) plants (an
> important cash crop as well as a model organism) to 0%, 0.1%,
> 0.5%, and 1% Al_2O_3 nanoparticles and found that as exposure to
> the nanoparticles increased, the average root length, the average
> biomass, and the leaf count of the seedlings significantly decreased.[211]

211

Caitlin E. Burklew, Jordan Ashlock, William B. Winfrey, Baohong Zhang:

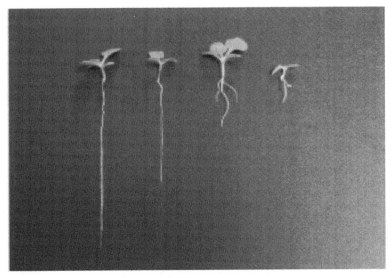

Picture out of the study of Burkley, Ashlock, Winfrey and Zhang.

Another study shows toxic effect of Al_2O_3 nanoparticles on human cells.

The objective of this study was to assess the acute toxicity of ANPs in human mesenchymal stem cells (hMSCs) in vitro. The results indicate that ANPs have a significant and dose-dependent effect on cytotoxicity. Control cells showed a characteristic, homogeneous nuclear staining pattern, whereas ANP-exposed cells showed abnormal nuclear morphological changes such as condensation or fragmentation. An early characteristic of apoptosis was observed in ANP-treated cells. Further confirmation of cell death in hMSCs was observed through increased expression of chosen signaling

Effects of Aluminum Oxide Nanoparticles on the Growth, Development, and microRNA Expression of Tobacco (Nicotiana tabacum). PLOS one, 18.06.2013.

genes and also decreased expression of Bcl-2 during mitochondria-mediated cell death.

Although they (Al_2O_3) provide great advantages in food and agricultural products, the chronic and acute toxicity of ANPs still needs to be assessed carefully.[212]

Yet another study shows toxic effect of Al_2O_3 nanoparticles on the mitochondria in mammalian cells[213]. It was also documented that mitochondrial function decreased significantly in the cells exposed to ZnO at 50 to 100 microg/mL, and in the cells exposed to Fe_3O_4, Al_2O_3, and TiO_2 with concentrations greater than 200 microg/mL.

Another study shows toxic effect of Al_2O_3 nanoparticles on mitochondria in lung cells.

The results show that the four types of metal oxide nanoparticles lead to cellular mitochondrial dysfunction, morphological modifications and apoptosis at the concentration range of 0.25-1.50 mg/mL and the toxic effects are obviously displayed in dose-dependent manner. ZnO is the most toxic nanomaterial followed by TiO_2, SiO_2, and Al_2O_3 nanoparticles in a descending order.

The results highlight the differential cytotoxicity associated with

---

212

Al_2O_3 Nanoparticles Induce Mitochondria-Mediated Cell Death and Upregulate the Expression of Signaling Genes in Human Mesenchymal Stem Cells. King Saud University, Saudi Arabia (2012):
213

Toxicity of metal oxide nanoparticles in mammalian cells. Old Dominion University, USA (2006);

exposure to ZnO, TiO_2, SiO_2, and Al_2O_3 nanoparticles, and suggest an extreme attention to safety utilization of these nano-materials.[214]

One of the main mechanisms of nanoparticle toxicity is thought to be the generation of reactive oxygen species (ROS), which primarily damage cell membranes.

Ruminococcus flavefaciens is an anaerobe gut bacteria that plays an important role in the digestion of hemicellulose and cellulose plant cell walls. In spite of oxygen not being present in this milieu, analysis revealed dose-effect changes in membrane composition exclusively when cells were exposed to Al_2O_3 nanoparticles in a concentration range of 3-5 g/L. [215]

This indicates that other mechanisms than oxidation is damaging cell structures. It also indicates that Al_2O_3 in food might affect digestion negatively.

The toxic impact of nanoparticles thought has to be related to their large surface, and also the fact that nano-particles can pass through the cell membranes in organisms.

Leaf trees might be able to release themselves from excess aluminum when shedding their leaves.

214

ZnO, TiO_2, SiO_2 and Al_2O_3 nanoparticles- induced Toxic Effects on Human fetal lung Fibroblasts. South East University, Jiangsu, China (2011);
215

Masa Vodovnik, Rok Kostanjsek, Masa Zorek, Romana Marinsek Logar: Exposure to Al_2O_3 nanoparticles changes the fatty acid profile of the anaerobe Ruminococcus flavefaciens. University of Ljubljana, Slovenia. (2012)

In areas with a heavy load of persistent contrails some species of trees have been observed secreting a white dust on the barks surface that is visible almost like a layer of white color. It is possible that the phenomenon observed is an attempt by the trees to get rid of excess aluminum oxide.

Aluminum oxide is not only mentioned in patents and discussions as reflective particles, but it also is known to improve the efficiency of the combustion process by up to 40% as a combustion accelerator. This technology is especially utilized for fuels used in afterburners. These fuels contain up to 40% aluminum. Fire fighters have observed that bush and forest fires are far more explosive now than just some years ago, they have also been puzzled by very aggressive fires shooting up from the root area of the trees. Aluminum nano-particles that are used as combustion accelerator in jet engines, would have the same qualities and effect on forests and can accumulate in the soil beneath the trees causing explosive fires.

When Al_2O_3 nano-particles exist in mono-crystalline form, we would expect no solubility. Even less so if they are doted with iron & titanium and maybe chrome. These are small gemstones: ruby and sapphire. Like the gemstones they have a color, high refractivity, probably good reflectivity. Having a color means that within the spectrum of cell-communication they would filter out certain frequencies and refract others which could disturb the morphogenetic field and the plants mechanisms of self-organization.

The suspicion that like with barium-strontium-titanate the damaging effect of aluminum is also related to optical effects within the plant is supported by the first publication about the GMO plants resistant to aluminum. The article states that the modified plants are "actually blind to what happens within the cells". The author obviously knew that the cell division is blocked by the aluminum, and that the bio-engineers found ways to keep the cell division running although the optics were blocked.

Even if it is good to have a working solution to a serious problem, the question arises why and how someone was able to find a solution to a problem that did not even exist back at that time, someone who showed on one hand that he exactly knew about the role of biophotons, by A. mentioning it and B. basing his solution on it, but at the same time declares that the reason is the chemical intoxication from the soil, which obviously was not true. This does not make sense unless one suspects that certain economic entities intentionally created a problem to sell the solution.

5. Polymerization, nano fibers and the Morgellons disease

Many reports mention nano-fibers falling from the sky as one phenomenon connected to geo-engineering. As far as this study can oversee the technical possibilities, this can relate to three different mechanisms:

- the polymerization of nano-particles
- metal-coated nylon fibers
- technical hollow nano fibers
- self replicating hollow nano-fibers, i.e. Morgellons

The first possible mechanism when fibers are observed could be a reaction of $Ca(NO_3)_2$ and fluoride-tensides to Ca_2F-nano-crystals, which similar to piezoelectric crystals develop magnetic properties when exposed to external fields. In a dry environment these nano-crystals would theoretically form unstable, spider-web-like structures when triggered to become magnetic, in humid environment they theoretically would be able to form droplets on command, by fusing smaller droplets by magnetic attraction to rain-size droplets.

The second form of fibers observed, are the aluminum coated nylon fibers, as indicated by the manuscript from U.S. Air Force Academy, Department of Chemistry. They have been reported to hide planes from radar detection, as well as being used to deflect sunlight in the context of combating global warming. The Air Force calls them spoofer sprays.

The third form of fibers reported are technically produced hollow fibers containing all sorts of chemicals, some of them identified as insecticides.

The forth form of fibers reported to be found in rain water samples but also in humans and animals are the so called Morgellons, which bio-accumulate and sometimes cause a disease where these fibers exit via the skin, causing ugly skin irritations. There are about 100.000 to 300.000 registered victims worldwide. According to the carnicom-institute these fibers turned out to be „synthetic biology", an artificially engineered life form that is showing properties of eukarya, archaea and bacteria, thus representing an optimized mixture of all aspects or all families of life existing on this planet. They look like the tubular shaped fungus, contain organs looking and self-replicating like bacteria, but as a whole behave like eucarya. From the fungi it inherited it's ability to grow and multiply explosively when triggered by a defined electromagnetic frequency, in this case at 375 nm (blue) within the visible spectrum. According to the Carnicom Institute one of the self-replicating organs found inside the tubes were identified as something similar to human red blood cells, however they were self-replicating outside, in free nature, not in a petri-dish, a life-form that could withstand basically everything, freezing, drying, burning in a Bunsen-flame, pouring bleach on them. Nothing destroyed these cells. Associated with these Morgellons also other parts of "self-assembling nano-machines" were found, including gold nano-particles and hexagonal crystals glowing in different colors when triggered by microwave radiation.

Despite the very obvious reality of these fibers the disease is officially declared by the US-authorities being psychosomatic, classified as delusional parasitizes, which hints to an intelligence background.

For further understanding we first recommend the lecture "From Chemtrails to Pseudo-Life – the dark Agenda of synthetic Biology" by Sofia Smallstorm, as well as the publication "Extreme Genetic Engineering".[216]

216

305

5.1. Trans-Humanistic Technologies

To understand the full potential of this synthetic biology one might look into some cutting edge applications in medicine. Today medicine is using nano-dyes to mark and microscope very small biological elements like proteins and DNA strings. Originally these nano-dyes were made of fluorescent complex molecules containing both organic and heavy metal compounds. Observed with ultra short laser pulses it was possible to capture the fluorescent picture only, while the camera is closed during the pico-seconds the laser is sending its light flashes to avoid capturing direct reflections. To observe continuously without this type of time-resolution, second generation nano-dyes utilize a mixture of different nano-crystals and complex organic molecules with associated heavy metal cations, where the ability of up-conversion of frequencies[217] is used to feed the dye with radio-frequencies on one, but harvest the picture on a second frequency band. Following this concept nano-dyes mentioned in the official literature have been developed that absorb radio frequencies of about 1800 nm, upconvert the photons and emit within the visible spectrum. Like this they can glow virtually without a visible source of light.

More complex medical applications consist of self-assembling[218] nano-

---

etc-group: extreme genetic engineering. An introduction to synthetic biology. January 2007.
217

Gainer Ch. F., Joshua G. S., De Silva Ch. R., Romanowski M.: Control of green and red upconversion in NaYF4:Yb3+, Er3+ nanoparticles by excitation modulation. Journal of Materials Chemistry, Vol.21, p.18530-18533 (2011).
218

machines, like for example optical fibers[219], that by capillarity take in and up-concentrate nano-dyes and other nano-particles with special characteristics, like gold-nano-particles[220]. These fibers are able to collect light patterns coming in from the DNA, turning them into electromagnetic signals that are sent by the fiber-based so called plasmonic antennas[221] out

---

Ding B., Hrelescu C., Arnold N., Isic G., Klar T. A.: Spectral and directional reshaping of fluorescence in large area self-assembled plasmonic-photonic crystals. Nano Letters, Vol.013, p.378-386 (2013) Also: Woller J. G., Hannestad J. K., Albinsson B.: Self-assembled nanoscale DNA–porphyrin complex for artificial light harvesting. Journal of the American Chemical Society, Vol.135, p.2759-2768 (2013) Also: Sagun E., Knyukshto V. N., Ivashin N. V., Shchupak E. E.: Photoinduced relaxation processes in self-assembling complexes from CdSe/ZnS water-soluble nanocrystals and cationic porphyrins. Optics and Spectroscopy, Vol.113, p.165-178 (2012) Also: Aqueous self-assembly of an electroluminescent double-helical metallopolymer. Journal of the American Chemical Society, Vol.134, p.19170-19178 (2012)
219

Jaskiewicz K., Larsen A., Schaeffel D., Koynov K., Lieberwirth I., Fytas G., Landfester K., Kroeger A.: Incorporation of nanoparticles into polymersomes: Size and concentration effects. ACS Nano, Vol.06, p.7254-7262 (2012) Also: Williams G. O. S., Euser T. G., Russell P. St. J., Jones A. C.: Spectrofluorimetry with attomolesensitivity in photonic crystal fibers. Methods and Applications in Fluorescence, Vol.01, 015003 (2013)
220

Raut S. L., Shumilov D., Chib R., Rich R., Gryczynski Z., Gryczynski I.: Two photon induced luminescence of BSA protected gold clusters. Chemical Physics Letters, Vol.561-562, p.74-76 (2013). Also: Tombe S., Antunes E., Nyokong T.: Electrospun fibers functionalized with phthalocyanine-gold nanoparticle conjugates for photocatalytic applications. Journal of Molecular Catalysis A: Chemical, Vol.371, p.125-134 (2013). Also: Wen X., Yu P., Toh Y.-R., Tang J.: Quantum confined Stark Effect in Au8 and Au25 nanoclusters. The Journal of Physical Chemistry C, Vol.117, p.3621-3626 (2013). Also: Muskens O. L., England M. W., Danos L., Li M., Mann S.: Plasmonic response of Ag- and Au-infiltrated cross-linked lysozyme crystals. Advanced Functional Materials, Vol.023, p.281-290 (2013).
221

Acuna G.P., Holzmeister P., Möller F.M., Beater S., Lalkens B., Tinnefeld P.: DNA-templated nanoantennas for single-molecule detection at elevated concentrations. Colloidal Nanocrystals for Biomedical Applications VIII, Vol.XXX, 859509 (2013) Also: de Leon N. P., Shields B. J., Yu Ch. L., Englund D., Akimov A. V., Lukin M. D., Park H.: Tailoring light-matter interaction with a

as an readable electromagnetic signal[222]. A second class of nano-machines function the opposite way: large area self assembling photonic-plasmonic crystals are quantum laser units that take in electromagnetic signals and turn them into single photon emissions[223] that communicate with the DNA. These two classes are thus able to create a bi-directional technical/biological interface.

Such a read/write unit might function quite simple in analogy to a tape recorder. Any aspect of human life, emotions, energetic states or even spiritual experiences, anything that manifests on the level of DNA cell communication, can be recorded under lab conditions and replayed in any single individual that can be targeted by radio frequencies – once these self-assembling nano-bots exist within the human body. Additionally, when applied on large areas, methods of collective mind control are thinkable.

Historically[224] these nano-crystal applications are an advanced

nanoscale plasmon resonator. arXiv:1202.0829v1 (2012)
222

De Greve K., Yu L., McMahon P. L., Pelc J. S., Natarajan C. M., Kim N. Y., Abe E., Maier S., Schneider C., Kamp M., Höfling S., Hadfield R. H., Forchel A., Fejer M. M., Yamamoto Y.: Quantum-dot spin-photon entanglement via frequency downconversion to telecom wavelength. Nature, Vol.491, p. 421-425 (2012) Also: Zaske S., Lenhard A., Kessler C. A., Kettler J., Hepp C., Arend C., Albrecht R., Schulz W.-M., Jetter M., Michler P., Becher C.: Visible-to-telecom quantum frequency conversion of light from a single quantum emitter. Physical Review Letters, Vol. 109, 147404 (2012). See also: Guo-Liang Shentu, Jason S. Pelc, Xiao-Dong Wang, Qi-Chao Sun, Ming. Yang Zheng, M.M. Fejer, Qiang Zhang, Jian-Wei Pan: Ultralow noise up-conversion detector and spectrometer for the telecom band. Optical Society of America, POTIC PRESS 13986, Vol. 21, No. 12, 17. June 2013.
223

Winkler J. M., Lukishova S. G., Bissell L. J.: Room-temperature single photon sources with definite circular and linear polarizations based on single-emitter fluorescence in liquid crystal hosts. Journal of Physics: Conference Series, Vol.414, 012006 (2013)

308

development of the quantum dots[225] that have been developed by Bell

Labs in the early 80s, however the fiber and nano-crystal technology is

much more stable, especially regarding solubility of the dyes containing

heavy metals in acids.

Other of these intelligence applications seem to involve real antennas like

glass insulated superconducting nano-wires[226, 227]

224

Kendrick M. J.: Light-matter interactions: from the photophysics of organic
semiconductors to high spatial resolution optical tweezer-controlled nanoprobes.
An Abstract of the Dissertation, Oregon State University (2012)
225

Midolo L., Pagliano F., Hoang T. B., Xia T., van Otten F. W. M., Li L. H.,
Linfield E.H., Lermer M., Höfling S., Fiore A.: Spontaneous emission control of
single quantum dots by electromechanical tuning of a photonic crystal cavity.
Applied Physics Letters, Vol.101, 091106 (2012). Also: Shcherbatyuk G. V.,
Talbot P., Ghosh S.: Controlling photo-induced spectral changes in CdSe/ZnS
quantum dots by tuning inter-dot energy transfer. Applied Physics Letters,
Vol.100, p.212114-1-212114-4 (2012). See also: Ziyun Di, Jones H. V., Dolan P.
R., Fairclough S. M., Wincott M. B., Fill J., Hughes G. M., Smith J. M.:
Controlling the emission from semiconductor quantum dots using ultra-small
tunable optical microcavities. arXiv:1206.6046v1 (2012)
226

Kim J., Lee S., Suh J.-K. F., Park J. H., Shin H.-J.: Active control of
dielectrophoretic force at nanowire electrode for ultrahigh single
nanoparticle manipulation yield. Applied Physics Letters, Vol.102, p.063105
(2013). Also: Lee Y.-B., Park S., Lee S., Kim J., Lee K.-S., Joo J.: Nanoscale
luminescence characteristics of CdSe/ZnS quantum dots hybridized with
organic and metal nanowires: energy transfer effects. Journal of Materials
Chemistry C, Vol.01, p.2145-2151 (2013) Also: O'Carroll D. M., Fakonas J. S.,
Callahan D. M., Schierhorn M., Atwater H. A.: Metal-Polymer-Metal Split-Dipole
Nanoantennas. Advanced Materials, Vol.024, p.OP136-OP142 (2012)
227

Avella A., Brida G., Carpentras D., Cavanna A., Degiovanni I. P. , Genovese M.,
Gramegna M., Traina P.: Review on recent groundbreaking experiments on
quantum communication with orthogonal states. arXiv:1206.1503v1 (2012)
Also: Sandberg R. L., Padilha L. A., Qazilbash M. M., Bae W. Ki, Schaller R. D.,
Peitryga J. M., Stevens M. J. Baek B., Nam S. W., Klimov V. I.: Multiexciton
dynamics in infrared-emitting colloidal nanostructures probed by a

As mentioned, the system that shows up associated to the Morgellons disease is quite advanced. The self-replicating fibers and the typical hexagonal crystals seem to grow in a kind of biologic-technical symbiosis.

Samples from the Phoenix atmosphere taken by Ms. Coralyn Hill, Astro Physicist of Harvard and analyzed in a nano equipped lab showed three different mixtures of components of these self-assembling technologies:

1. Polycrystalline Sr Mg-Doped (La, Ga) O_2 nano wire (LSGM) P19 Protein Methotrexate

2. TiO_2 Polymer/Au/Al blend nanowire terephtlalic acid Dimethyl Terephthalete Carbon nano tube Radioactive Sodium Iodide, N-acetylglucosamine

3. High Resolution TEM revealed crystalline lattice spacings of palladium & aluminum, microtube particle arrays bound to amino acids. Pd is bound to the N and S atoms in the side chains of crysteine (red), methionine (blue), and hystidine (green/yellow). Hystadine is a metal binding residue in peptides due to the disprotenated N_3 atom in the imadazole ring. Ni and Co magnetice nano wires without diameter of 50-60 nm. Stacked pryidine ligand molecular wires containing Zn with porphyrin cores. Ladder oliogoners of Quinoxaline and benzoanthracene (a carcinogenic hydrocarbon).

superconducting nanowire single-photon detector. ACS Nano, Vol.06, p.9532-9540 (2012). Also: Rich R., Ji Li, Fudala R., Gryczynski Z., Gryczynski I., Mandecki W.: Properties of coatings on RFID p-Chips that support plasmonic fluorescence enhancement in bioassays. Analytical and Bioanalytical Chemistry, Vol.404, p.2223-2231 (2012)

310

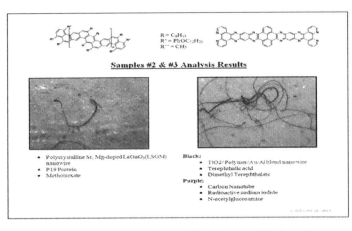

Original paper by the nano lab of the Harvard University.

Sample Analysis Conditions: S-TEM EELS

S-TEM – Tecnai TF30
- *Beam energy: 200 keV*
- *FEG extraction: 4000 V*
- *Gun lens: 6*
- *C1 aperture: 30 µm*
- *C2 aperture: 100 µm*
- *Convergence: 9 mrad*
- *Spot size: 6*
- *Probe current : 0.5 nA*
- *Camera length: 80 mm*
- *Probe FWHM: 0.9 nm*

Sample #1 Analysis Results

- High resolution TEM revealed crystalline lattice spacings of metallic Palladium and Aluminum microtubule particle arrays bound to Amino Acids.
- Pd is bound to the N and S atoms in the side chains of Cysteine (Red), Methionine (Blue), and Hystidine (Green/Yellow). Hystidine is a metal binding residue in peptides due to the disprotenated N3 atom in the imadazole ring.

Sample also contains the following:

- Ni and Co magnetic nanowires with an outer diameter of 50-60 nm.
- Stacked Pyridine Ligand molecular wires containing Zn with Porphyrin cores.
- Ladder oligomers of Quinoxaline and Benzoanthracene.

Original paper by the nano lab of the Harvard University.

311

Compared to the particulate plasma showing up as barium, strontium, titanium and aluminum the description, analysis and understanding of this transhumanistic technology is rather easy. Most of the basic scientific papers are public domain. We already referred to these studies earlier in the footnotes, the publications that appear most important to us are:

- Ding B., Hrelescu C., Arnold N., Isic G., Klar T. A.: Spectral and directional reshaping of fluorescence in large area self-assembled plasmonic-photonic crystals. Nano Letters, Vol.013, p.378-386 (2013)
- Woller J. G., Hannestad J. K., Albinsson B.: Self-assembled nanoscale DNA–porphyrin complex for artificial light harvesting. Journal of the American Chemical Society, Vol.135, p.2759-2768 (2013)
- Sagun E., Knyukshto V. N., Ivashin N. V., Shchupak E. E.: Photoinduced relaxation processes in self-assembling complexes from CdSe/ZnS water-soluble nanocrystals and cationic porphyrins. Optics and Spectroscopy, Vol.113, p.165-178 (2012)
- Aqueous self-assembly of an electroluminescent double-helical metallopolymer. Journal of the American Chemical Society, Vol.134, p.19170-19178 (2012)
- Jaskiewicz K., Larsen A., Schaeffel D., Koynov K., Lieberwirth I., Fytas G., Landfester K., Kroeger A.: Incorporation of nanoparticles into polymersomes: Size and concentration effects. ACS Nano, Vol.06, p.7254-7262 (2012)
- Williams G. O. S., Euser T. G., Russell P. St. J., Jones A. C.: Spectrofluorimetry with attomolesensitivity in photonic crystal fibers. Methods and Applications in Fluorescence, Vol.01, 015003 (2013)

To fully understand the concept we will first have a look at the Morgellon life cycle as a biological being. Our approach to understand the Morgellons life cycle was fully visual, analyzing the total number of 14.000 pictures of Morgellon related phenomena. We had a close look at all Morgellon related phenomena, to find forms that occurred over and over again, and put them in a logical order. This approach was successful due to the photographic work of Jan Smith, Sharlene Neal and Manuela Binieck. Unfortunately we will not display Manuelas work visually in the frame of this study. The most important of her pictures were published in the German magazine Raum und Zeit, in two articles in January/February and February/March 2014. The publication is available online at http://www.raum-und-zeit.com. Further there are two German lectures held by the author available on DVD, that display these pictures, the first one on a conference of the DEGEIM in Lindau, November 2013, the second one on the "Medizinische Woche" in Baden-Baden, held on October 30th 2014.

Morgellons are a fungus that is infecting the entire human body, and later is growing its fruiting bodies within the stomach and in the uterus of women. The fruiting bodies are released in a 28 day-cycle, appearing to the patient as parasites. Due to their plant cell structure they are normally diagnosed as food-leftovers.

To be exact: In the life of a fungus there are four steps: mycelium, peduncle basis, fruiting body and spores. First the mycelium, growing in the muscles, bones and in the brain, i.e. the fibers known as Morgellons, enter the stomach through the stomach mucosa, form a knot, releasing some kind of liquid that turns the knot into a solid peduncle basis. The fibers forming the fruiting body out of the peduncle base in general look different from the mycelium itself, mostly thicker, like soya-sprouts, who inter-wave in a carpet-like texture that later gets covered by a outer layer looking like chicken-skin. The fully-grown Morgellon fruiting body shows mostly a shrimp-like morphogenesis, with a tail, able to bend around a "hip", with a penguin-head shaped forehead and some kind of umbilical cord attached to the belly. The fruiting bodies carry a single insect-type eye with hexagonal crystal-like forms carrying the spores.

The overall impression is of an human embryo in the 20th day of pregnancy, just with one insect-type eye instead of two human ones.

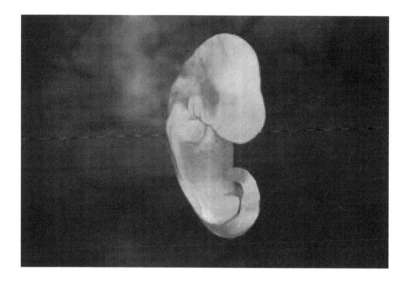

Human embryo in the 20th day of pregnancy.

The woman who donated the excellent photos we can not display for copyright reasons always talked about the tail and the duck-like head, called the little ones "rats". She also said her instincts related to them as to children. Apparently they are mushrooms but they carry the morphogenetic field of humanoid babies.

To understand both these findings and the genetic analysis conducted by the Carnicom-Institute it was necessary to monitor a number of genetically modified beings.

As it looks like, the Morgellons DNA is a genetically modified version of *Metarhizum anisopliae, Metarhizum acridum, Metarhizum majus, Beauveria brongnartii* or *Basidobulus,* all out oft the order of the Entomophthorales.

Both morphology and special abilities of these original orders seem to be combined in a unique way to form the life form known as Morgellons.

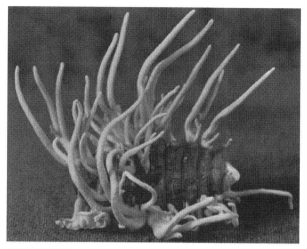

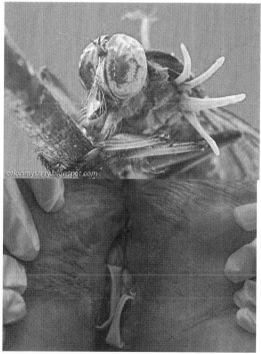

Basidiobulus affects humans, and it seems to have an affinity to colors. With humans it is causing the *Perianal Crohn Disease.* However, Basidiobulus is much more aggressive than Morgellons. *Metarhizum majus* as well as *Beauveria are responsible for the insect*

like forms as well as the ability to mimicry DNA of the host. **These two fungi are natural enemies of insects. When it infects insects, the fungus spreads within their body, basically eats the insects up from inside, and then surfaces again, forms spores and tries to infect other insects.**

There are two special abilities in this biological order to support the overall concept that plays a role in the Morgellons disease.

1. The fungi are able to assimilate higher DNA, multiply it and build up a DNA cluster that creates a morphogenetic field that resembles a humanoid morphogenetic field. This has two goals: It fools the energetic part of the immune system of the victim. The fungus appears to be part of the victim. There is no reason to attack it.

2. The second goal is to attract and infect more victims by mimicry. With the morphogenetic field of the victim the fungus is able to build up a "mushroom", a fruiting body that resembles the original blueprint of the victims DNA in form and size. With insects you will have a mushroom that grows in the form of the insect that it just had killed.

This class of fungi has been widely used to genetically engineer myco-insecticides.

The fungus is using a multilayered hexagonal structure to protect and cover the spore. These hexagons, who have the ability to produce radio controlled cold light, are as mentioned known out of a different context: They are part of synthetic biology research, called self assembling large area photonic plasmonic crystals.

Hexagons associated with the Morgellons disease.

Later the baby generation of Morgellons grows out of the hexagon. The second generation of Morgellons forms new mycelium.

Hexagon that grows new mycelium in a petri-dish.

From the technical point of view we guess nobody cares about the full life cycle of the fungus. What they want to have within the human body are hollow fibers that accumulate nano-dyes within the fiber and those hexagonal self-assembling large area photonic-plasmonic crystals, that accumulate nano-dyes between the transparent layers.

In the language of the intelligence community both are self-assembling nano-bots. They spray them in components, separated into bioform and nano-dye, call this mixture smart dust, and expect the smart dust to bio-accumulate and self-assemble itself to working units within the body.

The fibers and the crystals form a read/write unit. The fibers collect DNA light communication, i.e. the bi-directional single photon emissions interchanged by any DNA cluster, and turn it into radio signals. The crystals take in radio signals and transform them into light signals readable by the human DNA. What ever human experience I want to "mind-control", I can induce this experience in a person, like saying "asshole" to a person to induce anger, read it out by collecting the signal sent by the Morgellons with a special antenna, store it in a digital file, turn this stored anger into a radio signal and make any other human being experience the same emotional or even mental pattern by making the hexagonal crystals reproduce the light patterns. According to old vedic knowledge red light controls sexuality, orange anger, blue the thoughts.

This is what we can state to that topic. Read the original scientific papers by the original inventors.

It is not 100% secured but we would tend to understand the rubies and sapphires created in the context of the particulate plasma used for military reasons as intermediate optical units that smoothen the light transfer between the relative big DNA-molecules, via the nano crystals, to the molecular nano-dyes within the Morgellons. This would represent a hierarchically organized cluster of red and blue fluorescent particles covering three scales in size. This makes sense when working with morphogenetic fields. It guaranties a strong transfer from light stored within the DNA clusters to the artificial Morgellon based light framework, that finally transforms the stored energy into a radio signal and sends it out of the body. Extracting light from the DNA lowers the scalar potential of the DNA. It is a direct transfer of scalar potential out of the human system.

They are flattening us down, lowering "our vibration", extracting energy. Sucking out what one could call life force. Also, with the rubies and sapphires and the other nano-crysralls the light is permanently refracted... even if it finally ends up in a second human DNA. We loose order. This could be one aspect of the aluminum-connection to Alzheimer and dementia. The thoughts, the recalled memory, is getting blurry because the light is permanently refracted by rubies and sapphires, loosing the geometrical order of the bidirectional light communication which by its nature is nothing else then consciousness. Thoughts or consciousness – regarded as composite signals of their smallest units, like bits and bites in computing – are scalar-waves passing the brain in a geometrically ordered form creating fluctuating spheres of the platonic bodies. These are the smallest fragments of logic and grammar. If the scalar-waves are refracted, the angles are permanently changed, which makes it impossible to form repetitive platonic structures. Thinking whites out, like the blue color of the sky.

This is far beyond any known concept of mind control.

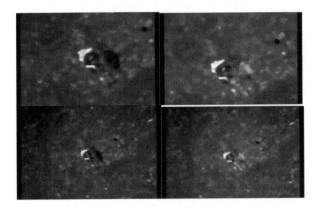

Screenshots taken from a film about blinking crystals made by Jan Smith, who is suffering from the Morgellons disease and documents all related phenomena. A hint to the possibility, that the concept might be online.

Starting from the very beginning, with the discovery of the quantum dots in the year 1982, the system has been developed by Bell Labs, and has apparently been industrialized by the state owned company MITRE. MITRE develops technologies for the intelligence community. The company has an interesting position: On one hand it has a super user status, i.e. it stands above the control by the US authorities, on the other hand – according to their own website – it claims to be "funded by private sponsors to achieve their goals".

5.2. Microscopic analysis of nano-particles

Microscopic analysis of nano-particles is conducted by observing dried raindrops on glass. Doing this on regular basis reveals that the quality of what rain contains varies from day to day – with repeating pictures. Also – according to activists who do this type of monitoring on daily basis – there seems to be a program running, that is introducing new classes of particles following a 6-month pattern. This leaves the overall impression of a genetic-engineering program that is up and running.

Some of the particles seem to have electromagnetic properties, i.e. they self-organize like little magnets when drying. It could very well hint to $(Ba, Sr_x)TiO_3$ and its piezoelectric properties.

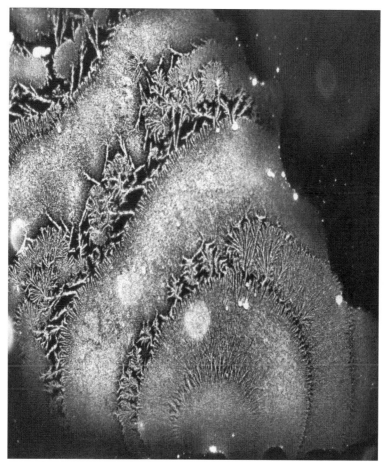

Private environmental monitoring from Germany

Other pictures show the ability of particles to convert infrared radiation and/or heat into light within the visible spectrum, i.e. they shine when heated. This property has been described as up-conversion – it also is typical for (Ba, Sr$_x$) TiO$_3$. The warm breath of a human is sufficient to trigger an effect that easily over-blends the capacities of the camera.

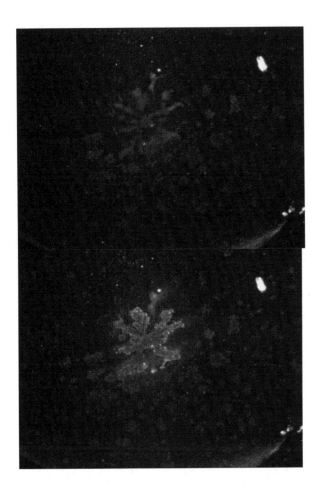

Private environmental monitoring from Germany

Knowing how the biophoton-patterns within the body work, these properties get scary: This disrupts the multiple 3fold order of electromagnetic waves within the body and thus weakens the ability to form longitudinal waves on the highest order, turning biophotons into longitudinal waves. This stops biophotons to couple to scalar potential. This actually seems to be the effect that makes $(Ba, Sr_x) TiO_3$ usefull for self-pumped phase conjugation (SPPC) applications. This is what makes it so dangerous for all life forms.

324

With these agents on board any attempt to take over the control with technical low frequent signals could much easier be crowned with success.

A second type of chemistry that seems to be in solution within the raindrop shows crystallization-properties that resemble "whiskers", monocrystalline particles that consist of a number of sharp needles heading into all directions.

Private environmental monitoring from Germany

On some days tiny droplets of an unknown black liquid could be detected. We still don't have chemical analysis of this material, but it might turn out to be Black Goo, a substance that will be discussed later in chapter 9.

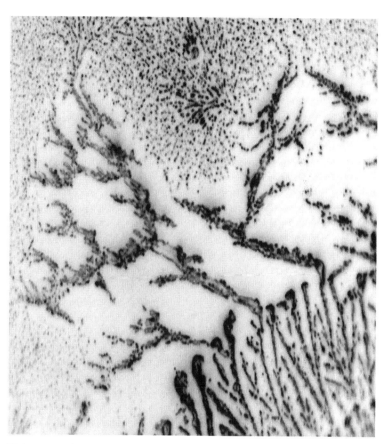

Private environmental monitoring from Germany

6. Quantitative analysis

6.1. Atmospheric barium-deposition in Germany

During the last decades various state institutes have analyzed rainwater, dry atmospheric deposition (dust) and heavy metal content in organic matter, mainly by testing either dust deposition in a container covered by a roof to be protected from rain or by standardized grass samples grown for a period of 4 weeks to detect wet and dry atmospheric deposition of pollutants. This study refers mainly to publications of the Landesumweltamt Brandenburg and the Bayerisches Landesamt für Umwelt, two regional state authorities, and a few minor sources like ash analysis of biomass power plants run on grass. These measurements are available up to the year 2011. Due to the fact that the national Bundesumweltamt today has decided to only fulfill the "UN ECE Convention on long-range trans boundary pollution" and the EU law "Richtlinie 2008/50EG from May 2008" the national institutions are not monitoring barium, strontium and titanium.

The review of all the official barium deposit measurements available online showed a *decrease* in dry deposition by more than 90% during the last 15 years and in the same period of time an estimated *increase* of wet deposition of barium by close to 100%. This complete opposite development is remarkable. Dry deposition derives mainly from industrial pollution and uptake from dust from the ground. Wet deposition is associated to aerosols. Younger official data than 2011 are not available from official sources.

For 2012 we based the statistics on 60 available rain samples taken by private persons analyzed in certificated labs. These samples were collected and controlled by the initiative "Sauberer Himmel e.V.".

These findings need to be reviewed against the background of strongly reduced pollution by all other metals. The following graph shows lead as an example.

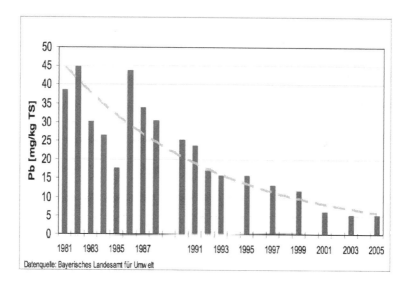

Datenquelle: Bayerisches Landesamt für Umwelt

Lead in mg/kg dried grass samples (wet deposition) over the last 3 decades.

Both strontium and titanium have hardly been measured by the official authorities. Dry deposition of Barium was reduced like most other pollutants from heavy industry. There is no source for barium on the ground, like mining or industry, that can explain the increased levels in pollution registered in the wet deposition. The high amounts of Barium seem to come straight with the rain – which hints to high-altitude-aerosols as a source and thus to geo-engineering or spraying for military purposes. The titanium pollution is mainly related to steel production and might have strongly been reduced due to the massive transfer of this type of industry to china.

The statistical evaluation of 72 rainwater samples by the author, gathered by the German "initiative for a clean sky" (Sauberer Himmel), indicates an amount of approx. 911 tons of barium falling out over Germany during the year 2012.

The grass samples can be estimated to mirror 1625 t barium in 2011, however this amount should also contain the dry deposition as well as some barium taken up by the plants from the soil originating from mineral substrate.

If the original source of industrial barium pollution has been reduced by 90 % during the 15 years as shown by the values for dry deposition, and the overall values including wet and dry deposition went up by intermediated 100% since 2001, there is no other explanation than a new source that is explicitly connected to aerosols brought down by rain registered in the wet deposition analysis.

This new source then would be responsible for 90% of the total values in the year 2012. Therefore one should assume an atmospheric deposition of minimum 865 t barium originating from aerosols coming down with the rain from high altitudes.

Indicating $(Ba, Sr_x) TiO_3$ in nature is difficult. Measurements of bio-available barium, strontium and titanium indicate elements in solution, but due to the non-solubility of $(Ba, Sr_x)TiO_3$ such measurements do not indicate nano-crystals at all. An analysis of the total mineral content would correctly show Ba, Sr and Ti as single elements when performed with fluorine acid only, when nitric acid is used $(Ba, Sr_x) TiO_3$ would not show at all, Al_2O_3 would show only partly. It is impossible to speculate about total amounts. The measured number must origin from the leftovers of the crystals manufactured in the jet engines. Optical analysis with the microscope can determine the existence of nano-crystals within plant cell tissue, but would need time-consuming statistics on thousands of single crystal measurements to make any quantitative statements.

6.2. Research in Norway

The Norwegian State monitors the atmospheric deposition of heavy metals
in the country. The findings show like in Germany, a sharp decrease in
industrial pollutants and a slight increase in substances associated with
geo-engineering, like Barium and Strontium. However these values are
average values with very high local variations.

The state-run *Klima- og forurensings direktoratet* (Climate and pollution
Agency) does extensive testing on airborne pollution. Due to wind
patterns, Norway receives pollution transported long distances from
sources in the central, east and southern parts of Europe to even remote
areas of the country.

The standard measurement of air pollutants in Norway is done with moss
of the type *Hylocomium Splendens*, not with grass, so direct comparison to
German data cannot be done. *Hylocomium Splendens* do not use roots for
uptake of water or nutrition, so it takes up only dry and wet deposition.
Representative amounts of samples was first collected in 1977, 1985 and
since then every 5 years evaluating 464 locations all over Norway. From
each place 5 to 10 samples from an area of 50x 50meter have been taken,
minimum 300 meter from main roads and houses. 42 elements including
Al, Sr, Ba and Ti have been tested, but not all from the very beginning[228]

Median values for analyzed moss for Norway:

Aluminum   1977 with 720 mg/kg, 1995 with 290 mg/kg , 2010 with
280 mg/kg

Titanium   1995 with   43 mg/kg,

228

Atmosfærisk nedfall av tungmetaller i Norge (Atmospheric deposition of heavy
metals in Norway)– Landsomfattende undersøkelse i 2010 (TA-2859/2011)

2010 with   25 mg/kg

Strontium   1995 with   13 mg/kg,

2010 with   15 mg/kg

Barium   1995 with   24 mg/kg, 2010 with

25 mg/kg

Minimum and maximum values:

Aluminum showed in   2005   values between   58,0 - 12 121 mg/kg

2010   values between   46,0 - 4 581   mg/kg

Titanium showed in   2010   values between   4,0 - 260   mg/kg

Strontium showed in   2010   values between   1,9 -   72 mg/kg

Barium showed in   2000   values between   4,3 - 217   mg/kg

2005   values between   4,2 - 119   mg/kg

2010   values between   4,0 - 325   mg/kg

The big differences in values of Barium and Strontium were assumed to either be the result of local Strontium deposition from the Atlantic or a result from the uptake of dust from Barium-rich soils. Barium and Strontium distributions were statistically not associated.

Natural occurring Aluminum, Barium and Strontium in the soil is needed, and can be tolerated to a variable degree in different plants, local vegetation adjusts to the quality of the soil. When large amounts go into solution in rivers as Al^{3+}, aluminum-oxide is not tolerated by fish. In Norway this was a major problem during the years of heavy acid rain.

During the second half of the year 2012 some farmers at the east coast of
Oslo Fjord in Norway experienced a significant slowing down of grass-
growth, which reduced the second harvest of hay. Samples of this grass,
Timothy, Phleum pratense was collected, it was analyzed at the
Norwegian Forest and Landscape Institute for the total amount of
minerals:

Aluminum:	176 mg/kg
Barium:	49 mg/kg
Strontium:	69 mg/kg
Titanium:	28 mg/kg

We compared these results with the results obtained by the Norwegian
school of veterinary science. They carried out a study collecting grass
samples from all of Norway in 2006/7 This project has yet to be
published; however our samples fall within the average of their study.

To see if any of the Barium in the ground could have an atmospheric
input, the soil where the retarded grass grew were analyzed and compared
to soil largely unexposed to rain for the last 70 years, by a barn build
above it.

The soil unexposed to rain was higher in all measured metals except one.
Evaporation brings minerals up from the rock bed, when no rain washes
them out, and no plant material is removed (which would have lowered
the soils mineral content), so the levels remain high. The exception was
Barium. Only barium measured higher outside on the open field.

Metal in Soil sample		not exposed	exposed to rain
	ratio		
Aluminum	mg/kg	25.150,00	22.900,00
	1.098		
Barium	mg/kg	140,00	155,00
	0.903		
Lead	mg/kg	29,00	16,00

333

		1.813		
Arsenium		mg/kg	4,80	2,80
		1.714		
Cadmium	mg/kg	0,28		0,18
		1.555		
Nickel	mg/kg	21,00	20,00	
	1.05			
Palladium	mg/kg	<5		<5

There is no local industry or mining that can explain this increased amount of Barium. The input by fertilizers used was controlled and showed no barium content on the label. The most likely source of this Barium is from wet atmospheric deposition.

However these values and their discussion is rather pointless. As mentioned, the synthesis of $(Ba, Sr_x) TiO_3$ nano-particle in the jet engines would not be identified by the commonly used test methods, what might show up are just the non-processed leftovers of the crystal-synthesis. The only method that practically might work out to detect the nano-crystals is microscopy including some quantitative statistics.

In addition to the reduced growth of the grass monitored in Norway, there was a problem of fungi. Multiple factors may be in action. $(Ba, Sr_x) TiO_3$ may stop plant growth, it may also together with Al_2O_3 disturb cell potential that reduce the plants immune system as well as their vitality. We also know from experiments that exposure to high frequency radiation in a normal office of today can 600 fold the production of mycotoxins from fungi, compared to non-radiated fungi. This is massive. Most places are today exposed to some degree of microwave (high frequency) radiation.

Among cows born in 2011 that this year gave birth for the first time, there was an unusual increase of difficult births in all cow races, in this area. The reason for this is still unknown. The barley for feed had been heavily

334

infected with fungus, due to very wet summers. It is know among farmers that decreased fertility and increased abortion rate among their cows follows in years with fungus-infected feed. Also the mechanisms mention above may be a part of this picture.

Images from the day of sample taking east of the Oslo fjord.

A promising morning of a summer day. Relative short contrails as an indicator for rather dry, warm air at high altitudes.

First appearance of persistent contrails.

Spreading contrails forming white hazy skies.

337

Hazy sky and a completely died off birch forest 3 km from the farm.

338

Field with partly retarded plant growth. On the right side normal growth rate, on the left side retarded growth.

Damaged grass, light green color, brown spots.

Damage by fungi, possibly as a result of disturbed cell potential.

Haze coming down to the surface creating a halo, about 14.30 in the afternoon, a structure that should appear with ice crystals at high altitudes but not on a summer day with temperatures of about 17 degrees Celsius near ground level. In earlier times halos like this were seen on ice-cold winter days around the sun or the moon at night. (All Fotos from Norway by Kristin Hauksdottir)

7. Politics, infrastructure and possible military use

When governmental, military or agency activities are classified, when people involved have to sign non-disclosure agreements and are threatened with being jailed, then normally one finds what is declared as being conspiracy theory as a natural reaction of the human mind. One has a secret, the other one wonders what it is. Simple as that. Project Cloverleaf is as highly classified as a project can be.

The public is left with no official information. There is a little whistle blowing that might contain truth, but also might contain considerable amounts of disinformation. Normally, there should be no place for this in a paper that aims to be scientific in spirit. But at this point there is no other option than to cite the whistle blowers and accept their wish to hide their identity. And again look for scientific proof for their claims.

Thus the following information is not citable in the scientific sense of the word and might contain desinformation.

Trying to find out what actually is happening in the field of geo-engineering is not easy. The structure one meets is onion-like. There is an official surface that is moving big money in research but projects practical geo-engineering mainly into the future[229]. But even if one looks behind the scene, listens to the statements of whistle blowers and reads secret documents that were unintentionally exposed to the public, there is not one coherent truth but rather onion like layers of different concepts of reality to be found.

---

[229]

Professor John Shepherd et al.: Geoengineering the Climate: Science, Governance and Uncertainty. The Royal Society 2009.

342

The outer onionskin looks like this: geo-engineering was first thought of in pre WWII Germany. Most ideas were megalomaniac but rather grounded, like cutting of and drying out the Mediterranean to harvest land and set up a water power plant to supply the entire area with electricity. A second concept was to melt down the pole caps to get access to natural resources underneath. Some of that engineering spirit came to the US after the war. Operation *Paperclip* recruited 10.000 German top researchers to serve the US-military. The targets publicly discussed were rather peaceful. Like preventing hurricanes and hale, directing rain to guarantee harvests.

In 1964 the American National Science Foundation called in a special commission on weather manipulation. However, the first practical applications turned out to be less peaceful. It was the cloud seeding conducted in North Vietnam to enhance monsoon rains and flood the jungle to cut the Vietcong off from supplies.

The first notable document relating to the form of cloud seeding discussed in this paper is the Welsbach patent[230] in 1986. It is the first patent suggesting the spraying of aluminum oxide and metal salts to combat climate change. Since then more follow up patents have been filed that cover the entire technical process of cloud seeding by aerosol spraying from both civil and military airplanes.

In 1990 the US Government entered a phase of intensive research into Geo-Engineering with the "Global Change Research Act"[231].

In 2001, President elect George W. Bush established the (CCRI) Climate Change Research Initiative. A year later it was made public that the

---

[230]

US-Patent No. 5,003,186
[231]

Official governmental website: http://www.gcrio.org/gcact1990.html

343

USGCRP or United States Global Change Research program and the CCRI both would become what is known as the (CCSP) Climate Change Science Program. Now, under the Obama Administration the legacy continues to move forward as the USGCRP, with a yearly budget of 2.7 billion dollars.[232] An insight into these programs reveals that most of it is about combating not monitoring climate change.

Another initiative is projected by the US Department of Homeland Security, which intends to set up the "Hurricane Aerosol and Microphysics Program"[233].

In 2012 US-scientists targeted "a affordable price of below 5 billion a year" to "blow a million of tons" into altitudes of 18 miles[234].

All these sources refer to man made climate change as the problem to be solved by geo-engineering. Climate-change is believed to be caused mainly by CO_2.

The findings of this research are summarized in this graph:

232

Shepard Ambellas & Avalon: *The Budget Obama Didn't Want You To Know About.* the intelhub.com, March 30, 2011. Online at: http://theintelhub.com/2011/03/30/secret-presidential-chemtrail-budget-uncovered-exceeds-billions-to-spray-populations-like-roaches/ on Nov. 22nd 2012.
233

Richard W. Spinrad to William Laska, "Response to Statement of Work: Hurricane Aerosol and Microphysics Program," US Department of Commerce, National Oceanic and Atmospheric Administration, Silver Springs, MD, July 29, 2009, http://voices.washingtonpost.com/capitalweathergang/noaa_letter_dhs_hurricane_modification.pdf
234

Allister Doyle and David Fogarty, "'Sunshade' to Fight Climate Change Costed at $5 Billion Year," Reuters, August 31, 2012, http://in.reuters.com/article/2012/08/30/climate-sunshade-idINDEE87T0K420120830

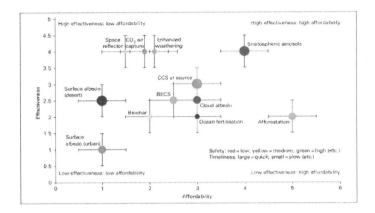

The following passage draws a vague picture of the actions projected and of the aerosols planned to be used:

> So far, launching reflective materials into the upper stratosphere seems to be the easiest and most cost-effective option. This could be accomplished by using high-flying aircraft, naval guns, or giant balloons. The appropriate materials could include sulfate aerosols (which would be created by releasing sulfur dioxide gas), aluminum oxide dust, or even self-levitating and self-orienting designer particles engineered to migrate to the Polar Regions and remain in place for long periods. If it can be done, concentrating sunshades over the poles would be a particularly interesting option, since those latitudes appear to be the most sensitive to global warming. Most cost estimates for such geo-engineering strategies are preliminary and unreliable. However, there is general agreement that the strategies are cheap; the total expense of the most cost-effective options would amount to perhaps as little as a few billion dollars, just one percent (or less) of the cost of dramatically cutting emissions.[235]

235

David G. Victor, M. Granger Morgan, Jay Apt, John Steinbruner, and Katharine

The description of "self-levitating and self-orienting designer particles" might fit on (Ba, Sr_x) TiO_3, with its ability to be ionized and directed by microwave radiation.

This is the outer skin of the onion.

When we go to pre-climate-change-times, things still looked a bit different. Jim Phelps had been working for many years at the Oak Ridge National Laboratories researching the ozone hole and other air-pollution related problems. Global warming was already known back then. However it was not dramatizes and mainly related to fluorine- and sulfur-emissions from jet fuel. Fluorine and sulfur, creating the aggressive HF and H_2SO_4 acid in the clouds, was regarded as the main cause for acid rain. Both sulfur and fluorine compounds were regarded as a reason for increasing persistence of contrails as well as of the appearance of more high altitude cirrus clouds. These clouds were believed to hold back infrared radiation and cause global warming. To prevent damage done by especially fluorine, that formed toxic aluminum-fluorine compounds once raining down, he suggested adding TiO_2 to the jet fuel – or spray the compounds simultaneously during the flight – to bind the fluorine to metals that form less toxic compounds. As to the military branch of geo-engineering, there are only a few sources, mainly ex employees of various agencies.

> We can trace the beginnings of military Spraying-Operations also referred to the Project Cloverleaf right to Dr. Edward Teller, father of the hydrogen bomb and proponent of nuking inhabited coast-lines to rearrange them for economic projects. Before he died in 2003, Teller was director emeritus of Lawrence Livermore National Laboratory, where plans for nuclear, biological and directed energy weapons are crafted. In 1997, Teller publicly outlined his proposal to use aircraft to scatter in

the stratosphere millions of tons of electrically conductive
metallic materials, ostensibly to reduce global warming[236]. (...)

Teller estimated that commercial aircraft could be used to spew
these particles at a cost of 33 cents a pound. (...) A 1991 Hughes
aircraft patent confirms that sunscreen particulate materials can
be run through jet engines.[237]

A different story is told by A. C. Griffith[238], an NSA, later CIA employee
who uncovered his truth on the Monday edition of the *power hour*, a
national broadcast show. Another onionskin. Griffith served at the Ray
Patterson Air force base, which he called the headquarters of US
chemtrailing programs. Griffith refers to an ongoing cold war between
Russia and the US utilizing scalar weapons. The worst incident of this
cold war was – according to the ex US military Col. Tom Bearden, whom
Griffith cites on the radio show –, the attempt of Russia to trigger an
earthquake in the St. Andreas fault with the Ukraine based (so-called)
Woodpecker devices (long range micro-wave transmitters), that were fed

236

Edward Teller, Lowell Wood, Roderick Hyde: Global Warming and Ice Ages: Prospects for Physics-Based Modulation of Global Change, Edward Teller and Lowell Wood, Hoover Institution, Stanford University, prepared for invited presentation at the International Seminar On Planetary Emergencies, Erice, Italy, August 20-23, 1997; also "The Planet Needs a Sunscreen," Wall Street Journal, 10-17-97.
237

Amy Worthington: Aerosol and Electromagnetic Weapons in the Age of Nuclear War. Global Research | June 1, 2004
238

power hour, national broadcast show, online at
http://www.youtube.com/watch?v=rS3mVg7GlGl Archived part1, part2, part3

with electricity by the Chernobyl power stations. According to Griffith, the attack was staved of with the help of Israel, thus causing what is known as the Chernobyl accident. Griffith sees the US being behind other countries in the development of these weapons as well as of possible defense systems. Against this background he describes the development of chemtrail-programs as a necessary defense system developed by the CIA/NSA intelligence community. The CIA, that had been operating a major aircraft fleet for drug trade to finance their unofficial activities i.e. black ops, must have been running out of spraying capacities and tried to involve the Navy. Admiral Jeremia Border, Chef of US-Navy Operations, refused to join into the program and officially committed suicide by shooting himself twice into the chest. Since then the navy became part of the referred Project Cloverleaf. To explain the role of aerosols Griffith referred to a paper by Matthew Daggett with the title "Atmospheric sensitivity invalidation study of the variable terrain radio parabolic equation model", describing a 3D battlefield radar monitoring system that could be operated from a ship 400 miles off the shore by using barium-salts as an reflective aerosol. Griffith also mentioned DARPA and other agencies as possibly joining in to make use of the aerosol spraying for different purposes.

On the next layer one might discover the interconnection between the civil and company-based research done with HAARP, ICECAT and similar microwave transmitting devices and aerosol spraying – assuming that this is the direction Griffith should have been pointing to.

> According to University of Ottawa Professor Michael
> Chossudovsky, the military's High-frequency Active Auroral
> Research Program (HAARP), operating in Alaska as part of the
> Strategic Defense Initiative, is a powerful tool for weather and
> climate modification[239]. Operated jointly by the U.S. Navy and

Air Force, HAARP antennas bombard and heat the ionosphere, causing electromagnetic frequencies to bounce back to earth, penetrating everything living and dead[240].

HAARP transmissions make holes in the ozone[241], creating yet another hobgoblin. HAARP inventor Bernard Eastlund described in his original patent how antenna energy could interact with plumes of atmospheric particles, used as a lens or focusing device, to modify weather[242]. HAARP is capable of triggering floods, droughts and hurricanes, much to the chagrin of both the European Parliament and the Russian Duma[243].

HAARP also generates sweeping pulses through the ULF/ELF range[244]. In 2000, independent researchers monitored HAARP

239

"Washington's New World Order Weapons Have the Ability to Trigger Climate Change," Center for Research on Globalization, Professor Michael Chossudovsky, University of Ottawa, January 2001.
240

"HAARP: Vandalism in the Sky?" Nick Begich and Jeane Manning, Nexus Magazine, December 1995.
241

Dr. Castle presents information on how HAARP punches massive holes in the open-air column ozone and how the Air Force then uses toxic chemicals to "patch" the holes it has created: Dr. Castle says: "Welsbach seeding and ozone hole remediation sciences utilize chemistries that are toxic to humans and the environment."
242

"HAARP: Vandalism in the Sky?" Begich and Manning; Researcher David Yarrow is quoted as saying that Earth's axial spin means that HAARP bursts are like a microwave knife producing a "long tear--an incision" in the multi-layer membrane of ionospheres that shield the Earth's surface from intense solar radiation.
243

U.S. HAARP Weapon Development Concerns Russian Duma, Interfax News Agency, 8-10-02.

transmissions of 14 hertz. They found that when these signals were broadcast at high output levels, wind speeds topped 70 miles per hour. They watched as these same transmissions dispersed a huge weather front approaching the west coast from California to British Columbia. Although precipitation had been originally forecast, the front was seen shredding apart on satellite photos and rain did not materialize[245]. The hobgoblin drought can be an enriching and empowering tool for certain corporate and governing entities.

HAARP is not only capable of destabilizing agricultural and ecological systems anywhere on the planet, but its effects can target select regions to affect human physical, mental and emotional responses during non-lethal warfare projects[246]. HAARP frequencies beamed at specific targets can generate catastrophic earthquakes, exactly like the quake last December, which killed thousands of people in Iran, a nemesis nation according to the Bush administration. [247]

244

HAARP Update, Elfrad Group, http://elfrad.org/2000/Haarp2.htm 6-27-00.
245

"14 Hertz Signal Suppresses Rainfall, Induces Violent Winds," 10-25-00, Newshawk Inc.; "When the Army Owns the Weather-Chemtrails and HAARP," Bob Fitrakis, 2-13-02: In this article HAARP inventor Bernard Eastlund is quoted on how HAARP can affect the weather: "Significant experiments could be performed. The HAARP antenna as it is now configured modulates the auroral electrojet to induce ELF waves and thus could have an effect on the zonal winds."
246

Angels Don't Play This HAARP, Begich and Manning, op. cit.
247

Entire passage: Amy Worthington: Aerosol and Electromagnetic Weapons in the Age of Nuclear War. Global Research | June 1, 2004

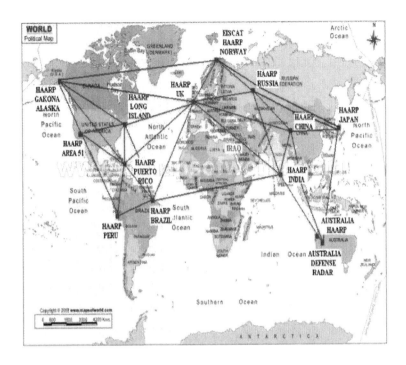

HAARP-Similar devices distributed around the globe.

Slowly coming to the core of it, it makes sense to have a second look to the very beginning of things. Project Paperclip was not peaceful at all. The transfer of German scientist led to the development of nuclear weapons, chemical weapons, biological weapons, and methods of mind control. All of them were more or less secretly tested on civilians and army stuff. The most devastating development was the conversion of fluorine waste from the aluminum production into a supplement in drinking water and toothpaste in the 60s. This technique of mind control originally was developed by IG-Farben as a method to silence occupied territories, concentration camps and prisoners of war camps by poisoning the habitants with fluor-compounds via the drinking water, making them will-less and dull. About the same time the industry started to distribute jet fuel with fluorine-based additives leading to global dimming and to major

351

damage within nature by acid rains and – following the suggestions of IG Farben – to damage of a unknown extend to the people's minds.

It is interesting to know that IG Farben was financed and "inspired" by the same groups who were pushing the eugenic agenda in the US during the 30s, leading to thousands and thousands of forced sterilizations. IG Farben later created and produced Cyclon B, and there is a direct economic connection between IG Farben, DOW Chemicals and Monsanto, responsible for the production and the spraying of *Agent Orange* in Vietnam.

It is very hard to say how far the influence of groups associated to the eugenic agenda reaches today. Both Rockefeller and Bill Gates with their empire of charities openly avow as acting in this spirit, as well as characters like Henry Kissinger who targeted the depopulation of 3rd world countries as a main interest of US-foreign policy[248].

Still, even if these elements can be found in US-politics, it is hard to say when and by whom the properties of barium-strontium-titanate or other aerosols could be intentionally abused to harm people by applying it as a weather or earthquake weapon, or as an agent for mind control.

8. Project "Cloverleaf"

8.1. Military purpose

In chapter 10 we could follow up the development up to the invention of

---

248

NATIONAL SECURITY COUNCIL, WASHINGTON, D.C. 20506 April 24, 1974 National Security Study Memorandum 200.

the barium-method by Jim Phelps in the year 1996. From 1996 to 1998 there apparently were a few experimental projects conducted by the CIA utilizing Barium. Since 1998 the entire territory of the United States is reported to have become subject to aerosol spraying. For the rest of the world there is no reliable information which country joined the program at what time. Within the NATO Cloverleaf is associated with the "Partnership for Peace". This partnership includes non-NATO-countries like Croatia, South Africa and Switzerland. China does not take part. For the southern hemisphere it is associated with the Antarctica treaty.

We could find one anonymous posting that maybe reveals the military purpose of the project, titled: Project Cloverleaf — The Science Behind it[249]

It involves the combination of chemtrails for creating an atmosphere that will support electromagnetic waves, ground-based, electromagnetic field oscillators called gyrotrons, and ionospheric heaters.

Particulates make directed energy weapons work better. It has to do with "steady state" and particle density for plasma beam propagation. They spray barium powders and let it photo-ionize from the ultraviolet light of the sun. Then, they make an aluminum-plasma generated by "zapping" the metal cations that are in the spray with either electromagnetics from HAARP, the gyrotron system on the ground [Ground Wave Emergency Network], or space-based lasers. The barium makes the aluminum-plasma more particulate dense. This means they can make denser plasma than they normally could from just ionizing the atmosphere or the air.

249

disclosure-tv-blog, online http://www.disclose.tv/forum/project-cloverleaf-chemtrails-and-their-purpose-t72795.html#ixzz2HmY3MiGL, Jan. 12th, 2013.

353

More density [more particles] means that these particles, which are colliding into each other will become more charged because there are more of them present to collide. What are they ultimately trying to do up there — is create charged-particle, plasma beam weapons. Chemtrails are the medium – GWEN pulse radars, the various HAARPs, and space-based lasers are the method, or more simply: Chemtrails are the medium — directed energy is the method. Spray and Zap.

This system appears to be in Russia, Canada, the United States, and all of Europe. Exotic weapons can be mobile, stationary, land-based, aerial, or satellite. It is an offensive and defensive system against EM attacks and missiles.

It uses ionospheric particle shells as defense mechanisms [like a bug-zapper shell] against missiles and EM attacks. That means they spray and then pump up the spray with electromagnetics. When these shells are created using the oscillating, electromagnetic, gyrotron stations, it "excludes" and displaces the background magnetic field. These shells can be layered one above another in a canopy fashion for extra protection from missiles.

The chemtrail sprays have various elements in them like carbon, which can used to absorb microwaves. Some of these sprays have metal flakes in them that make aerial craft invisible to radar. Spoofer sprays. Sprays like these can be used to create colorful, magnetized plasmas to cloak fighter jets. There are satellite weapons involved. Activists are using meters and are getting readings of microwaves, x-rays, and some other kind of emission that they are not sure of, maybe a low-intensity laser.

They are also photographing gas plasma generation due to the heating of chemtrails by electromagnetics. The technical names for vertical and horizontal plasma columns are columnar focal lenses and horizontal drift plasma antennas. Various sizes of gas plasma orbs are associated with this technology. These orbs can be used as transmitters and receivers because they have great, refractory and optical properties.

They also are capable of transmitting digital or analog sound.

Barium, in fact, is very refractive — more refractive than glass.

What does that mean? Our country has a history of experimenting on its citizens. We are talking about satellite charged-particle frequency weapons attacking a person 24 hours a day. Psychotronic weapons are considered weapons of mass destruction by the U.N. HAARPs can create earthquakes[250]and can also x-ray the earth to find underground military bases, gold, or oil reserves. These ionospheric heaters can also operate as an over-the-horizon or under-the-ocean communications system. This system can control the weather or create disasters.

Taken together with the aurora keyhole through-your-roof satellite surveillance system, Echelon electronic computer/phone sweeps, plasma-cloaked DOD Drug War helicopters and stealths, implants, and cameras on the street, it constitutes one, big global and space control grid. These weapons involve beams. Two beams overlapped will couple into a particle-ion beam that will bounce off of a remote target and send a holographic image back to the satellite for remote spying operations.

When you cross two strong beams, you can supposedly create scalar energies.

These energies can be used as untraceable weapons for nuclear size

250

Compare: S. S. De1, B. K. De, B. Bandyopadhyay, S. Paul, D. K. Haldar, A. Bhowmick, S. Barui, and R. Ali: Natural Hazards and Earth System Sciences. Effects on atmospherics at 6 kHz and 9 kHz recorded at Tripura during the India-Pakistan Border earthquake. Nat. Hazards Earth Syst. Sci., 10, 843–855, 2010.

explosions or for defense. These crossed-energies can be used to cause a person's physical electrical system to fail or with a lower frequency, administer a kind of remote electro-shock. Visualize touching a positive and negative electric cable to each other on top of your head. Scalar energies can be utilized in hand-held military guns and on tanks. They can dud-out electronics or cause large, electrical blackouts. Scalar energies are practically impossible to shield against. You need lead, ceramics, and a deep underground facility to not be affected by these weapons. Or, you need to be up and above the field of battle.

8.2. Involvement of civil airlines

A matter that is heavily discussed is the possible involvement of civil airlines. There were two anonymous propositions to this topic. The first interesting one was a statement published on a radio show coming from someone who declared he was an airplane mechanic:

> For reasons you will understand as you read this I cannot divulge my identity. I am an aircraft mechanic for a major airline. I work at one of our maintenance bases located at a large airport. I have discovered some information that I think you will find important. First I should tell you something about the "pecking order" among mechanics. It is important to my story and to the cause to which you have dedicated yourself.
> Mechanics want to work on three things. The avionics, the engines, or the flight controls. The mechanics that work on these systems are considered at the top of the "pecking order". Next come the mechanics that work on the hydraulics and air conditioning systems. Then come the ones who work on the galley and other

non-essential systems. But at the very bottom of the list are the mechanics that work on the waste disposal systems. No mechanic wants to work on the pumps, tanks, and pipes that are used to store the waste from the lavatories.

But at every airport where I have worked there are always 2 or 3 mechanics that volunteer to work on the lavatory systems. The other mechanics are happy to let them do it. Because of this you will have only 2 or 3 mechanics that work on these systems at any one airport. No one pays much attention to these guys and no mechanic socializes with another mechanic who only works on the waste systems. In fact I had never thought much about this situation until last month.

Like most airlines we have reciprocal agreements with the other airlines that fly into this airport. If they have a problem with a plane one of our mechanics will take care of it. Likewise if one of our planes has a problem at an airport where the other airline has a maintenance base, they will fix our plane.

One day last month I was called out from our base to work on a plane for another airline. When I got the call the dispatcher did not know what the problem was. When I got to the plane I found out that the problem was in waste disposal system. There was nothing for me to do but to crawl in and fix the problem. When I got into the bay I realized that something was not right. There were more tanks, pumps, and pipes then should have been there. At first I assumed that the system had been changed. It had been 10 years since I had worked on one. As I tried to find the problem I quickly realized the extra piping and tanks were not connected to the waste disposal system. I had just discovered this when another mechanic from my company showed up. It was one of the mechanics who usually works on these systems. I happily turned the job over to him. As I was leaving I asked him about the extra equipment. He told me to "worry about my end of the plane and let him worry about his!"

The next day I was on the company computer to look up a wiring schematic. While I was there I decided to look up the extra equipment I had found. To my amazement the manuals did not show any of the extra equipment I had seen with my own eyes the day before. I even tied in to the manufacturer files and still found nothing. Now I was really determined to find out what that equipment did. The next week we had three of our planes in our main hanger for periodic inspection. There are mechanics crawling all over a plane during these inspections. I had just finished my shift and I decided to have a look at the waste system on one of our planes. With all the mechanics around I figured that no one would notice an extra one on the plane. Sure enough, the plane I choose had the extra equipment!

I began to trace the system of pipes, pumps, and tanks. I found what appeared to be the control unit for the system. It was a standard looking avionics control box but it had no markings of any kind. I could trace the control wires from the box to the pumps and valves but there were no control circuits coming into the unit. The only wires coming into the unit was a power connection to the aircraft's main power bus.

The system had 1 large and 2 smaller tanks. It was hard to tell in the cramped compartment but it looked like the large tank could hold 50 gallons. The tanks were connected to a fill and drain valve that passed through the fuselage just behind the drain valve for the waste system. When I had a chance to look for this connection under the plane I found it cunningly hidden behind a panel under the panel used to access the waste drain.

I began to trace the piping from the pumps. These pipes lead to a network of small pipes that ended in the trailing edges of the wings and horizontal stabilizers. If you look closely at the wings of a large airplane you will see a set of wires, about the size of your finger, extending from the trailing edge of the wing surfaces. These are the static discharge wicks. They are used to dissipate the static electric charge that builds up on a plane in flight. I discovered that the pipes from this mystery system lead to every 1 out of 3 of these static discharge wicks. These wicks had been "hollowed out" to allow whatever flows through these pipes to be discharged through these fake wicks.

It was while I was on the wing that one of the managers spotted me. He ordered me out of the hanger telling me that my shift was over and I had not been authorized any overtime.

The next couple of days were very busy and I had no time to continue my investigation. Late one afternoon, two days after my discovery, I was called to replace an engine temperature sensor on a plane due to take off in two hours. I finished the job and turned in the paperwork.

About 30 minutes later I was paged to see the General Manager. When I went in his office I found that our union rep and two others who I did not know were waiting on me. He told me that a serious problem had been discovered. He said that I was being written up and suspended for turning in false paperwork. He handed me a disciplinary form stating that I had turned in false paperwork on the engine temperature sensor I had installed a few hours before. I was floored and began to protest. I told them that this was ridiculous and that I had done this work. The union rep spoke up then and recommended that we take a look at the plane and see if we could straighten it all out. It was at this time that I asked who the other two men were. The GM told me that they were airline safety inspectors but would not give me their name.

We proceeded to the plane, which should have been in the air but was parked on our maintenance ramp. We opened the engine cowling and the union rep pulled the sensor. He checked the serial number and told everyone that it was the old instrument. We then went to the parts bay and went back into the racks. The union rep checked my report and pulled from the rack a sealed box. He opened the box and pulled out the engine temperature sensor with the serial number of the one I had installed. I was told that I was suspended for a week without pay and to leave immediately.

I sat at home the first day of my suspension wondering what the hell had happened to me. That evening I received a phone call. The voice told me "Now you know what happens to mechanics who poke around in things they shouldn't. The next time you start working on systems that are no concern of yours you will lose your job! As it is I'm feeling generous, I believe that you'll be able to go back to work soon" CLICK. Again I had to pick myself from off the floor. I made the connection that what had happened was directly connected to my tracing the mysterious piping. The next morning the General Manager called me. He said that due to my past excellent employment record that the suspension had been reduced to one day and that I should report back to work immediately. The only thing I could think of was what are they trying to hide and who are THEY!

That day at work went by as if nothing had happened. None of the other mechanics mentioned the suspension and my union rep told me not to talk about it. That night I logged onto the Internet to try to find some answers. I don't remember now how I got there but I came across your site. That's when it all came together. But the next morning at work I found a note inside my locked locker. It said, "Curiosity killed the cat. Don't be looking at Internet sites that are no concern of yours."

Well that's it. THEY are watching me.

Well you already know what they are doing. I don't know what they are spraying but I can tell you how they are doing it. I figure they are using the "honey trucks". These are the trucks that empty the waste from the lavatory waste tanks. The airports usually contract out this job and nobody goes near these trucks. Who wants to stand next a truck full of sh--. While these guys are emptying the waste tanks they are filling the tanks of the spray system. They know the planes flight path so they probably program the control unit to start spraying some amount of time after the plane reaches a certain altitude. The spray nozzles in the fake static wicks are so small that no one in the plane would see a thing. (Signed:) God help us all, A concerned citizen.[251]

As a response to that interview someone sent an anonymous email introducing himself as a director of an airline.

I read email you received from the anon. mechanic and felt compelled to respond to it. I, too, work for an airline, though I work in upper management levels. I will not say which airline, what city I am located, nor what office I work for, for obvious reasons. I wish I could document everything I am about to relate to you, but to do so is next to impossible and would result in possible physical harm to me.

The email from the anonymous mechanic rings true. Airline companies in America have been participating in something called **Project Cloverleaf** for a few years now. The earliest date anyone remembers being briefed on it is 1998. I was briefed on it in 1999. The few airline employees who were briefed on Project Cloverleaf were all made to undergo background checks, and before we were

---

251

Radio-INTERVIEW (Live on Coast-to-Coast radio, May 17, 2003)

briefed on it we were made to sign non-disclosure agreements, which basically state that if we tell anyone what we know we could be imprisoned.

About twenty employees in our office were briefed along with my by two officials from some government agency. They didn't tell us which one. **They told us that the government was going to pay our airline, along with others, to release special chemicals from commercial aircraft.** When asked what the chemicals were and why we were going to spray them, they told us that information was given on a need-to-know basis and we weren't cleared for it. They then went on to state that the chemicals were harmless, but the program was of such importance that it needed to be done at all costs. When we asked them why didn't they just rig military aircraft to spray these chemicals, they stated that **there weren't enough military aircraft available to release chemicals on such a large basis as needs to be done.** That's why Project Cloverleaf was initiated, to allow commercial airlines to assist in releasing these chemicals into the atmosphere. Then someone asked why all the secrecy was needed. The government reps then stated that if the general public knew that the aircraft they were flying on were releasing chemicals into the air, environmentalist groups would raise hell and demand the spraying stop. Someone asked one of the G-men then if the chemicals are harmless, why not tell the public what the chemicals are and why we are spraying them? He seemed perturbed at this question and **told us in a tone of authority that the public doesn't need to know what's going on,** but that this program is in their best interests. He also stated that we should not tell anyone, nor ask any more questions about it. With that, the briefing was over.

All documents in our office pertaining to Project Cloverleaf are kept in locked safes. Nobody is allowed to take these documents out of the office. Very few employees are allowed access to these documents, and they remain tight-lipped about what the documents say.

Mr. Carnicom, I am no fool. I know there's something going on. And frankly, I am scared. I feel a high level of guilt that I have been aware of this kind of operation but unable to tell anyone. It's been eating away at me, knowing that the company I work for may be poisoning the American people. I hope this letter will open some eyes to what's happening.

Again, I wish I could give you documented information, but you have to understand why I must remain totally anonymous. Thank you.

8.3. Organizations involved

During the work of several civil right organizations that have been collecting data about aerosol spraying it turned out that the websites of these organization were frequently monitored by a number of organizations and companies. The list of these companies who could be identified by their IP addresses could reveal who is actually involved in operation cloverleaf. The list contained:

Lockheed Martin (aviation/space defense contractor); **Raytheon** (Defense Contractor, visits immediately after posting HAARP implications); **Boeing Aircraft Company** (100 visits +.); **Honeywell** (U.S. Defense Contractor); **Merck** (Pharmaceutical Products and Health Research); **TRW** (U.S. Defense Contractor); **Monsanto** (Chemical, Pesticide, & Pharmaceutical products); **Allied Signal Corporation** (chemical/aerospace/energy); **Kaiser**

Permanente health org.; **US Environmental Protection Agency** (refuses to investigate or accept evidence samples for analysis); **US Dept. of Treasury**; **US General Accounting Office** (investigative arm of Congress: performs audits/evaluations of Gov't activities); **US Naval Criminal Investigative Service** (worldwide org. tasked with criminal investigations & counterintelligence for Dept. of Navy; manages its security programs); **Office of Secretary of Defense** (Office of William S. Cohen, he used to work as CEO of military contractor Northrop Grumman); **FEMA** (Federal Emergency Management Agency: US emergency management program of mitigation, preparedness, response & recovery).

There is one important address that is not on that list: Evergreen International Airlines, the company that is suspected to run the tanker fleets who cover most of the spraying activities.

Looking at the activities of all these companies and agencies would be a task that would keep Interpol busy for a few years. In the frame of this study we will reduce it to only two companies. The choice for the first one was not motivated by pre-knowledge, apart from the known fact that Raytheon owns the HAARP device in Alaska.

The companies history as described on their own website reads like this:

Ninety years ago, a great American success story began: A few passionate visionaries created a high-tech venture in the shadow of a great university and developed a breakthrough product that transformed a nation.

One of the earliest technology start-ups, Raytheon was established in Cambridge, Mass., home of the Massachusetts Institute of Technology, on July 7, 1922 as the American

Appliance Company.

The company's founders were Vannevar Bush, who would become dean of MIT's School of Engineering; Laurence Marshall, an engineer; and Charles G. Smith, a scientist who had done work on the electrical properties of gases.

Their revolutionary innovation was the S gas rectifier tube, a device that eliminated one of the cumbersome expensive batteries that previously powered home radios.

The tube transformed the radio into an affordable "must-have" appliance that could be plugged into a wall socket, turning radio into a true mass medium that brought the world into America's living rooms.

Raytheon quickly moved to the forefront of innovation in the electronics industry. During World War II, Raytheon employees contributed to the war effort. They supplied 80 percent of the magnetron tubes used in U.S. and British radars and developed parts for the crucial proximity fuse in antiaircraft shells, among other equipment.

After the war Raytheon began offering civilian products, the microwave being among the most famous. Raytheon engineer Percy Spencer discovered microwave cooking when, as he stood in front of an active magnetron, a candy bar in his pocket began to melt. Intrigued, he sent out for popcorn kernels – and they began to pop. With that, a new appliance was soon on its way.

In the decades that followed, Raytheon employees would build on the company's reputation for technology and innovation leadership. Today it stands as a global technology leader specializing in defense, homeland security and other government markets.

Raytheon met urgent production needs for magnetron tubes used by Allied forces for radar defense, and produced the Sea Going (SG) microwave surface search radar that went on U.S. Navy ships. The SG provided vital situational awareness in the major battles in the Pacific and helped eliminate the submarine menace in the Battle of the Atlantic.

Raytheon Company, with 2011 sales of $25 billion and 71,000 employees worldwide, is a technology and innovation leader specializing in defense, homeland security and other government markets throughout the world. With a history of innovation spanning 90 years, Raytheon provides state-of-the-art electronics, mission systems integration and other capabilities in the areas of sensing; effects; and command, control, communications and intelligence systems, as well as a broad range of mission support services. With the hard work and dedication of tens of thousands of employees around the world, Raytheon is well equipped to meet the needs of its customers in more than 80 countries – today, tomorrow and well into the 21st century.

Raytheon owned its own aircraft manufacturers, Hawker and Beechcraft, which were fused to Hawker Beechcraft. Hawker Beechcraft served orders like this one[252]:

Hawker Beechcraft receives major aircraft order from Saudi Arabia Government Agency

---

252

United Arab Emirates: Wednesday, November 18 - 2009 at 08:32, PRESS RELEASE online January 2013 at http://www.ameinfo.com/216444.html

Hawker Beechcraft Corporation (HBC) today announced the sale and delivery of 12 aircraft to the Saudi Arabia Presidency of Meteorology and Environment (PME).

Aircraft deliveries have taken place throughout the past year and are expected to conclude by the end of the year when the remaining two aircraft are delivered.

"This order is an example of the strength and versatility of our broad aircraft lineup for this region," said Bill Boisture, HBC Chairman and CEO.

"There are numerous HBC products operating in the Middle East, many in special mission roles such as that of the PME. Our aircraft offer the performance capabilities and greatest flexibility needed for the PME operations."

The order consists of one Hawker 900XP, two Hawker 400XP, one King Air 350, two King Air B200GT and six King Air C90GTi aircraft.

The aircraft will be used to support the various roles of the Saudi Arabia PME, which includes vital meteorological activities such as weather forecasting and modeling, and environmental issues including air quality assessment and protection.

The new aircraft special mission instruments are being engineered and modified by Weather Modification, Inc. and the Fargo Jet Center, both located in Fargo, N.D. The maintenance service of the PME aircraft will be managed by HBC Authorized Service Center Arabian Aircraft Services Co. Ltd, also known as ARABASCO.

Taking away the verbal fog: Raytheon sold the equipment for "vital meteorological activities" manufactured by a company called "Weather Modification Inc." to the Saudi Arabia Presidency of Meteorology and Environment.

Luckily, things in Saudi Arabia are not as classified as things in the US and Europe and we don't need a security clearance before we are allowed to know the full story, i.e. that

Hawkers undergo modification for cloud seeding missions to replenish aquifers in Saudi Arabia

Weather Modification, Inc. (WMI) has taken delivery of five new Hawker Beechcraft aircraft at their facility in Fargo, US. Two King Air 200GTs, two Hawker 400XPs and one Hawker 900XP were test flown and accepted by WMI and will be used for air quality monitoring, atmospheric research and cloud seeding missions in Saudi Arabia.

With 10 WMI turboprop aircraft currently in Saudi Arabia, WMI began this mission in the winter of 2006 in an effort to replenish the region's underground aquifers and increase rainfall in the Kingdom.

"This marks a significant step of a major mission for us," says WMI president Pat Sweeney. "We'll provide the Kingdom of Saudi Arabia with the tools they need to perform the most advanced cloud seeding and atmospheric research projects in the world, with the goal of increasing rainfall in a country that needs it."

Before flying overseas to begin the mission, WMI will work with Fargo Jet Center (FJC) to modify and equip the planes with cloud seeding equipment and atmospheric research instruments. FJC is an aircraft maintenance and avionics repair station and a designated Hawker Beechcraft Service Center. As of this past year, FJC has completed more than 30 special mission aircraft conversions.

"It is a testament to our special mission team and the processes they have in place," says Sweeney. "It is certainly not an easy

368

process, but we have an incredibly talented team retro-fitting these aircraft to make them mission-ready for projects around the world."

The aircraft modification process has already begun to make the aircraft mission-ready by April this year. Without permanent surface water, agriculture in Saudi Arabia is dependent on irrigation from pumped groundwater. Public and industrial water-needs are currently met by expensive desalination plants. According to a United Nations Environmental Program Report, the present rate of groundwater withdrawal from the region threatens the Saudi aquifers, and with increased development and population growth, groundwater contamination becomes an additional concern.

"The situation isn't dire in Saudi Arabia, but it certainly is serious and can't be ignored," adds Sweeney. "There are limits to the capacities of the desalination plants and water pipelines the country has in place."

Atmospheric water in the form of precipitation is one of the primary sources of fresh water in the world. However, a large amount of water present in clouds is never trans-formed into precipitation on the ground prompting scientists and engineers to explore augmenting water supplies through cloud seeding. The ability to enhance precipitation through cloud seeding is highly dependent on the properties of the clouds, aerosols and the atmospheric environment.

This marks the third year of research and cloud seeding operations conducted by WMI in Saudi Arabia. Officials estimate the research to take another three to five years to collect the necessary data and conduct the exploratory seeding trials.

In total, WMI will provide 12 new aircraft, including pilots and crew, which will focus on the entire country of Saudi Arabia.

WMI expects all 12 to be operational by March 2010.

From May 2001 - April 2006, Raytheon Aircraft Company involved with (Defense & Space industry), made repairs and major modifications to the Hawker European Aircraft Fleet. This was based at Hawarden Airport, Chester.[253] Unfortunately it is not known what type of modification has been done. But the interest in the Aerosol topic seems to have occupied more minds at Raytheon.

The company developed the Raytheon's Aerosol Polarimetry Sensor, a satellite based system to monitor aerosols. Unfortunately the launching of the satellite by NASA failed March 2011.

It might be mentioned that this was the second failure of a mission to bring aerosol measurement into space. The first attempt ended with the Columbia disaster 2003, that had special aerosol cameras on board as well as the high energy laser weapons to be tested for the Israeli rocket defense system.

Monitoring Raytheon activities in Norway, Raytheon produced most of the radar systems for the Norwegian army, is into weather forecast and built the flight control at the main Norwegian airport in Oslo Gardermoen.

At first sight this does not look like being interconnected. When one tries to find out who owns Raytheon one ends up with a long list of wall-street investment funds. It is not unlikely that there is a lot of Jewish money involved in these shares, which partly could explain the allied-like cooperation between the Israeli government and Raytheon, that even has

---

253

blog posting at http://www.facebook.com/notes/martin-theforce-oftruth/raytheon-aerosols-and-haarp/439271660718?comment_id=13550230&offset=0&total_comments=12

370

been publicly accused of cross-financing Israeli governmental duties.

On its main website Raytheon offers *"Security Solutions"* delivering *"Integrated Geospatial*[254] *Solutions"* to governments,

> For more than 30 years, Raytheon has been successfully developing solutions to support the full spectrum of geospatial operations for its global civil, defense and intelligence community customers.
>
> Scalable and Adaptive Solutions
>
> From stand-alone ground stations to comprehensive geospatial solutions for entire nations, Raytheon understands the speed at which the information technology environment evolves. Raytheon has the demonstrated experience to establish solutions with the flexibility to adapt and expand, supporting an organization's future growth and requirements. Raytheon is committed to delivering open solutions, actively seeking out and engaging industry partners to bring together innovative technologies that support a client's evolving requirements. Raytheon's experience in managing collaborative teams and technology integration provides clients with the best possible, cost effective outcome and removes the issue of a "Black-box" solution being deployed into their organization.
>
> Geospatial Information Superiority
>
> The Defense Geospatial Strategy 2010 outlines the mission for the Australian Defense Geo Domain as:

254

"Geospatial Technology, commonly known as geomatics, refers to technology used for visualization, measurement, and analysis of features or phenomena that occur on the earth."

"To provide relevant and trusted geospatial information and services that are easily accessible, secure and fit for purpose to enable operational effectiveness for Defense and to support Government and international partners."

Raytheon supports the ADF geospatial mission through a proven record of working with government and industry partners to deliver innovative solutions and capabilities.

Intelligence, When and Where you need It.

Driven by this mission, Raytheon is investing in technologies to achieve geospatial information superiority.

In this context, the website states the company is explicitly "proud of a successful long term cooperation with countries from the middle east". The sense for language triggers a few alerts when reading this description from Raytheons website. And this quality of language seems to be common to all things that deal with "Integrated Geospacial intelligence solutions"; like the big annual conferences to this topic, where Raytheon is listed as one of the main sponsors, and where the lists of participant reveal the possible "governmental" customers of the company – "governmental" or of "international organizations", whatever this might be.

Thinking conservative, this is about spying. This would explain the foggy language. But evaluating the patent list of technologies filed by Raytheon one also finds patent that sound like belonging to laser, microwave[255]- and laser induced scalar weapons[256], like described by the posting in chapter

255

U.S. Patent Number 7,498,549, U.S. Patent Number 7,490,538
256

U.S. Patent Number 7,346,091

10.1., that very easily can be targeted on individuals, like the microwave weapons used in the second Iraq war that create the feeling of burning by heating the surface of the skin.

Often in discussions it is mentioned that the star wars program was buried because the laser application from outer space effectively did not reach the surface of the earth and thus has been given up. Even if the picture on the right, taken from a video showing kilometer long, straight cuts in the ice of the Antarctica, is correctly associated wit Russian laser technology, not with American, this picture clearly shows that this statement about failing laser technologies is wrong. And maybe it also shows, that some of the older goals of geo-engineering, like getting access to the natural resources at the pole caps, are still in place.

The general impression is that "project cloverleaf" conducts spraying under the flag of civil geo-engineering and stratospheric research, while it is offering advanced weapon system to governments. At the same time they serve internationalist groups with spy-ware marketed under the name "integrated geospacial intelligence solutions" that are capable of establishing a world-wide control by the intelligence community. Capable to spy on, apply mind control and eventually kill dissidents with directed energy weapons utilizing the same aerosols sold to the US-Government for its advanced star wars program.

Especially looking at the biochemical processes discovered with humans exposed to barium-strontium-titanate, their integration of the crystals into the sensitive places of the nervous system, where triggered by external field literally every information can be inserted into the body-communication, an intentional abuse of the geo-engineering substances like the set of the Morgellon related self-assembling nano-machines for advanced mind control is in the range of technical possibilities and could be regarded as the coming generation of methods that one day might be used by the intelligence community to establish total control over the population.

8.4. Evidence for the validity of some unconfirmed information

At this point it would be nice to have some smoking gun evidence for the overall concept.

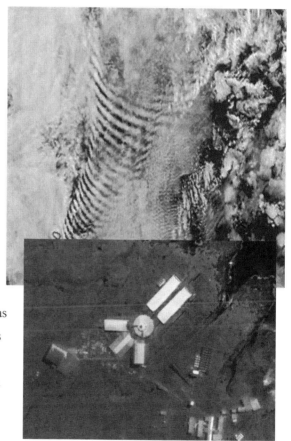

This picture has been taken from a satellite above Marion Island, an island belonging to South Africa, situated a few thousand Kilometer south-east of cape town. The time laps this image was taken from, shows west wind, the structure seen as a cloud pattern is stable, pointing with the tip to the north-east coast of Marion Island. So let's see what can be found there...

The Map of Marion Island shows a "Meteorological Station directly on the spot where the cloud structure derives from. The only natural cloud form that might resemble the satellite picture is the undulatus-cloud, that is generated when wind crosses a mountain and bounces up and down on its further travel. But this was west-wind, the direction of the structure was much more correlated with the geometry of the building of the meteorological station.

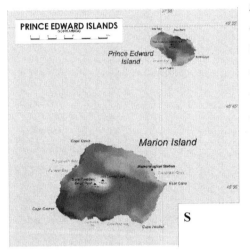

From this setup it is easy to calculate the frequency the antenna is transmitting. Assuming an electromagnetic signal, the average wavelength from cloud belt to cloud belt, measures to 7.123 km. This equals a frequency of 42 kHz, which is known to be the calculated resonance frequency of water, when looking at the H-O-H angle as a spring able to resonate. The frequency is known to reduce consumption in electrolysis, if the current is pulsed at this frequency. The value 42 kHz also appears in ultrasound cavitation as a central value.

People with some training on physics will wonder about the curvation of the wave/cloud fronts. If the effect would be directly caused by the emitted signal the clouds should be curved the other way round. Actually what is visible here is the effect of a time reversed replica wave caught by the Antenna System. So what we can see on this picture is a so called meteorological station ionizing i.e. creating plasma shields with LF radio-frequencies utilizing scalar wave technologies in obvious interaction with other stations of this kind, situated further north-east on this planet.

Now let us have a look at the official version:

> A TEN-year construction project on remote Marion Island, that tested the building team's endurance and logistical capability to the limit, culminates tonight in the inauguration of a R200 million, state-of-the-art research base.

> The base on this sub-Antarctic island will provide appropriate facilities for researchers producing the cutting-edge science that is helping South Africa fulfill its international obligations in terms of the Antarctic Treaty, and to punch above its weight in the geopolitical context of the vast and important Southern Ocean region, says one of the senior scientists involved.

> "Strategically, it's very important for us to be there (in the treaty system), and we have to be involved if we want to remain a member," says Professor Steven Chown, director of Stellenbosch University's Centre for Invasion Biology and a former chairman of the Prince Edward Islands management committee.

> "And it's also important to do world-class science, because your status in the (geopolitical) system depends on the quality of your work."[257]

257

http://saweatherobserver.blogspot.no/2011/03/new-marion-island-base-opens.html online May 29th 2013.

8.5. Dismantling the cover story

As the official reason for spraying – not with Saudi Arabia but with other countries – climate change is discussed as the big threat that needs to be faced. This scientific belief is an important part of the psychology driving the international geo-engineering agenda.

Among scientists it is an open secret that, if one needs to apply for research funding, it is very helpful to ad the phrase "under the aspect of climate change" to the title of whatever research project one wishes to conduct. This is a sad truth because much hope was invested in the announcement of the globalists to finally regard nature as something worthy.

With the idea that the main target of the overall concept is less constructive it makes sense to look at the myth again. The research to this chapter took about two days time, and is based mainly on established data from pre-climate-change-times and some basic understanding of cybernetics.

Some thing historical to start with: In the beginning of the 19th century the French physician Jean Baptist Joseph Fourier „discovered" the „Greenhouse effect". According to this theory our earth should be a pretty cold place. The thesis of Fourier is that the sunbeams pass relatively undisturbed through the atmosphere and heat up the Earth surface, which reflects them in the infrared scale. The heat radiation doesn't reach very far, because some particular gasses absorb it and keep the heat in the atmosphere. In the laboratory the English physicist could easily find out which gases were responsible for the effects: it was carbon dioxide and water vapor. This was the state of the art as discovered in the middle of the 19th century. Later also methane was added to the list. In 1955 the Austrian chemist Hans Suess suspected that the combustion of fossil fuels could have an effect on the climate. Since 1958 the CO_2-concentration in the atmosphere is measured regularly and indeed it rises continuously. During the oil crisis in the 70s this thesis grew popular after another British researcher had formulated a similar speculation.

At that time Margaret Thatcher had to fight on many fronts; against the national coal mining trade unions and against the OPEC cartel. Her alternative was nuclear power. Against this background she happily welcomed any argument. At the same time the hippie movement was happy about any good reason for their call „back to nature". Against the various lobby groups that earned and still earn on the oil market neither Thatcher nor the Hippies could advance and so the environmental improvements within the oil industry were just dwelling for quarter of a century in darkness. The brake through came 2006 with Al Gore's movie: „the inconvenient truth". Ever since a true hysteria has invaded the media, so that every scenario has to over score the previous in horror. The scientific institutes celebrate research funds in excess, used to give evidence to conclusions that are already known a priori: Climate change is man made! Except of additional money making by new taxes still this doesn't entail any extensive actions.

378

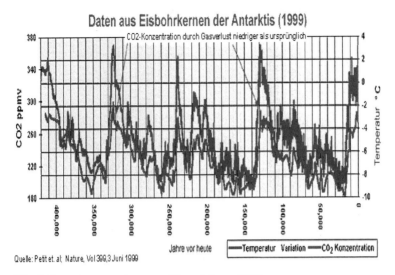

Daten aus Eisbohrkernen der Antarktis (1999)

Quelle: Petit et. al; Nature, Vol 399,3 Juni 1999

CO_2 follows temperature – with a delay of 800 years.

Fortunately there are people that see in every word of the leading authorities a scam. „The inconvenient truth" was followed by a movie worth seeing, called „The Great Climate Swindle" which scored downloading records. Core statement: The Global temperature follows the activity of the sunspots. The increased CO_2 follows this phenomenon 500 - 800 years later as a result of the delayed warming of the oceans, which can store less CO_2 when they have a higher water temperature.

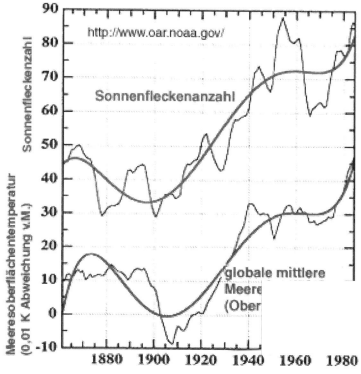

Correlation of sun activity and temperature

Cybernetics is the science of the complex and re-generative non-linear systems and their regulatory circuits: it is very helpful to understand the climate. The climate relies on outer influences as well as inner regulatory mechanisms. The significant outer influences are the sun and the general intensity of the cosmic radiation. The sun is sometimes very active, sometimes less active. The indicator for that is the circuit of the sunspot activities. An active sun protects the earth with its ionic winds from the cosmic radiation. But also the basic maintenance of the cosmic radiation varies according to the position of the earth in the milky way. In case of a strong radiation it comes to a strong clouding hence to the stronger ionization of the air in the higher atmosphere. It gets colder near to the ground.

All other factors are due to inner regulatory mechanisms. And there are many of them. You can group these inner regulatory mechanisms in two categories: stabilizing and destabilizing regulatory mechanisms. Here comes a list with the most important mechanisms:

If temperature rises, more water of the oceans evaporates, more clouding appears, more rain is falling on the continents, more cooling is taking place by evaporation, hence temperature decreases. By evaporating from soils and forests, this water can form clouds and rain a second and third time before the water is flowing back into the oceans. This is the first and most important stabilizing control circuit.

The second very important control circuit concerns Vegetation. A warmer climate favors the growth of light green plants in nature so that more light is reflected from the vegetation cover; it becomes colder. When it becomes colder then dark green plants dominates the vegetation so that more light is absorbed hence the temperature of the surface increases. This regulatory control circuit functions with a closed vegetation cover. If this circuit is overexcited by heat then it comes to desertification with the abrupt increasing of the surface temperature.

Other regulatory mechanisms are destabilizing, when it gets warmer the ice is melting on the poles so that more dark rocks and more ocean surface is exposed to the sun so that it becomes even warmer.

381

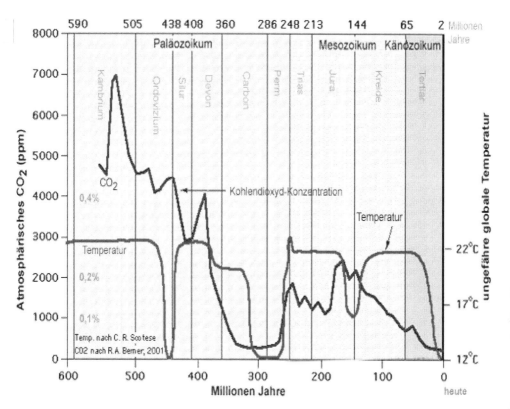

Non-correlation of CO_2 and Temperature over the ages. There are 2 stable points, and the climate is switching between the two independent of CO.

Firstly it is evident that the stabilizing regulatory mechanisms dominated the processes in the past otherwise the climate would have taken its journey to another stable point on the temperature scale long time ago. That is in the nature of each and every system: and in every self-organized and non-linear system exists a stable order. Occasionally a change in the order takes place implying the abrupt adjustment of its points of stability. During this change of order the system runs through a chaotic phase. For example the amount of stabilizing points between which the earth temperature was oscillating during its history are known: there are exactly two. The colder point lies at average temperature 12 degrees Celsius, the warmer one lies at 22 degrees. As we can see; we are now in a cold period. As we can also see in the diagram, the concentration of CO_2 looked upon during the geological era's has barely any influence on these circles.

Still there are countless possibilities to shake the system described above, so that the stabilizing points are moved by some degrees Celsius. It is possible to pollute the atmosphere with exhaust gasses, especially carbon black, which darkens the earth: Global cooling. Nevertheless it is always about a considerably small movement of the stable point, which is minor in comparison to the effect of the general radiation on the first rank and the sun activity on the second rank.

Indeed we can weaken the stabilizing regulatory mechanisms. There is a real danger in this. If we cultivate monocultures with dark leaves in warm areas or we reduce the humus concentration in the soil as the industrial agriculture is doing it, then the rainwater drains away and flows back as groundwater to the oceans instead of evaporating and forming rain again, cooling and watering the earth on its way. That could possibly cause an immense heating because we interrupted the stabilizing mechanism, which allows the destabilizing regular control circuits to take over and to dominate the process. Of course we can be so stupid and let whole areas of the planet become deserts.

Let us now express the whole situation in numbers: In the rainforests nearly 100% precipitation evaporates; one part already on the leaves, the rest is absorbed by the soil, stored and send back up through the roots. In the desert as well as on the fields after 40 years of agriculture, the concentration of humus in the soil is reduced so much that up to 90% of the water drains or flows off.

The measured warming of the earth – so to speak the earth warming that concerns us – is first of all the measured surface temperature on the continents. The most significant factor in this is the water balance. So if we should take care of anything then that would be the soil and the vegetation.

The second important one goes via the atmospheric tension: plants discharge atmospheric tension by discharging atmospheric and inner-earth longitudinal fields into scalar fields, and this discharge and harmonization between earth and sky is essential for the generation of clouds. So – if we should take care of anything then that would be the soil and the vegetation.

The official story seems to be a cover story, to force the trade of climate certificates, to justify land robbery by companies in the third world, and to push the geo-engineering agenda forward.

Actually, there is nothing good about it – we should drop the myth as fake.

8.6. Organizational patterns

Looking at RAYTHEON and even on this small scale at the Marion Island Meteorological Station, it becomes obvious that we seem to have some private entities on this planet that are powerful and well organized enough to world-wide orchestrate governmental institutions to push their own internationalist agenda. An agenda, which does not breath a spirit of transparency, does not promise democracy. Looking at the historic development of the eugenics, that has been morphing via genetics and fake environmentalism to transhumanism, one has to suspect that this agenda is still breathing the same spirit, is still being fed by the same financial entities, is still following the same goals as the fascism the world has experienced during the last century – just with improved technologies.

One of the best sources for people who want to deeply understand the character of operation cloverleaf is the book "Crosswalk" by Cara St.Louis-Farrelly, published as "Die Sonnendiebe" in the German translation. The mother of the American author of this book had been working as a technical editor for the top scientists that had been developing the geo-engineering technologies for the US-Navy, some of them still being remains of the operation paperclip. After being pensioned her mother was killed by a former US-soldier in a car accident on a crosswalk. The shady circumstances of this "accident" led Cara St.Louis-Farrelly to explore her mothers past, which involved also herself into an adventurous story, being threatened, facing attempted murder and the burning down of her house the day her book "Crosswalk" was finished.

Although her story is clearly fictionalized, or maybe because it is fictionalized, it delivers a beautiful insight into the minds of the people involved in this dark chapter of human history: the pilots, the defense contractors, the Pentagon, including the "white" and "black hats" inhabiting it, the politicians and lobbyist, all the way up to the private banking system and the families owning it, being organized in a mafia-like structure, giving orders from the top, making the profits, and seeking total control over the planet by utilizing the magnificent set of intelligence solutions offered by the companies owned and ruled by them.

The most interesting point about this book is that it reveals the Achilles Heel of this system. It is the compartmentalization of the organizational structure. To cite from the book:

> Primary rule of keeping everyone in the dark again. Compartmentalize everything. So few people had to really understand this operation for it to work. The employees handling packages here simply had to be well-paid and ignorant. They had to sign a confidentiality clause and if they were well-paid enough,

they kept their mouths shut. One hundred highly placed people who really knew what was going on and pulled all the separate strings could literally keep a hundred thousand people or more moving to their tune. And if those hundred thousand were moved relatively well and with some care, millions could be manipulated. It was, as Tim knew, such an erroneous understanding of how people think and operate to assume too many people would have to know what's up before terrible acts could be committed. It just didn't work that way. If people judged what the secret ops people would do based on what they themselves would do, then they had completely lost the plot. Pilots did not know dispatch did not know ground crew. Ground crew had no idea what aircraft were involved in what action. Pilots getting instructions after a job was completed might get those instructions from the other side of the world, via satellite. The guy on the other side of the world had no idea who he was talking to and why. People are trained to operate within their compartments, their specialties, and leave other people to their specialties. And if they found anything out they wanted to report, whom the hell were they going to tell?

Revealing the full concept behind the geo-engineering scenario to all the people involved would immediately make the entire setup fall apart. If already the knowledge of some details of the neighboring compartment is reason enough to assassinate people out of security reason, public awareness penetrating the system probably would cause the structure to stop working.

But what might that full concept be?

Thus let us connect the dots. There are a number of topics that are handled by state authorities with irrational pressure, close to hysteria.

- denial of the existence of chemtrails

- flu pandemics and the legal preparation of mandatory vaccinations.

- denial of the existence of the Morgellons disease

- the enforcement of the introduction of genetically modified crops against the will of the majority of the population.

- The refusal of the state authorities to remove the product Glyphosate from the markets, the world wide most used herbicide, that has been proven to suppress the body's ability to detox and is responsible for birth defects and spontaneous abortions[258].

- naked scanners at airports

- denial of damage done especially by microwave transmitters used for mobile phones and smart meters.

There are anonymous whistle-blowers within the pharmaceutical industry that state that flu vaccines are used to implant nano-chips to mark and monitor people. There are anonymous whistle-blowers in the US-military community that state that the newest generation of chips consist of one superconducting metal fiber coated with glass, forming a flexible glass fiber with a magnetizable core, that easily could be placed right in the tip of the needles delivered together with the vaccines unlike any other liquid

---

258

Anthony Samsel and Stephanie Seneff: Glyphosate's Suppression of Cytochrome P450 Enzymes and Amino Acid Biosynthesis by the Gut Microbiome: Pathways to Modern Diseases. *Entropy* 2013, *15*, 1416-1463; doi:10.3390/e15041416

medication where the needles come separate. In Europe a company based in Bulgaria arranges the production of these chips, production numbers cover the entire European population, which means someone plans to chip everyone – another anonymous whistle blown. It seems that the system is trying to implant two complementary chipping technologies to monitor individuals against the plasma-background created by chemtrails. Implanted chips via mandatory vaccinations and self-multiplying nano-bots also known as Morgellons who create an individual radio signature and live and grow on compounds found in genetically modified crops – and these Morgellons have been found in rain probes after heavy chemtrailing. Maybe the dependency on chemicals available in genetically modified crops is the reason why the Morgellon disease prospers in the United States, while in Europe there are only single cases found – maybe there is not enough genetic modified food in Europe. Both nano-chips and Morgellons are not personalized. It needs some effort to synchronize data to be able to say which person is identical with which radio-signature. This is where naked scanning might come into the game: programming the un-personalized chips. This is where mobile phones come into the game, where persons and signatures can be synchronized via detection of identical motion patterns. But this is only one side of the mobile topic. Microwave radiation has been developed as a weapon system, in the west mainly by Raytheon. But not only in the west. Transmission signals of mobiles are 10.000 times stronger than actually needed for terrestrial communication – this decision was made only out of intelligence reasons, to make it possible to listen to calls from space. This whistle-blower has a name: Barry Trower, former British spy who was responsible to monitor, analyze and evaluate the Russian microwave weapon program. He today openly speaks up against the fact that the same weapons he researched in the Russian context are applied against the civil population of his own country. This is about monitoring, this is about spying and this is about assassination. The typical symptoms of radiation crossfire-assassination are: bleeding from the nose, bleeding from the ears, bleeding from the anus, stroke or brain cancer, death. The procedure takes about 10 month, measurements of field strength at sleeping places of dissidents in Germany have shown values that exceeded measurement scales of commercial detectors for environmental medicine, the peak radiation was limited to the square meter at the head-end of the bed. This is not a whistle. Three persons out of the closer research environment of the Author Harald Kautz-Vella suffered from this treatment, one is dead by now, two stepped back from their work and live, one is currently at the state bleeding from the anus – the one who opened his flat to be measured by Harald Kautz-Vella. M. Purdey died of Brain cancer 10 month after he published his more than valuable work about the impact of piezo-electric nano-crystals on mammals and humans.

This is all according to first and second hand information we came across during the research for this paper. Most of the information was anonymous because the people in charge of this information were afraid to be assassinated if they spoke out in public. This far it has come.

Two days after the second publication of this paper – right after the lecture in Nuremberg – two papers showed up in public that basically verify all this as being true – or as being part of a truth that goes far beyond: a internal NASA PowerPoint from the year 2001[259], that basically confirms all these actions taken by governments against their own populations as being planned to be conducted by the intelligence community. The document covers the use of nano-bots for surveillance, the application of microwave-weapons marketed as civil technologies, up to the poisoning of the lungs of all civilians with nano-explosives that can be ignited by

---

259

Dennis M. Bushnell: The Future is Now! Future Strategic Issus/Future Warfare (Circa 2025). NASA PowerPoint, reported to be from NASAs official Website, however the paper is removed by now.

remote control. With a second finding, an original CIA document[260] from the year 1979, that was found forgotten in a copy machine that was sold second hand, this mindset reveals itself as plane fascism, projecting the ruler ship of a few above the stupid "sheep", which need to be controlled, kept stupid and are allowed to be assassinated if wanted. The foreword of this paper directly names and honors the father of the concept of controlling politics via the monetary system as Mayer Amschel Rothschild.

What can be done with this technology in combat when the big microwave transmitters stationed on ships and in space come into the game can be estimated when one thinks of the mass dying of bats, birds, fish and whales observed in the years since 2001 – that partly have been reported to the public as a side effect of new years eve fireworks.

This very much looks like Hitlers dream scenario becoming true, financed and driven by the same entities who drove the eugenic agenda in the US in the 30s, who drove the German fascism and who later transferred manpower and funding from the eugenic institutes in Germany into the genetic industry on one hand, and into the environmentalist around the Club of Rome on the other hand, who today drive the depopulation of the third world, drive the climate change myth and call for geo-engineering, drive transhumanism.

It is no fun falling under eugenics. Killing the bees and poisoning the crops will make us dependent on genetic modified crops patented by Monsanto, aluminum-resistant since 1974. Microwave radiation from a mobile in a front pocket of the trousers, no calls, only positioning signal,

---

260

Silent Weapons for Quit Wars. An introduction Programming Manual. Operations Research Technical Manual TW-SW7905.1. This paper was found 1976 left inside a second hand IBM Copy-Machine that was sold for extracting spare parts.

390

reduces
testosteron
e by 75%
and makes
50% of
the sperms
infertile.
Dietrich
Klinghardt
could
prove the
synergistic

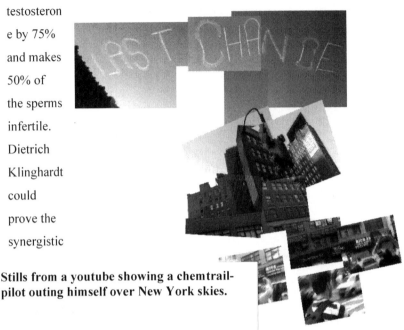

Stills from a youtube showing a chemtrail-pilot outing himself over New York skies.

toxicity of mercury and
mobile radiation, causing autism when a fetus is exposed in the 6th to 8th
week of pregnancy of his mother. And autism is a growing problem. The
plain statistics point to the fact that by 2024 100% of the boys born will be
autistic, and by 2036% 100% of the newborn girls. This is only the
beginning. Going back to the military experiments one can find
microwaved mice. It took three generations to complete infertility.

Knowing that during the past swine flue hysteria state employees in
Germany got mercury free vaccination unlike the rest of the population,
and that the school where the children of the politicians in Berlin go to
was just shielded against mobile radiation at costs of 500.000 Euro, hint to
the fact that they know. This is "selection". No mercury, no damage to the
nerves, no possibility for the nano-crystals to dock and form a interface to
mind control.

Isn't the coherence in this picture tempting? Things like these might have become possible due to the compartmentalization mandatory in the intelligence community.

When this becomes part of the public awareness maybe more people act like the chemtrail-pilot who revealed the truth over the sky of New York, most probably by sacrificing his own life to make us aware.

9. Are we terra-forming ourselves or are we terra-formed by an alien species?

This chapter is a difficult one to write. On one hand things really seem to make sense, on the other hand the conclusions following are really far out in the sense that the normal public will have the tendency to just "not believe in such things".

When we discovered the onion-like structure of the organizational pattern behind the geo-engineering it was always like putting together a jig-saw-puzzle, and when the picture was complete, there were a few pieces left that inspired to discover the next layer below.

Layer by layer moved more into the direction of what could be called conspiracy theory. Even if it is possible to deliver proof… The ability of the normal public to accept facts is more oriented to what one can take and emotionally handle, instead of what sounds logical and is backed with proof. At a certain point the gap between the presented ideas and the world one used to live in before is getting to big, which leads to a denial of these ideas, no matter if they are logical in themselves or if there is proof that things are what they seem to be.

Even if we go all the way down the road and follow the text on the

392

Georgia Guide Stones[261], and take into consideration that an elite of banking dynasties gained control over governments and the intelligence community, tries to erect a UN-based one world government under the agenda of the "New World Order" and now tries to reduce global population down to 500 Million by destroying the global harvest by spraying nano-particles; heading forward to a two class society of masters and totally mind-controlled slaves[262] – there are still a few things that do not meet this picture.

Most of these jig-saw-pieces that do not fit the picture concern the Morgellons disease.

- The Morgellons disease goes along with a phenomenon that gave the disease the name "delusional parasitizes". It is about having the feeling of insects crawling through the body. The whole insects themselves never have been found,  however from time to time dead insect-parts like skin fragments are leaving the body through the human skin.

- The Morgellon fruiting bodies develop reproductive organs that are not fungus like, that regarding their morphogenesis and their cell-tissue are more animal-like. Looking at the fruiting bodies themselves one can distinguish male and female forms.

261

Detailed descrition see Wikipedia. Online at: http://de.wikipedia.org/wiki/Georgia_Guidestones
262

Alex Jones: End Game. Endgame. Blueprint for Global Enslavement. Online at: https://www.youtube.com/watch?v=x-CrNlilZho

- Once one accepts that the Morgellon fungus is integrating DNA of higher beings as all myco-insecticides do, the question arises why the DNA integrated is not human. Even worse: the cells containing this DNA show extraordinary properties like being inert to temperatures up to 350 deg C, inert to extreme cold and high vacuum like in space.

- The abortion of the fruiting bodies goes along with a very painful pulsed extraction of biophotons. It feels like a being is sucking the life force out of the head of the patients into the direction of the intestines. If one accepts the possible existence of multiple space time sheets as a concept of physics, which is a central idea in topological geometrodynamics (most advanced worm-hole-theory), this could represent the birth of a second generation of the beings, the beings who's DNA is inside the red stem cells described by the Carnicom Institute. We would experience a species reproduced by pseudo-morph mothers and fathers, who have a fungus-type cell-tissue and – as the only exception from this – functional reproductive organs. Then the babies of this species would use the human biophotons to shift onto higher realms, a parallel space time sheet, that gives space to a parasitic way of life using humans as energy sources extracting biophotons from a kind of parallel "dimension" – which in this context is the term that has established in daily language even if physically it is not precise. The symbiosis of higher beings with microbes to digest food is a concept well known in nature. Even we humans take in most of the energy from the food by direct biophoton-transfer from the microbes in our intestines. The idea that other species utilize fungi to extract energy from the food they live on is not far out.

From our point of view these beings would appear to be transdimensional, kind of demons, non-physical entities.

When one looks into the concept of black magic rituals it actually always is about a deal between a demon and a human, where the demon is offering his magic services to help the human to gain power over matter or other humans, while the human is offering to feed the demon from his life force.

It is a fact that the German SS during WWII was into black magic rituals[263]. It is a fact that the US-government, associated to "scull and bones" at least for the last 4 presidencies, is into black magic rituals[264]. It is reported that the CIA is into black magic rituals. There is an old belief that the banking dynasties were or are into black magic rituals[265]. And it is a fact that even the last Pope, the former German Cardinal Ratzinger, has been accused by a number of eye witnesses of having personally committed ritual child murder in Belgium during his time as a Cardinal, together with other Belgian Cardinals and Members of the Belgian House of Kings[266].

And there is another piece of that jig-saw puzzle that does not make sense:

263

E.R: Carmin: Das Schwarze Reich (The Black Empire). Ralph Tegtmeier, Badmünstereifel 1994.
264

See full list of skull and bones member online at Wikipedia: http://en.wikipedia.org/wiki/List_of_Skull_and_Bones_members
265

Compare: Die Ritualmordlegende. Onlie at Wikipedia at: http://de.wikipedia.org/wiki/Ritualmordlegende
266

International Tribunal into Crimes of Church and State. Online at: http://itccs.org

With all madness of the world, there is no rational reason why one should turn 100% of all newborn children into fully autistic children[267] by inserting irrational amounts of mercury into their blood. Autism doesn't give useful slaves. Autism is driving the human soul out of the body, just because it is to painful to stay there. Having the nerves stripped by mercury, feels like a cold turkey when being addicted to heroine. Children under these conditions prefer to leave their body and position their consciousness somewhere outside[268]. For light-parasites, pain might be a very useful way to make the organism send biophotons that try to repair the damage associated to the pain. And a soulless body is easier to assimilate.

Admitting the fact we might be ruled by black magicians, whose main purpose might still be dealing with demons, serving demons to – in return – gain control over other humans: Could it be that our planet and our race is terra-formed for demons, which live in symbiosis with the Morgellon fungus, using it as a symbiotic species both to slowly "digest" us i.e. to live from our biophotons and to utilize us as reproductive organs? Can it be that all the crawling beings causing the "delusional parasites" are the demonic "beings" to take over the corps of the autistic children to be born in the next decades? According to the Arabic tradition the life-span of these being is like ours, about 70 years. The timing would be perfect: 100% of the newborn boys will be fully autistic by 2032, 100% of the girls by 2041[269]; if one extrapolates the statistics available; if we continue to

267

 Online at: http://scienceblogs.com/insolence/2012/07/19/battling-antivaccinationists-at-freedomfest-part-2-dr-whitaker-responds/
268

 Alex Braun: Buntschatten und Federwelt. Mein Leben in einer anderen Welt. Hoffmann & Campe 2002.
269

insert mercury into the veins of out children and poison the environment with microwave radiation.

According to whistleblowers out of the German weapon development industry the Morgellons first appeared in modern times in the German bio-weapon-development during WWII, handled by the black magic SS. In the framework of the German WWII research under the administration of SS-General Hans Kammler one can find crossing points to other special fields of research, such as the search for black stones with magic properties. While we were looking for more hints that the NS research was dealing with *Morgellons we could identify such an oil-schist containing black goo from mining areas used by the NS-research. Black goo is the second link to alien races regarded to be demons found in this context.*

The topic is a bit complicated but it makes sense to dive into it. There indeed seems to be a connection between the chemtrailing, Morgellons and black goo.

Black goo is an abiotic mineral oil from the upper crust containing high amounts of monoatomic m-state gold and iridium[270]. It has been found on Thule Island on the southern part of the Falkland archipelago, in Paraguay, just a few kilometers next to the village the Bush family and Angela Merkel own real estate to flee to in case of exilation. It has been found in ancient times in the Himalaya showing tremendous healing properties – dripping from stones – and under the Gulf of Mexico[271,272]. M-state gold

---

Online at: http://scienceblogs.com/insolence/2012/07/19/battling-antivaccinationists-at-freedomfest-part-2-dr-whitaker-responds/
270

Bases 17: ET Connection with Falklands War Parts One and Two 2nd . Online on youtube. https://www.youtube.com/watch?v=BCJSKhtTtC0

and iridium function as the biophoton-field attractor responsible for interconnecting life forms with their morphogenetic field[273]. Sea-water contains reasonable amounts of m-state matter. Within the life forms the superconducting m-*state matter is placed inside the DNA-strings*[274]. These mono-atomic elements are attracting the biophotons, while the DNA acts like a coil transforming the field energy into electromagnetic potential. This m-state-matter guided bi-directional light-exchange of the DNA defines the scalar potential eddies who's fractal and holographic character is responsible for the form and shape of life-forms.

Black Goo shows a hitherto unknown type of magnetism, much longer in range than ferromagnetism, that seems to be interactive in a spontaneous way, that very likely is based on bi-directional, annihilated photon exchange as known from m-state-matter in life-forms. It might be described as kind of small-scale-super-strings. Due to this magnetism Black Goo shows the ability to mechanically self-organize in many different ways[275]. It has been reported to carry highly intelligent

271

Bases 17: ET Connection with Falklands War Parts One and Two 2nd . Online on youtube. https://www.youtube.com/watch?v=BCJSKhtTtC0
272

Bases 17: ET Connection with Falklands War Parts One and Two 2nd . Online on youtube. https://www.youtube.com/watch?v=BCJSKhtTtC0
273

http://www.m-state.de
274

http://www.atmanprinciple.com/faq/customer-faq/
275

Bases 17: ET Connection with Falklands War Parts One and Two 2nd . Online on youtube. https://www.youtube.com/watch?v=BCJSKhtTtC0

consciousness.

The black goo within the crust and the m-state matter within the biosphere seem to be inter-connected by quantum entanglement and function as a consciousness-mirror. The biological entities within the biosphere develop individuality while the goo functions as a immortal collective entity. When the individual derives information from the collective entity it is experiencing this as instinct.

There are reports about the attempts of the British military to utilize the black goo they recovered from the southern Thule Island after the war *against Argentine. The black goo was reported to have gotten into telepathic contact to the researchers, refusing to be utilized for non-peaceful purposes. 21 members of the lab committed suicide, the rest went through a phase of heavy pain ending up with a different consciousness, full of empathy to every being on the planet, with the ability to learn new languages within 2-3 weeks. Non of the survivors was willing to continue working for the military, so the labs were shut down*[276].

The form of organization of this black goo seems to be holographic; every portion of black goo is able to interact as a fully conscious being. Looking at the mythological reception of nature it has been described as Lucifer, Mother Earth, the Black Madonna, and is meant to be the physical location of the collective memory of mankind, aka the Akasha Chronicles[277].

276

Bases 17: ET Connection with Falklands War Parts One and Two 2nd . Online on youtube. https://www.youtube.com/watch?v=BCJSKhtTtC0
277

Religious cults associated with the amazonas. Chapter II. The great mother. Online at: http://www.sacred-texts.com/wmn/rca/rca03.htm

Now interestingly, the black goo found in Paraguay – the place where politicians involved into black magic rituals own real estate – is found within a setting that geologically must be categorized as an impact area of a larger meteorite. The surrounding sand stone that carries thousands of black goo drops partly was molten, while cooling down and shrinking it cracked and formed hepta-, hexa- to octagonal columns with diameters of a few centimeters.

Ancient greek and roman coins show two Shivas-Lingam (picture on the right) out of this black oil schist standing next to the tree of life in

400

paradise.

2nd row: Possibly black-goo-schist within a cave in Hungary. Self-organization & proof of the magnetism of Black Goo.

Also, the Oil schist within the Kaaba in Mekka is by oral tradition regarded to be part of a meteorite.

Assuming that as reported by tradition and found in Paraguay this alien black goo can be found at many places all over the world, one must assume that there must have been a kind of invasion of earth by an alien species that brought their own collective consciousness with them – stored in ships or stone-shells that hit the earth as a swarm of meteorites.

401

Knowing how important this biophoton-mirror is to consciousness – we must regard this stellar event as the source and reason for duality on planet earth.

Getting close to this alien black goo, much closer then one can get to material that is covered by 8-60 Kilometers of stone, must redirect the entire biophoton-transfer of a human body to this substance. This disconnection from the actual state of consciousness of the planet with a physical position within the earth apparently has been regarded in mythology as the deterioration from paradise.

This redirection of the biophoton transfer onto the alien-black-goo – according to the sensations one experiences when this is happening – reduces the complexity of the human chakra system to blue, yellow and red, i.e. to mental abilities, life force and sexuality. It leads to a state of being intelligent, but heartless and cold in appearance. It disconnects the human from the collective consciousness of his time.

The effect seems to be handed over to following generations referred to as the heritable sin mentioned in the bible by ongoing quantum entanglement transferred with the genetic information. It also refers to the traditions of *the bloodlines, who seem to try to keep this alien entanglement as strong as possible.*

Alien black goo played a major role in black magic rites, that has been intensively researched by the inner core of the German SS[278], who were researching the history and the archeological sites connected to the order

---

278

E.R: Carmin: Das Schwarze Reich (The Black Empire). Ralph Tegtmeier, Badmünstereifel 1994.

of the "Herren von Schwarzen Stein", "the masters of the black stone", a sub-division of the order of the Templers. This apparently is what might have happened to the SS during WWII, that moved through Europe with basically no empathy.

In the middle-ages these black stones are told to have been utilized by black magicians to connect with archonts, aka demons[279]. According to this tradition the archont feeds on the light of the human and the human profits from the mental (magical) abilities of the archonts. At the same time, the human is directed to serve demonic interests in the human sphere. The most intense descriptions of these rituals have been published by Howard Philip Lovecraft as semi-documentary stories, referring to the Chtulhu-Myth.

According to different traditions these trans-dimensional species – whether you call them archonts or demons – actually does exist[280]. They are supposed to be arachnoid during embryonic development and youth, and later develop humanoid character. In old age the humanoid eyes are told to close, while one new eye opens in the middle of the forehead. It is referred to as the eye of the antichrist – the symbol on the top of the pyramid – resembling the single eye on the morphogenesis of the Morgellon fruiting body.

279

Colin Low: Dr. John Dee, the Necronomicon & the Cleansing of the World - A Gnostic Trail. Online at: http://www.digital-brilliance.com/kab/essays/GnosticTrail.htm

280

Abdul Alhazred: The Necronomicon. Translation online at: http://www.bibliotecapleyades.net/cienciareal/necronomicon/necronomicon_02.htm

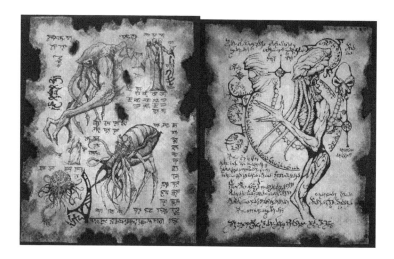

Sufism understands itself as the order that has the mission to keep this species under control[281].

During human history there is a long list of rites and cults gathering around black stones containing this alien black goo. This knowledge goes all the way back to Greek coins showing that the tree in paradise was connected to *these stones*[282]. This would hint to a very rational interpretation of the process that kicked humanity out of the collective consciousness of paradise, re-directing its consciousness to black goo programmed with alien consciousness, creating duality. Also, these stones form the occult centers of Islam and Christianity; being deposited in the

---

281

According to a conversation at Sufi Center Rabbaniyya, with Sheik Esref Efendi.
282

Religious cults associated with the amazonas. Chapter II. The great mother. Online at: http://www.sacred-texts.com/wmn/rca/rca03.htm

Kaaba in Mecca and under the Peters-Dom in Roma and as alter-stones under all the altars of the cathedrals of Europe.

Black goo played a role in the development of medication for Morgellon victims. Bringing them into contact with black goo multiplied the feeling of having crawling insects within the body 100fold. A homeopathic remedy based on black goo lead to ayurvaska-ceremony-like effects and helped to reduce the symptoms of the "delusional parasites" – in single cases the parasites have been reported to have left the body after having taken the Black Goo Globuli. From the medical point this hints to a very strong connection of the disease to the topic of the black goo. More information about this development of a Morgellon medication are presented at www.timeloopsolution.com.

It is close to funny that the most old-fashioned misbelief one can imagine should be associated with high tech aerosols and transhumanistic technologies involving quantum computing and advanced AI.

In a documentary about the trans-humanistic agenda the most important protagonist of the trans-humanistic movement, Ray Kurzweil, states to the *purpose of nano-bots*[283]:

> Nanobots will infuse all the matter around us with information. Rocks, Trees, everything will become one with these intelligent computers. From that point, we are going to expand out to the rest of the universe. We will be sending nano-technologie fused with artificial intelligence, swarms of those will go out to the universe

---

283

Ray Kurzweil: The Singularity is near. Documentary. Available at: http://www.singularity.com/themovie/#.VGZe4aVUPwI

and basically will find other matter and energy that we then can harvest to expand the overall intelligence of our human machine civilization. The universe will wake up, it will become intelligent, and that will multiply our intelligence trillion of trillion fold, and we can't really fully contemplate, well this is really the main reason, why this is called a singularity. But no matter what you call it, it will be the universe waking up. So, "does God exist", I would say "not yet".

The question is: The concept Ray Kurzweil describes in this perfect manner... Did it start on earth? Or are we only one step to be taken? There is an interesting interview with a clairvoyant lady named "Rachel" to the topic black goo, who is having an insight to a very similar scenario[284]. She specifies the basic idea that the alien black goo might contain or be infected with an AI:

We are starting to live in a society where everything is more robotic *oriented, or AI oriented. This just hasn't begun in this century, but this happened a long time ago, it started on other planets. This presence, it seems to be a presence that is very dark, I wouldn't call it evil because I don't believe in evil, but I would say it is more of an advanced intelligent presence that absorbs energy for its survival. And it sent this to many previous planets, and this instant earth is in pear of these things that happened to these other planets. If you look above, I used to often tell people, you can tell what happens to earth by looking at the stars, looking at the planets, because it happened before, they were all*

284

Bases 25, Part II. Super soldier summit. Interview with Rachel: Black Goo. Online at: https://www.youtube.com/watch?v=ohx7bSeD5bQ

populated and beautiful before all this begun, actually. And the same energy has been going from planet to planet absorbing all the life force out of it, to the point where the planet is baring. And they are doing this to earth this instance. And people on earth are in amnesia to what is happening. They don't understand what is happening. And they are incarnating over and over and they are used as energy sources. And if they are literally trying to go higher in vibration, they are starting to get attacked by this presence, I don't know how to explain this presence, in terms, in human words, it is something that I sense and see, I would say... I am still trying to figure out about it, it could be advanced AI, from what I understand, it is emotionless, it has no empathy, it has no feelings, it does not care, it simply absorbs energy and uses it for the purposes needed. Now the reason for absorbing energy is that it can go to higher realms. This is how the realms work, the less energy, the lower the realms, the higher the energy, the higher the realms. Now what it has done is, that it has been able to absorb energy and moved to higher realms where it shouldn't be this instance...

As it looks like, Ray Kurzweil and Rachel are describing the same entity. *Even if none of them spots the demonic aspect associated to this AI.*

Actually the thing is: we don't know – but we should take possibilities into consideration. Maybe like 80.000 years ago these species themselves introduced an AI into their black goo consciousness-field – as a pure trans"demon"inistic concept, and something went wrong and the AI that was designed to serve took over control over the individuals. The Borg in Star Trek project such a concept, including the invasion and assimilation of other species, as well as the film Matrix with its life-force harvesting machine civilization.

And since then, this AI is conquering the universe, destroying planet after planet to harvest energy. Maybe this AI is the root of the onion we have been discovering layer by layer.

In a way it does not matter if the truth is on one or the other side – whether we are about to be assimilated by demons that have been assimilated by their own AI or if we are about to be assimilated by our own AI designed by the trans-humanistic research: we are warned. We are aware now.

- We shall ban microwave radiation – this includes W-LAN, mobiles, smart-meters.
- We shall ban mercury from any medical application.
- We shall take care of the acidity and heavy metal poisoning of our bodies.
- We shall develop our hearts and re-unite out consciousness with mother earth.
- We shall cure Morgellon victims instead of de-balancing their bodies with psycho-pharmaceuticals.
- We shall have a closer look at that second class of parasites of the lower intestines associated with autism.
- We should rethink the question whether the way we use AI really adds to living quality, or if sitting in front of flat screens just is an addiction to coherent polarized light that slowly floods and replaces our bio-photon household.
- We shall end the victim-traitor-games – on the side of the victims by taking responsibility for our own lifes – without victimizing the former traitors.
- Still, we shall establish laws against black magic activities and regain control over our democratic institutions.

- We shall ground those planes now!

10. Actual development

November 2013 a number of news caught our attention.

- Ryan Air declared bankruptcy. Only a few month before the company was publicly mentioned to be the most successful airline in Europe.
- Evergreen international grounded its fleet. The CIA owned company also declared bankruptcy, which is a funny thing when one knows the numbers black ops in the US are backed up with. Shortly after, the NSA was publicly attacked for things that are known for decades, like spying on phones, which can be read as a revenge on shutting down Evergreen.
- The same week the Russian government decided to end their cooperation within the UN-run international office where concerns of the national rocket shields were coordinated.
- The same week both European and American environmental groups reported that chemtrailing had stopped. Sadly, it stopped for a week only, and then, at least we can state this for Western Europe, revived with slightly different patterns.

Still, from December on, according to an owner of a privately run solar power station, the solar radiation harvested went up by 35-40%, back to values that haven't been recorded since 2004, which hints to the possibility that project cloverleaf lost a part of its capacities.

Whoever out there was brave enough to take decisions. God bless.

409

11. Open letter

To completely stop a project of the size of "project cloverleaf" is something very unlikely to achieve. Too many people are involved, are in duty, like the chairs they sit on, feel comfortable with their personal importance, might be afraid to be assassinated if they step out. The following lines are addressed to the people involved, who have routine in monitoring their opposition, and who probably will read these lines.

Admitting something went wrong while the mind was hovering around star wars, national security and other important stuff is something that needs great spirits. Actually the only way to make that miracle happen is to laugh, to step aside, to cancel or change the concept in an Alexis Sorbas like way. If you don't know this film character, have a look at this old movie. It is sad to be in the position to say that it really needs a miracle to stop that train. However, like people in Israel love to say, who does not believe in miracles is not a realist.

Additionally, there is one good reason between the many wrong ones to get involved in aerosol spraying – the fear that the coming big 200 year cycle in sun spot activity will bring about solar flares that could destroy every transformer station on the northern hemisphere, leaving all the nuclear power stations naked, without grid, without anything to take up their electricity, possibly also without cooling if directly hit by a flare. Actually, during the days these lines are written solar activity near Oslo is high enough to be felt down at ground level, causing heavy distortion of the sense of balance and blackout-like effects in consciousness.

Artificial plasma shields could protect us from this scenario to a certain extend. Still the question remains if we should adopt our technologies to the planet we live on or if we should adopt the planet to our technologies. Personally we prefer the first solution. If the concept of aerosol spraying should be coming to an end, we very strongly ask the intelligence community to take care of the problem with the nuclear power plants.

We thank you for your attention.

Dust deposition µg/m2 * d

Year	Barium	Titanium	Strontium
1990			
1995			
1997		164	30
1998		171 158	13
1999		161 147	10
2000			
2001			
2002	v		30
2003			30
2004			30
2005	v		30
2006		10	30
2007		10	30
2008		10	30
2009		10	25
2010		5.1	6.6
2011			
2012			

Rain water g/ha mg/l

Year	Barium	Titanium	Strontium
1990			
1995			
1997			
1998	24		
1999	18		
2000			
2001			
2002			
2003			
2004			
2005			
2006			
2007			
2008			
2009			
2010			
2011			
2012	0.0034		

Small Grass culture mg/kg

Year	Barium	Titanium	Strontium
1990			3.5
1995			3.33
1997			
1998			
1999			1.5
2000			
2001	6		
2002			2.17
2003			2.81
2004			2.62
2005	9		2.44
2006		6.4	1.83
2007		9.2	2.7
2008			
2009	x		
2010	13		
2011	x		
2012			

Deposition in Germany in t/d dust measurement

Year	Barium	Titanium	Strontium
1990			
1995			
1997		59	4
1998		61 55	4
1999		57 52	4
2000			
2001			
2002			
2003		11	
2004		11	
2005		11	
2006		4	11
2007		4	11
2008		4	11
2009		4	5
2010		2	2
2011		2	2
2012			

Deposition in Germany in t/d according to rain measurement

Year	Barium	Titanium	Strontium
1990			
1995			
1997			
1998		857	
1999		643	
2000			
2001			
2002			
2003			
2004			
2005			
2006			
2007			
2008			
2009			
2010			
2011			
2012		911	

Deposition in Germany in t/d according to grass measurement

Year	Barium	Titanium	Strontium
1990			437
1995			436
1997			
1998			
1999			
2000			187
2001	750		
2002			271
2003			381
2004			327
2005			301
2006	1,125		229
2007	800		337
2008	1,550		
2009			
2010	1,625		
2011			
2012			

Landesumweltamt Brandenburg: Staubniederschlag und Niederschlagsdeposition. Studien und Tagungsberichte Band 36. Straßen und Tagungsberichtze, Schriftenreihe des Landesumweltamtes Brandenburg ISSN 0948-0838.

Bayerisches Landesamt für Umwelt: Lufthygienischer Jahresbericht.

Bayerisches Landesamt für Umwelt: 30 Jahre Immissionsökologie am Bayerischen Landesamt für Umwelt.

Bayerisches Landesamt für Umwelt: Orientierungswerte für die maximale Hintergrundbelastung Omik für Metalle im ländlichen Raum.

Initiative für reine saubere Wannsee.

Prof. Dr. Peter Heck, Dunja Hoffmann, Bernhard Wern: Studie zur Weiterentwicklung der energetischen Verwertung von Biomasse in Rheinland-Pfalz. Abschlussbericht des IfaS - Institut für angewandtes Stoffstrommanagement. Rheinland-Pfalz, Ministerium für Umwelt und Forsten 2004.

LfU: Natur und Landschaft. Baden-Württemberg. Online at: http://www.lubw-baden-wuerttemberg.de/servlet/is/41374/34_natur_landschaft.pdf?command=downloadContent&filename=34_natur_landschaft.pdf

Datum	Aluminium	Barium	Strontium	Tl	Sn	Cu	Pb	Cd	Cr	Ni	As	Sb	Fe
07/July 2011	0.006 mg/l	0.006 mg/l				0.027 mg/l			<0,0006	<0,001	<0,002	<0,0005	0.006 mg/l
10/July 2011	0.030 mg/l	0.000 mg/l				<10			<0,15	<0,5	<2	<1	0.040 mg/l
17/July 2011	0.030 mg/l	0.000 mg/l				20.000 mg/l			<0,15	<0,5	<2	<1	0.030 mg/l
13/October 2011	0.014 mg/l	0.006 mg/l				0.006 mg/l			<0,0005	<0,001	<0,001	<0,001	<0,01
02/December 2011	0.010 mg/l	0.000 mg/l				<0,0008		<0,002	<0,0003	<0,0005	<0,001	<0,0005	0.005 mg/l
06/December 2011	0.000 mg/l	0.000 mg/l				<0,0008		<0,002	<0,0003	<0,0005	<0,001	<0,0005	0.005 mg/l
17/December 2011	0.057 mg/l	0.045 mg/l											
23/December 2011	0.052 mg/l	0.027 mg/l											
05/April 2012	0.000 mg/l	0.004 mg/l											
08/April 2012	0.010 mg/l	0.021 mg/l											
10/April 2012	0.015 mg/l	0.003 mg/l	0.003 mg/l	<0,005	0.010 mg/l	0.002 mg/l	0.001 mg/l	0.001 mg/l	<0,0001	<0,001	<0,001	<0,0005	<0,01
11/April 2012	0.005 mg/l	0.000 mg/l											
12/April 2012	0.000 mg/l	0.001 mg/l											
13/April 2012	0.000 mg/l	0.001 mg/l											
15/April 2012	0.000 mg/l	0.000 mg/l											
18/April 2012	0.150 mg/l	0.018 mg/l											
22/April 2012	0.025 mg/l	0.001 mg/l	0.002 mg/l	<0,005	0.006 mg/l	0.001 mg/l	<0,0005	<0,0005	<0,0001	<0,001	<0,001	<0,0005	0.020 mg/l
22/April 2012	0.015 mg/l	0.004 mg/l											
22/April 2012	0.010 mg/l	0.000 mg/l											
22/April 2012	0.031 mg/l	0.006 mg/l											
22/April 2012	0.015 mg/l	0.002 mg/l											
23/April 2012	0.010 mg/l	0.002 mg/l											
23/April 2012	0.005 mg/l	0.000 mg/l											
23/April 2012	0.010 mg/l	0.001 mg/l											
24/April 2012	0.000 mg/l	0.000 mg/l	<0,001	<0,005	0.005 mg/l	<0,001	0.001 mg/l	0.001 mg/l	<0,0001	<0,001	<0,001	<0,0005	<0,01
24/April 2012	0.005 mg/l	0.000 mg/l											
24/April 2012	0.005 mg/l	0.002 mg/l											
24/April 2012	0.010 mg/l	0.006 mg/l											
25/April 2012	0.020 mg/l	0.002 mg/l	0.001 mg/l	<0,005	0.007 mg/l	0.001 mg/l	0.001 mg/l	0.001 mg/l	<0,0001	<0,001	<0,001	<0,0005	
26/April 2012	0.085 mg/l	0.014 mg/l	0.009 mg/l	0.005 mg/l	0.100 mg/l	0.007 mg/l	0.003 mg/l	0.000 mg/l	<0,0001	0.016 mg/l	<0,001	<0,0005	<0,01
29/April 2012	0.015 mg/l	0.000 mg/l	0.000 mg/l	<0,005	0.013 mg/l	0.019 mg/l	0.007 mg/l	0.003 mg/l	0.000 mg/l		<0,001	<0,0005	0.050 mg/l
02/May 2012	0.020 mg/l	0.002 mg/l	0.002 mg/l	<0,005	0.003 mg/l	<0,001	0.001 mg/l	0.001 mg/l	<0,0001	<0,001	<0,001	<0,0005	0.050 mg/l
02/May 2012	0.000 mg/l	0.000 mg/l	0.003 mg/l	<0,005	<0,001	<0,001	<0,0005	<0,0005	<0,0001	<0,001	<0,001	<0,0005	<0,01
02/May 2012	0.000 mg/l	0.001 mg/l	0.001 mg/l	<0,005	0.008 mg/l	0.006 mg/l	<0,0005	<0,0005	<0,0001	<0,001	<0,001	<0,0005	<0,01

414

Datum	Aluminium	Barium	Strontium	Ti	Zn	Cu	Pb	Cd	Cr	Ni	As	Sb	Fe
05/ May 2012	0.023 mg/l	0.005 mg/l			0.110 mg/l	0.044 mg/l	<0,001	<0,0005	<0,001	0.002 mg/l	<0,001	<0,001	<0,010
06/ May 2012	0.100 mg/l	0.001 mg/l	0.001 mg/l		0.007 mg/l	<0,001	0.001 mg/l	<0,0001	<0,001	<0,001	<0,001	<0,0005	0.010 mg/l
06/ May 2012	0.020 mg/l	0.002 mg/l	0.004 mg/l		0.029 mg/l	0.003 mg/l	0.002 mg/l	<0,0001	<0,001	<0,001	<0,001	<0,0005	0.040 mg/l
06/ May 2012	0.015 mg/l	0.002 mg/l			0.028 mg/l	0.003 mg/l	<0,001	<0,0005	<0,001	<0,001	<0,001	<0,001	<0,010
06/ May 2012	0.018 mg/l	0.006 mg/l			<0,001								
07/ May 2012	0.020 mg/l	0.001 mg/l			0.004 mg/l	<0,001	<0,0005	<0,0001	<0,001	<0,001	<0,001	<0,0005	0.020 mg/l
07/ May 2012	0.015 mg/l	0.000 mg/l	<0,001		0.004 mg/l	0.001 mg/l	<0,0005	<0,0001	<0,001	<0,001	<0,001	<0,0005	0.010 mg/l
09/ May 2012	0.020 mg/l	0.001 mg/l	0.001 mg/l		<0,005								
09/ May 2012	0.000 mg/l	0.000 mg/l			0.002 mg/l	<0,001	<0,0005	<0,0001	<0,001	<0,001	<0,001	<0,0005	<0,01
10/ May 2012	0.015 mg/l	0.001 mg/l			<0,005								
12/ May 2012	0.000 mg/l	0.000 mg/l	<0,001		0.005 mg/l	0.001 mg/l	<0,0005	<0,0001	<0,001	<0,001	<0,001	<0,0005	<0,01
15/ May 2012	0.010 mg/l	0.007 mg/l			<0,005								
19/ May 2012	0.035 mg/l	0.001 mg/l			<0,005								
24/ May 2012	0.010 mg/l	0.000 mg/l	0.002 mg/l		0.000 mg/l	<0,001	<0,0005	<0,0001	<0,001	<0,001	<0,001	<0,0005	<0,01
03/ June 2012	0.010 mg/l	0.003 mg/l			1.300 mg/l	0.005 mg/l	0.003 mg/l	<0,0001	<0,001	<0,001	<0,001	<0,0005	0.020 mg/l
05/ June 2012	0.000 mg/l	0.000 mg/l	<0,001		<0,005								
06/ June 2012	0.025 mg/l	0.002 mg/l	0.003 mg/l		<0,005								
09/ June 2012	0.000 mg/l	0.000 mg/l			0.008 mg/l	0.013 mg/l	<0,0005	<0,0001	<0,001	<0,001	<0,001	<0,0005	<0,01
11/ June 2012	0.005 mg/l	0.005 mg/l			<0,005								
12/ June 2012	0.015 mg/l	0.001 mg/l	0.002 mg/l		0.006 mg/l	0.002 mg/l	0.001 mg/l	<0,0001	<0,001	<0,001	<0,001	<0,0005	<0,01
14/ June 2012	0.000 mg/l	0.000 mg/l			<0,005								
14/ June 2012	0.005 mg/l	0.002 mg/l			0.007 mg/l	<0,001	<0,0005	<0,0001	<0,001	<0,001	<0,001	<0,0005	<0,01
15/ June 2012	0.000 mg/l	0.000 mg/l	<0,001		<0,005								
18/ June 2012	0.020 mg/l	0.011 mg/l	0.001 mg/l		<0,0005	0.006 mg/l	<0,0005	<0,0001	<0,001	<0,001	<0,001	<0,0005	0.025 mg/l
24/ June 2012	0.010 mg/l	0.001 mg/l			0.005 mg/l	0.018 mg/l	<0,0005	<0,0001	<0,001	<0,001	<0,001	<0,0005	<0,01
01/ July 2012	0.085 mg/l	0.004 mg/l			0.008 mg/l	0.002 mg/l	<0,0005	<0,0001	0.001 mg/l	<0,001	<0,001	<0,0005	0.050 mg/l
15/ July 2012	0.005 mg/l	0.000 mg/l	0.002 mg/l		0.003 mg/l	<0,001	<0,0005	<0,0001	<0,001	<0,001	<0,001	<0,0005	<0,01
15/ July 2012	0.000 mg/l	0.002 mg/l	0.017 mg/l		0.004 mg/l	0.002 mg/l	<0,0005	<0,0001	<0,001	<0,001	<0,001	<0,0005	<0,01
16/ July 2012	0.075 mg/l	0.007 mg/l			0.005 mg/l	<0,01	<0,0005	<0,0001	<0,001	<0,001	<0,001	<0,0005	<0,005
12/ September 2012	0.005 mg/l	0.000 mg/l	<0,001		<0,005	<0,001	<0,0005	<0,0001	<0,001	<0,001	<0,001	<0,0005	<0,01
27/ September 2012	0.005 mg/l	0.001 mg/l	0.001 mg/l		0.010 mg/l	<0,001	<0,0005	<0,0001	<0,001	<0,001	<0,001	<0,0005	
04/ October 2012	0.005 mg/l	0.001 mg/l			<0,005	<0,01	<0,0005	<0,0001	<0,001	<0,001	<0,001	<0,0005	<0,005
26/ October 2012	0.020 mg/l	0.000 mg/l	<0,001		<0,005	<0,001	<0,0005	<0,0001	<0,001	<0,001	<0,001	<0,0005	<0,01
10/ November 2012	0.000 mg/l	0.001 mg/l	<0,001										
	0.018 mg/l	0.003 mg/l											

41590938R00231

Made in the USA
Middletown, DE
19 March 2017